LIBRICIDE

*The Regime-Sponsored Destruction
of Books and Libraries in the
Twentieth Century*

Rebecca Knuth

Westport, Connecticut
London

Library of Congress Cataloging-in-Publication Data

Knuth, Rebecca, 1949–
    Libricide : the regime-sponsored destruction of books and libraries in the twentieth
century / Rebecca Knuth.
        p. cm.
    Includes bibliographical references and index.
    ISBN 0–275–98088–X (alk. paper)
        1. Censorship—History—20th century—Case studies.   2. Libraries and state—
    History—20th century—Case studies. 3. Libraries—Censorship—History—20th
    century—Case studies. I. Title.
    Z659.K58 2003
    363.31'09'04—dc21   2002044542   323.445

British Library Cataloguing in Publication Data is available.

Library of Congress Catalog Card Number: 2002044542
ISBN: 0–275–98088–X

First published in 2003

Praeger Publishers, 88 Post Road West, Westport, CT 06881
An imprint of Greenwood Publishing Group, Inc.
www.praeger.com

Printed in the United States of America

The paper used in this book complies with the
Permanent Paper Standard issued by the National
Information Standards Organization (Z39.48–1984).

10   9   8   7   6   5   4   3   2   1

CONTENTS

PREFACE

"Questions are the engines of intellect. . . . There can be no
thinking without questioning, no purposeful study of the past,
nor any serious planning for the future."

(Fischer 1970, 3).

Books and libraries occasionally fall victim to disaster. They are, after all,
fragile material objects. In 1966 floods in Florence damaged two million
books, many of them rare and precious manuscripts. In 1988, a devastating
fire claimed 3.6 million books in Leningrad's Academy of Sciences Library. While we are saddened by such catastrophes and feel a sense of
loss, we respond differently to the destruction of books in "natural" disasters than to the deliberate violation of books. In natural disasters, human agency is, at most, a secondary force at play, and damage to cultural
materials does not raise questions about the basic order of society. The
case is entirely different when books and libraries are systematically
looted, bombed, and burned, for then a deliberate and calculated attack
on the culture of a group is launched, and the world responds from a sense
that the whole of human culture has come under attack. In the pages to
come, I will argue that this is, in fact, the case, and for this reason a look
back at the twentieth century's plague of book destruction is critical if we
are to understand such behavior and, subsequently, take active steps to
protect the common cultural heritage of the world.

My project began with these two questions: What really distinguishes those who mourn the destruction of books and libraries from those who willingly, even joyfully, throw books into the fires? And how can the ideals of human progress be reconciled with the mass violence and destruction of culture that characterized the twentieth century? In formulating these questions, I was seeking to address what seems to me a lack of analysis in accounts of the destruction of books and libraries. Often emotional and bewildered, witness accounts describe the damage, and then proceed to attribute the violence—a violation of something they consider to be inherently good—to latent barbarism and a specialized evil. This is a seductive but non-productive mindset because it fails to come to grips with two critical factors: the political nature of written records and the fact that such destruction follows a common pattern. Far from being a mere product of evil, the destruction of textual materials was goal-oriented and carefully rationalized within struggles between competing worldviews that wracked the last century. Seeking Utopia, extremist regimes crossed every imaginable boundary as their belief systems metamorphosed into radical ideologies.

In the chaos achieved by extremist aggression, genocide and ethnocide emerged as recognizable phenomena, clearly linked to ideas, and I propose that a third pattern, libricide, exists and falls within the same theoretical universe. "Libricide" is defined in the Oxford English Dictionary as a rare term, denoting simply "the killing of a book." It combines the idea of book and slaughter (in the same way that "homicide" refers to the murder of a person) and its etymology reflects a link to genocide and ethnocide. In this book I have chosen to use "libricide" to refer specifically to the twentieth-century, large-scale, regime-sanctioned destruction of books and libraries, purposeful initiatives that were designed to advance short- and long-term ideologically driven goals; libricide is an identifiable secondary pattern or sub-phenomena occurring within the framework of genocide and ethnocide. Like other kinds of sociocultural violations committed during war or civil unrest, libricide has remained largely invisible at the same time as technological advancements, centralized leadership, extreme ideologies, and modern mentalities of war have enabled this kind of violation to become systemic. It is because of its social consequences that probing the dynamics of libricide is of immediate importance.

To establish a rudimentary sense of this dynamic, I have begun in Chapter 1 with an exploration of reactions to book destruction, building a case that libricide exists, and establishing its connection with genocide and ethnocide. Chapter 2 discusses the evolution and functions of libraries and links libraries to history, collective memory, belief systems, nationalism, and societal development. While most of the literature on librarianship focuses on the operational aspects of libraries—i.e. the retrieval, preservation, and dissemination of information—this chapter identifies their social and political functions, which are key to their becoming the targets of violence. In Chapter 3 the stage is set for the five case studies by the proposal of a theoretical framework for libricide in which beliefs, co-opted by extremists and transformed into ideologies, rationalize the identification of textual materials as tools of the enemy or as enemies themselves. The trigger factors that activate common patterns worldwide are identified.

Chapters 4 through 8 contain cases that were selected to demonstrate the viability of the framework and illustrate the dynamics of such destruction: libricides committed by Nazis, Serbs in Bosnia, Iraqis in Kuwait, Maoists during the Chinese Cultural Revolution, and Chinese Communists in Tibet. The choice of these cases was influenced by access to source materials, issues of geographical and political representation, and the ability of the case to advance understanding of the perpetrators' motivation and demonstrate the varying permutations of the phenomenon. Nazi Germany was selected because it is the prototypical case of libricide by a racist, right-wing, and nationalist agent; also, a plethora of materials was available. A study of Imperialist Japan was excluded because the motivation was similar to that of the Nazis and there were fewer resources. Bosnia was an essential case because of its currency, and because of insights to be gleaned from ethnic cleansing; I chose to focus on Serbian atrocities rather than Croatian because Serbia far surpassed Croatia in the scale and intensity of damage to books and libraries. I wanted to include a case from the Middle East and decided against the Turkish destruction of Armenian texts during World War I in favor of the more contemporary Iraqi invasion of Kuwait, which had an interesting mixture of ideological motivations. While probing left-wing or Communist libricide, it became evident that the Soviet Union, in the interest of extinguishing national identity among its constituent nations, was guilty of some of the most egregious cultural destruction; however, the necessary information has yet to be mined from Soviet archives. China, therefore, represented the best route to understanding left-wing or revolutionary destruction; further, the fate of books and libraries during the Cultural Revolution is an astonishingly compelling story. I collected information about Cambodia during Pol Pot's regime, but decided that the more significant and complex story was the Communist annihilation of the cultural materials of the quasi-medieval Tibet. More space has been devoted to China and Tibet than to the other cases in order to do justice to the complexities of the Cultural Revolution and establish the full scope of Tibet's written heritage before addressing its destruction. The book concludes in Chapter 9 with an exploration of deeper issues and attention to the development of international law and mechanisms for the prevention of libricide. It argues that twentieth-century libricide reflected battles between extremist ideologies and democratic humanism and internationalism.

Perhaps the most difficult theoretical dilemma I encountered was the handling of the immense destruction of books and libraries by Allied bombing in World War II. The Germans lost between one-third and one-half of their books during the war, the majority as a result of British carpet-bombing of cities. The Japanese lost about half of their books in the Americans' firebombing of Japan's cities. There are some who equate these strategic bombing campaigns with genocide (Markusen and Kopf 1995); however, most scholars hesitate to label these campaigns as genocidal because the Allies were motivated by self-defense and were not targeting groups *per se* for extinction. The Allies' campaigns did not fit my definition of libricide either: the damage to books and libraries in urban bombing raids was collateral, and the Allies' tactics were dictated by short-term defensive *objectives* rather than long-term political *goals*. However, the questionable pairing of human and cultural damage haunted me, and I subsequently wrote a paper that probed these bombings, particularly in terms of intense militarism and the logic of total war (Knuth, unpublished manuscript).

Libricide is informed by materials and perspectives from history, political science, psychology, ethics, communications, library and information science, international relations, and literature. The book's cross-cultural scope and comparative methodology made the identification of general patterns possible but dictated a reliance on secondary sources. In *Libricide* I was concerned with assembling and analyzing diffused, interdisciplinary source material and subsequently fashioning a compelling argument.

Great care was taken to avoid the jargon or highly specialized terms and positions that often characterize intra-disciplinary monographs. This is an inclusive work that is aimed at a broad community of scholars and intelligent people in general, based on my belief that there is a public interest in moving beyond emotionality to the mechanisms of systemic destruction. After all, the way in which the fate of books and libraries was entwined with that of human casualties is one of the great stories of the twentieth century.

While the overall framework (and some portions of the case studies) would not be new to political scientists, specialist historians, or genocide scholars, I think they might be interested in the comparative scope and the application of theories of political violence to a previously under-explored topic. In writing the book, I am aware that I violate a scholarly taboo against comparative genocide (and, by extension, comparison of related phenomena). However, I stand with Israel Charny (1996, xi) in the belief that "all cases of genocide are similar and different, special and unique, and appropriately subject to comparative analysis." Genocide studies as a whole, especially the "uniqueness" arena, need to move beyond remembrance, denial, and factionalism to a truly comparative approach, which focuses on the universality of the phenomenon (Knuth 1999).

To avoid terminological minefields, I have tried to construct operational definitions of contestable terms such as ideology, race, and imperialism. Except for "libricide," I used common terms with a history of usage that was appropriate to my subject. Nevertheless, a few terms benefit from advance clarification. I have used "books" to refer to any long written or printed works, and "libraries" to signify all informational materials (including books, documents, manuscripts, maps, photographs, archival records, electronic databases, etc.) that have been gathered together and preserved. A library can be the millions of items in a national library collection, the working library of a scholar, a small personal library that includes genealogical records, an archive, a government records collection, or a shelf of holy texts. When I use the word "destruction," I am referring, in the case of a book, to its physical destruction (usually through burning or pulping) or to gross damages. When used with reference to libraries, "destruction" may refer to the physical destruction of its collection, or to the dismantlement and dispersal of a collection through looting or widespread purging. The destruction of a library involves not only loss or damage to its material contents, but curtailment of its ability to serve personal, sociocultural, and political functions. To the greatest extent possible, I have, in the case studies, presented the functional losses as well as quantifying the physical losses.

Reliable figures on losses, however, are hard to come by for several reasons. First, the varied format of items, particularly those in archival and historical collections, resists quantification. Second, catalogues and documentation may never have existed—or may have been lost with the books. Because libricide usually occurs during war or massive civil unrest, books and even entire collections become flotsam as they undergo general looting, random vandalism, combat conditions, and urban bombing. In addition, calculations can be conflated by political factors, such as post-war revenge or cultural restitution motives or ongoing authoritarian controls on information. For example, the Soviet Union claimed immense losses of books and libraries at the hands of the Nazis, but never compiled lists and documentation. In order to portray their country as an innocent victim of fascism, the Communist Party quickly imposed absolute secrecy on Red Army seizures of trophy collections, as many as eleven million books, in the final days of the war (Simpson 1997). These cultural items "disappeared" for forty years and corroboration of their existence is just now emerging. Secrecy often is a norm in closed societies and makes estimates of loss problematic. I have sought to provide as much information as possible on the *extent* of damage in all cases, while keeping my emphasis on identifying libricidal patterns within extremist regimes. My primary goal is to explain *why* regimes and their followers destroyed books and libraries and to address the far-reaching effects of such destruction.

Within the nine chapters, choices concerning language, theory, and cases reveal my political and social orientation. Someone once wrote that no scholar can escape his "original condition"—his own national, cultural, political, and social prejudices are bound to be reflected in his work. I know mine are. I am oriented toward democratic, liberal humanism, and I believe in intellectual freedom and the importance of libraries as bulwarks of culture and identity. This book is an exploration of (among other things) the reasons libraries are important, why political regimes destroy them, and why their destruction is a threat to world culture and multiculturalism. The sentiments I express about cultural destruction are very close, if not identical, to those flowing from the United Nations; indeed, sanctions against the destruction of culture is an agenda item within the international community.

No book is written without the support of family, friends, and colleagues. Particular thanks go to Barbara Parker, Ed Knuth, Edith Kays, and Edith and Art Wartburg. My gratitude also goes to Harbhans Bhola, Daniel Callison, John Cole, Martha Crosby, Michael Hoffman, David Kaser, Anthony Marsella, Edward McClellan, James Raven, Britain Washburn, and George Whitbeck for their faith and interest in the project or the opportunities and support that they provided at various critical points in my career. Special aloha to Donna Bair-Mundy, Lynn Davis, Carol Langner, Gail Morimoto, Diane Nahl, Helen Nakano, Deborah Nelson, Sunyeen Pai, Luz Quiroga, Miriam Reed, and Zoe Shinno. And I want to thank my students in the Library and Information Science Program at the University of Hawaii for providing feedback and encouragement. These in particular stand out: Susan Johnson, Colleen Lashaway, Joyce Yukawa, and Donna Bair-Mundy. Special thanks also go to David French, who suggested the appropriateness of the word "libricide," Ellen Chapman, who prepared the index, and Alfonso Eugene Molcilo who provided invaluable support. Most importantly, I wish to thank and acknowledge Charlene Gilmore, whose personal editing and insights immeasurably improved the quality of the book.

REFERENCES

Charny, Israel. 1996. Foreward to *Is the Holocaust Unique?: Perspectives on Comparative Genocide*, ed. Alan S. Rosenbaum. Boulder, Colorado: Westview Press, ix–xi.

Fischer, David Hacker. 1970. *Historians' Fallacies: Toward a Logic of Historical Thought*. New York: Harper Perennial.

Knuth, Rebecca. "The Destruction of Libraries in World War II: Total War, Libricide, and the Bombing of Cities." [unpublished manuscript]

Knuth, Rebecca. 1999. *"Understanding Genocide: Beyond Remembrance or Denial."* (paper presented at International Law, Human Rights, and Refugee Health and Wellbeing Conference, Honolulu, Hawaii, November 14–18).

Markusen, Eric, and David Kopf. 1995. *The Holocaust and Strategic Bombing: Genocide and Total War in the Twentieth Century*. Boulder, Colorado: Westview.

Simpson, Elizabeth, ed. 1997. *The Spoils of War: World War II and Its Aftermath: The Loss, Reappearance, and Recovery of Cultural Property*. New York: H.N. Abrams.

Chapter 1

BOOKS, LIBRARIES, AND THE PHENOMENON OF ETHNOCIDE

"Man can commit atrocities, or incite others to commit them, not because of a personality disorder, but because of his belief in ideas that provoke and justify atrocities."

(Anzulovic 1999, 118)

Many people respond to the violent destruction of books and libraries with deep emotion. The sadness and fear in eyewitness accounts convey a sense that the destruction of texts signifies not only the immediate breakdown of order and peace, but also a compromised future. The victims' sense of loss, shared by many throughout the world, is tied to the perception that books and libraries are the living tissue of culture; the burning of books (as burning is often the means to their end) thus violates ideals of truth, beauty, and progress—and civilization itself. For centuries, the metaphors of writers have suggested "the human race may have converted books or the essence of books anthropomorphically into human beings. . . . . [They argue for] the prevalence of a deep-seeded mythic view that books are living beings" (Stern 1989, 14–15). Accounts of destruction often express this personification in their titles. Some examples of this would be the Croatian Library Association's 1993 booklet, *Wounded Libraries in Croatia,* and Hilda Uren Stubbings's book *Blitzkrieg and Books: British and European Libraries as Casualties of World War II.* While the English language, which presents life as biologically centered, is profoundly inadequate in expressing the animation and life-essence that exists in literature, poems, and other written works, witnesses often defy these limitations in their attempts to describe some vital entity that dies when books are destroyed. In a lecture on Nazi book burning, Guy Stern (1989) drew upon his experience as a witness to the fires and quoted Milton: "Books are not absolutely dead things, but do contain a potency of life in them to be as active as that soul was whose progeny they are. . . ." This poignant description of the burning of the National Library in Sarajevo is by a former librarian, then Bosnia's assistant minister for science: "The attack lasted less than half an hour. The fire lasted into the next day. The sun was obscured by the smoke of books, and all over the city sheets of burned paper, fragile pages of grey ashe (sic), floated down like a dirty black snow. Catching a page you could feel its heat, and for a moment read a fragment of text in a strange kind of black and grey negative, until, as the heat dissipated, the page melted to dust in your hand" (Bakarsic 1994, 14).

In addition to their innate vitality, books animate societies, and libraries collect the stories that give shape and meaning to our lives, helping individuals and cultures to orient and know themselves, to connect with each other, "self to self, past to future, and future to past. Our stories are the link across the gulfs of time and individuality. Indeed, human trauma may be defined as the *blow which interrupts the story,* whether personal or collective, breaking the continuity of time and human relations, and thus blocking the ongoing formation of a meaningful whole" (Wheeler 1993, xvi). Over centuries, many have arrived at the belief that culture and human advancement are the "result of a long, painful, massive, ceaseless accumulation of records" (Besterman 1946, 174)—that a living, developing community is inseparable from its records, and that destruction of these records reduces cultural viability and influences retrogression. Thus, mixed with laments over intentional destruction, expressions of outrage and anger also exist. Victims often attribute assaults on books to a fanatic and crazy hatred of life, learning, memory, and civilization and frequently typify the perpetrators as barbaric or Stone-Aged. In an article about the Nigerian Civil War, the damage to Nigeria's libraries was compared to the barbarians' indiscriminate sacking of Medieval Roman collections (Oluwakuyide 1972). A Croatian characterized the destruction of Zadar's historic monuments and libraries in a similar way:

> . . . in old Glagolitic documents, books and inscriptions, they [the Serbs] saw only enemies that should be destroyed to make place for their own books and monuments of the Balkan cultural and civilization level, the only one they could reach. Everything above that level should be destroyed or

plundered, as the Barbarians had destroyed the Roman cities and the Latin written word towards the end of the Classical Age. *Furor barbaricus* now at the end of the twentieth century has its Balkan counterpart in Croatia—*furor Serbicus.* (Stipcevic 1993,7)

Sadness and anger are twin responses to the shadow cast by violence and abnormality, the absence of order and security, and the apparent senselessness of the destruction. Cultural heritage has been assaulted; religious and cultural identities have been violated. Gone are the physical artifacts that link a people to a region or to a system of beliefs, and in their place grows the fear that society and humanity will cease to exist altogether (Fulford 1993). Indeed, the historical record draws a clear correlation between the decline of libraries and the decay of civilization. Libraries flourish best when civilizations are at a summit of high culture (Wallerstein and Stephens 1978). Their destruction undermines mankind's expectations of progress and, when enacted on a large scale, reminds us of the potential for self-destruction that lurks in every society. World war and ecological degradation have fostered an awareness of the interdependence of all societies, in which the self-destructiveness of one nation affects the well-being of all. This may well be the premise for legal definitions of the destruction of libraries as a criminal act and a direct threat to the values of culture, and civilization itself. We acknowledge, perhaps subconsciously, that where literature exists, there is civilization; without books, civilization falters.

The systematic destruction of books and libraries illustrates the reality that barbarism and the threat of civilization's breakdown cannot be consigned to history books—a realization that only compounds the trauma for contemporary societies. The disintegration of Yugoslavia shattered international complacency in an abrupt demonstration that "the terrible European past remained a part, a potential, of the European present" (Pfaff 1993, 83). The agent—in this case, the Serbs—tried to destroy a people "by obliterating all records, monuments of the past, creative works, and fruits of the heart written down in books or engraved in stone" (Balic 1993, 75). In Bosnia, when the material artifacts of Muslim presence were expunged, multiculturalism—"the singular, defining character of Bosnia itself"—was also under attack (Balic 1993, 75). In twentieth-century Asia, the Communists also took ideology to the brink. The Chinese attacked all that was traditional in their own civilization and, in Tibet, launched campaigns against Buddhism and its texts as part of a generalized assault on the independent and cohesive Tibetan civilization. In Cambodia, radicals under Pol Pot denied all modern structures of recorded knowledge, dumping books as if they were waste materials, smashing eyeglasses, and killing all those who could read. Such fanatical attacks on the fabric of modernity compromised the identity and security of millions of human beings.

When we speak of "modernity," we are referring to the phase in post-Renaissance Western cultural development that emerged in response to outdated social, economic, and political systems. The engine behind its advance, the printing press, provided the means by which religious hegemony could be broken. A proliferation of print resources and the subsequent spread of information enabled science and technology to flourish, new notions of individualism and human rights to develop, and a new unit of group identity—the nation—to emerge. Each nation was a geographically defined entity bound together by a common culture (a fabricated one, if need be) and a sense of unity referred to as "nationalism." Substituting a consensual identity for the homogeneity previously enforced by religion and tribes, nationalism facilitated the development of civil societies, industrialization, and the further spread of literacy. But nationalism took a toxic turn when its orientation in key countries shifted from identification to entitlement and became linked with militarism and imperialism. As advances in weaponry and communications technology accelerated, the lethal trilogy of nationalism, militarism, and imperialism became counterproductive to modernity, human progress, and peace.

In the twentieth century, during periods of social trauma and depleted resources, nationalists and revolutionaries seized power, consolidated their control, and imposed state ideologies that invested political policies with the sanctity of holy mandates. The benefits of national identity were transformed into dangerous rationales for cross-cultural competition as totalitarian governments of both the left and right imposed orthodoxy internally, and then externally. The world was divided into adherents or enemies and any individual or member of a group in the latter category had to be negated. The fact that political ideologues target their enemies' identity, which, though intangible, is witnessed by material culture, ensured that twentieth-century warfare would include attacks on more than military targets. Thus, extremist regimes subjected their enemies to ethnocide, the destruction of a group's culture, because no individual or group had any merit or entitlements outside of the extremists' collective vision. Totalitarian regimes demanded complete adherence, with the ideology practiced fervently as a secular religion and superseding all other commitments, including moral and ethical ones. Evidence of ties to traditional religions or loyalty to alternate social or political creeds was considered as markers of enemies of the state.

Those who rejected such absolutism drew sustenance from either a religion, such as Buddhism, or from humanism, an alternate belief system that resisted extremism by focusing on the individual rather than the collective (as its Latin root, *humanus,* "centered on human beings," indicates). Early humanists of the fourteenth and fifteenth centuries had rejected the intellectual censorship of the Roman Catholic Church. During the eighteenth-century Enlightenment period, humanists intensified their insistence on the need to pry "intellectual activity away from the shackles of religion and to irradiate human life not with assurance of God's mercy but with knowledge" (Jackson and McLeish 1993, 356). The legacy of the Enlightenment was an emphasis on individual intellectual and cultural achievement rather than dogma; this very shift is responsible for introducing the idea of free inquiry and, by extension, science. By the twentieth century, humanism had come to be associated with democratic societies, where it took the form of generalized ideas and ideals such as equality, pluralism, individualism, tolerance, and human rights. Though humanistic regimes were capable of callous measures when threatened (as when the Allies, avowed humanists, employed carpet bombing against the Nazis and Japanese Imperialists), such twentieth-century regimes usually eschewed attacks on cultural institutions—and more generally true—supported international laws that prohibit the gratuitous destruction of cultural artifacts.

Popular historian Barbara Tuchman's 1980 address at the Library of Congress describes the humanist's attitude toward books: "Books are the carriers of civilization. Without books, history is silent, literature dumb, science crippled, thought and speculation at a standstill. Without books, the development of civilization would have been impossible. They are engines of change, windows on the world, and (as a poet has said) 'lighthouses erected in the sea of time.' They are companions, teachers, magicians, bankers of the treasures of the mind. Books are humanity in print" (Tuchman 1980,13). This notion is a cornerstone of twentieth-century humanism. The well-being and future of people is linked with the well-being and future of books and libraries. Like an article of faith, Tuchman's words have emotional and rational resonance. The angst in humanists' accounts of the destruction of libraries carries a sense of personal trauma akin to accounts of the destruction of groups of people (especially of children). Books, like children, are objects of affection, vessels for society's hopes and aspirations, links between past and future, and barriers to mortality. While this analogy may seem labored, the kinship between books and humans provides a theoretical framework for libricide, the regime-sponsored, ideologically driven destruction of books and libraries, that is illuminating and meaningful. Libricide, in fact, shares the same theoretical universe as genocide, government-authorized mass murder that is the most horrific aspect of twentieth-century political history. This book asserts that regimes that commit genocide also destroy the material expressions of their victims' culture, books and libraries.

Let us now explore the phenomenon of mass destruction. The twentieth century has been called the bloodiest of all centuries. Government-authorized mass murder of *civilians*—not soldiers—accounted for most of the deaths that occurred throughout the century, from the Germans' extermination of the Herreros of South Africa from 1904–1907 to the ethnic cleansing of Muslims by Serbs in the 1990s. Along with an increase in human casualties, state-sponsored destruction of culture rose dramatically. New terms, genocide and ethnocide, were coined to describe these practices, but definitions of the two terms have remained in a state of flux, beleaguered by political and semantic issues. The five instances of twentieth-century political violence involving libricide discussed in this book (in Nazi Germany, in China during the Cultural Revolution, in Tibet, in Kuwait during Iraq's occupation, and in Bosnia) present a case for the relationship between the destruction of books and libraries in the twentieth century and the practice of genocide and ethnocide. "Libricide" is used to refer specifically to a component of ethnocide and suggests the shared character of the two. In this book, the proposed framework for libricide is drawn from a variety of sources, but owes a special debt to Ervin Staub's (1989) application of the dynamics of mass violence to explain genocide.

The terms "genocide" and "ethnocide" are products of the twentieth century, but they describe practices that have occurred throughout history. Governments have long been perpetrators of mass murder (most often during war) and have destroyed the culture of other groups under various circumstances: through colonization, as collateral war damage, to express dominance or impose orthodoxy, or to take revenge. However, many of these events were not recorded, either because of the totality of the annihilation or because of the control exercised by the perpetrators over information about the atrocities. Attempts to conceal mass destruction in this century are no less prevalent, but modern communication systems now convey images and texts that give unflinching testimony to violence that might otherwise be hidden from the world.

It was the truly unprecedented annihilation of six million Jews by the Nazis that led to the use of a new term, "genocide," which combined the Greek *genos,* meaning "race" or "tribe," and *cide,* meaning "killing." Coined in the 1930s by Raphael Lemkin, an émigré jurist who later lost seventy family members in the Holocaust, the term spread rapidly after Nazi atrocities were revealed. It was institutionalized in a 1946 United Nations resolution (96-I) that condemned genocide and in a 1948 convention that banned it. Unfortunately, the new law lacked a means of enforcement, and the United Nations has either ignored occurrences of genocide (as in the Hutus' massacre of Tutsis in Rwanda in 1994) or passed toothless resolutions of condemnation that fell short of advocating deterrence. For example, UN resolutions in 1960, 1961, and 1965 condemning the Chinese government's human rights violations in Tibet had no effect on ongoing policies aimed at the destruction of traditional Tibetan culture; indeed, political and social violence accelerated in the decade of the Cultural Revolution, from 1966 to 1976. Only in the 1990s, after the disintegration of Yugoslavia, did the United Nations begin to experiment with legal actions against perpetrators of genocide by launching the International War Crimes Tribunal.

This recalcitrance has stemmed in part from the United Nations' deviation from Lemkin's definition, brought on by intense lobbying by colonialists and Communists. Lemkin had characterized genocide broadly as the state's deliberate and systematic annihilation of a national, religious, or racial group. By his definition, the significance of genocidal acts extends beyond the loss of lives, for the destruction brings about the disintegration of the targeted group's political and social institutions, culture, language, national feelings, and religion, as well as its economic structure. From this perspective, genocide might be seen as a composite that would include even nonlethal actions that diminish the viability of a group. This definition would encompass the destruction of a group's books and libraries, among other cultural materials and institutions. However, the United Nations' 1948 convention narrowly defined genocide as actions, involving *bodily harm and physical circumstances,* committed with the intent to destroy, in whole or in part, a national, ethnic, racial, or religious group.

This definition excluded attacks on a group's culture or institutions. Thus, the term "ethnocide" was unofficially introduced to describe the organized commission of specific acts with intent to extinguish *culture,* utterly or in substantial part. This could include deprivation of the opportunity to use a language, to practice a religion, to create art in customary ways, to maintain basic social institutions, to preserve memories and traditions, and so on (Beardsley 1976). Genocide, then, is the "denial of the right of existence of entire human groups, as homicide is the denial of the right to live of individual human beings" (General Assembly Resolution 96-I), while ethnocide is the destruction of a culture without necessarily

killing its bearers (Kuper 1981). While the precedent for banning destruction of cultural institutions exists in international law (for instance, the
1954 Hague Convention for the Protection of Cultural Property in the
Event of Armed Conflict), progress toward substantive prohibitive mechanisms, sanctions, and legal retribution has been minimal. However, in
1999 the crisis in the former Yugoslavia resulted in the addition of a new
protocol to the Hague Convention and the formation of the UNESCO-
linked Committee of the Blue Shield, which took its name from the Hague
Convention's symbol for protected cultural property.

The coining of the terms "ethnocide" and "genocide" reflects a dis-
tinctly modern, analytical understanding of complex atrocities as phenomena with recognizable patterns. But it also opens the door to misconstruing
events that are remotely similar. The terms "ethnocide" and "genocide"
have come to be used loosely, and often acts of ethnocide are labeled as
genocide (echoing Lemkin's ideas). Confusion also has arisen because
genocide and ethnocide often occur sequentially (ethnocide serving as a
precursor to genocide, as in Nazi Germany) and simultaneously (as in
Tibet and Bosnia). And, toward the end of the century, the use of the terms
became increasingly erratic and conflated, especially when used by politicians, activists, and the public as general terms to express moral outrage
(Andreopoulos 1994).

With any complex phenomenon, common elements and causal mechanisms emerge when events are compared and analyzed in an historical
context (Maier 1988), but research into genocide and ethnocide has been
problematic where the politically charged issue of definitions is concerned.
Scholars cannot achieve consensus on qualifying conditions; politicians
are hounded by debate over semantics because of the implications of labeling cases with these grave but vague terms. International law clearly
labels genocide as criminal, but the burden of enforcement is costly in
political and financial terms. Ultimately, political considerations deflect
attention from condemning specific incidences, identifying genocide as a
universal problem, and addressing deeper issues involved in mass genocide and ethnocide, such as sovereignty, agency, and responsibility for
prevention, retribution, or reconciliation.

Despite the obstacles discussed in the previous paragraph, in the fifty
years since the United Nations offered its definition of genocide, research
on the subject has made some progress, particularly in establishing a connection between modern genocide and ideology. In 1976 Irving Horowitz
(1976) wrote of genocide as "a structural and systematic destruction of
innocent people by a state bureaucratic apparatus," as policy implemented
in an effort to assure conformity with its ideology and model of society.

Since then, "ideological" has been frequently cited in typological studies. In Helen Fein's (1984) typology, the fourth category is named "ideological," citing violence against those who are cast as enemies of the state's "hegemonic myth." Many scholars now view ideologically motivated genocide as the most prevalent form occurring in the twentieth century. Evidence of Communist genocides engineered by Stalin, Mao, and Pol Pot strengthened the ideological connection and revealed another flaw in the United Nations' definition: the omission of political groups as certifiable victims. Scholars have moved to address the issue of excluded groups; for example, in Frank Chalk and Kurt Jonassohn's 1990 study, *The History and Sociology of Genocide,* genocide is defined as "a form of one-sided mass killing in which a state or other authority intends to destroy a group, *as that group and membership in it are defined by the perpetrator*" [emphasis added] (Chalk and Jonassohn 1990, 23).

Though the subject of ethnocide has not received the depth of attention given to genocide, theories applied to the latter also may be applied to the destruction of a group's culture for the simple reason that these acts stem from the same impulse towards negation. Either the group and/or its cultural expressions are perceived as threatening and standing in the way of extremists' goals. The word "libricide," to date used rarely—and, then, vaguely—to refer to the "murder" of a book, becomes useful when it looks to genocide and ethnocide as parent terms and distinguishes that which targets books and libraries from other state-sponsored cultural destruction. Used in this sense, it becomes a more precise category, delineating patterns that occur within the larger context of ethnocide. As the voice and memory of the targeted group, books and libraries are central to culture and identity. Texts, especially when part of diverse collections, are vital in sustaining a group's uniqueness and protecting the group from the homogeneity promoted by extremists. To those who align themselves with extreme political ideologies, books and libraries are either tools of the regime or enemies of the state—the weapon of those who wish to undermine the government. Libricide (as well as genocide and ethnocide) is *not* the sum of spontaneous crimes of passion committed by barbarians, as is commonly thought, but a method of problem-solving that is deliberate and systematic. It is a solution that employs violence and compromises human rights in serving a collective good that is narrowly defined by ideology.

To those who value human rights and define humanity as a community extending beyond national and ethnic boundaries, the destruction of any one group or its culture has devastating ramifications for the entire species. Organizations like the United Nations, operating in the interests of human rights, multiculturalism, and world peace, deliver this disapproval through resolutions, conventions, and coalitions. But the dilemma of sovereignty versus human rights still dominates foreign affairs, even among international organizations and political structures professing multiculturalism. As a result, genocide, ethnocide, and libricide remain prerogatives of power. With little or no enforcement of conventions outlawing mass murder, it is not surprising that the destruction of culture, especially books and libraries, commands even less attention. The real issue linking the two is that mass violence, whether targeted at physical or cultural entities, weakens the human race. As Tibet and Cambodia have taught us, cultural destruction effectively turns individuals into ghosts and slaves, depleting the world's intellectual and spiritual reservoirs and diminishing the cultural heritage of the species.

In a century shaped by global self-consciousness, extremist ideologies (such as communism and exclusionary nationalism) have been the mobilizing force behind attacks on value systems such as humanism, democracy, and multiculturalism. Extremist ideologies are linked with anti-cosmopolitanism and anti-intellectualism, as illustrated by this story.

> In 1987, troops on a Soviet Army Base in Lithuania cleaned out a warehouse and dumped into a nearby field a store of rare books looted from a Prussian noble's library after World War II. The books included the 1534 Wittenberg Bible (a first edition of Martin Luther's translation of the Bible into German), a first edition of Mercator maps of Eastern Europe, and a 1785 volume of string quartets with a dedication by Mozart to Haydn. After a year in which the collection was exposed to rain and snow, Lithuanian librarians fearfully asked permission to salvage it. The officer's chilling response was: "You want those old books? Take them. They are shit." (Lesley 1994, 582)

The ignorance and provincialism of the officer has a disturbing effect on most educated people, who are shocked that someone with no appreciation of such materials should come to have power over them. However, in the spectrum of barbaric acts (progressing from ignorance to random destructive tendencies, spite or revenge, domination, negation, and finally annihilation) this incident is hardly significant. But the officer's disdain for old books does trigger memories of the destruction of the Alexandrian Library, an event long associated with a barbaric aversion to written culture (Thiem 1979). Those holding attitudes associated with modernity and humanism might judge the officer as malicious; on the other hand, behavior involving overt destruction has been labeled "evil." The mass murders perpetrated by extremist ideologues (Hitler, Stalin, Mao, Saddam, and Milosevic) raise doubts in bystanders about human nature. Indeed, the breach of taboos concerning the connection between people and their written records demands that evil and psychopathology be contemplated.

By the onset of World War II, man could be perceived as turned upon himself, deliberately striving to destroy the instruments of the mind, including books and libraries (Staub 1989). To intellectuals of the time, such as Archibald MacLeish (1942), mankind (as represented by the Nazis) appeared to be sick and writhing in the throes of ignorance and envy, seduced by propaganda that presented all learning, all enlightenment, and all distinction of the mind as false and foolish. MacLeish knew that it was often the intellectuals, the artists, the writers, and the scholars who were sought and killed by the Nazis. When he contemplated the books that were banned or burned or sequestered, the teachers who were silenced, the publications that were shut down, he found it difficult to insist that the world of art and learning existed apart from the revolution of the times. MacLeish was not alone in insisting that the revolution was against the mind and its offspring—a revolution of ignorance, violence, and superstition against the city of truth. For the humanist, World War II was evil rampant. Poets such as W.H. Auden knew that in those years, "Maps can really point to places/Where life is evil now; Nanking; Dachau."

Cultural and genocidal violence did not end with World War II. They have persisted as a function of the politics of both the right *and* the left. The violations committed by Communists have been less visible, acknowledged, and documented than those of the Fascists; information from such closed societies has been less readily available. But whispers of Stalin's destruction of national and ethnic groups circulated for years. Escapees brought tales of a maniacal revolution in Mao's China in the 1960s that savaged not only traditional printed culture and intellectuals, but also the entire Chinese population. An international network publicized conditions in Tibet where an ancient culture and its manuscripts were decimated. The world discovered to its horror that in the 1970s Pol Pot's regime killed off all vestiges of literacy and modernity in addition to massacring one-sixth to one-seventh of all Cambodians. But in each of these cases, knowledge of the acts against humanity reached the global public after the fact. As a result, it was horrifying to have the implosion of Yugoslavia in the 1990s played out in real time on the nightly news. Global audiences were exposed to "ethnic cleansing" in which groups obliterated each other's heritages and triggered vicious cycles of retaliation.

Questions of pathology emerged. Margaret Thatcher referred to "evil" in connection with the slaughter in Srebenica in 1993 (Pfaff 1993). Journalist Peter Maas (1996) wrote about a "wild beast" that was neither animal nor human, but a spirit of evil that exists in all animals, all people, all societies: "Bosnia can teach about the wild beast, and therefore about ourselves." Such comments (and, of course, the systemic violence itself) raised questions about whether extreme destructiveness is a latent component in all peoples or whether particular groups could be uniquely possessed by evil. Is the veneer of civilization so thin as to be easily stripped away? The violence in Yugoslavia caused many observers to revert to the assumption that a specific people, temporarily possessed by evil, commits genocide, and indeed, the extremism of the Serbs seemed to require this explanation. Too often, essential though it is, the subject of evil has dominated discussion of twentieth-century events. Using the notion of evil to explain atrocities easily becomes a distraction from confronting and struggling with the human capacity for extreme violence. For the most part, academics have hesitated to use the word "evil" because it infuses discussion with emotionality, subjectivity, and the incalculable, and it short-circuits the exploration of the multitude of factors that precipitate and sustain the kind of violence under study. Nevertheless, the sheer scale and malignity of the events of this century did cause some academic psychologists to consider the possibility of "cultural pathology" and attribute the violent behavior of groups to specific societal conditions and responses. Still, the focus remained on the individual. These psychologists agreed that, under the stresses of sociocultural violence, individuals could reject previously held values, assume extremist beliefs, and become pathological. Chinese writer Ba Jin described such an experience during the Cultural Revolution:

> [Literary classics were destroyed] as if they were rats crossing the streets. I myself destroyed books, magazines, letters and manuscripts which I had kept as treasures for years. . . . There was a time when I really believed that only a few formulistic stories were literature. All the rest were garbage. I totally and completely negated myself. I lost the sense of right and wrong. I saw neither the past nor the future. I had no opinion of my own, and I lived without using my mind. I lowered my head. . . . I was really bedeviled. . . . I completely negated myself, literature and beauty. . . . I even believed that an ideal society was one where there was no culture, no knowledge, and of course no literary resources. I was in a trance. (as quoted in Ting 1983, 148)

In the last half of the twentieth century, Western mental-health professionals and scientists, believing that problems originate in the minds of individuals, extrapolated from psychological research on the individual in order to explain motivations for social phenomena. Findings from Stanley Milgram's (1974) electric-shock studies, in which subjects were induced through incremental steps, sanctioned by authority figures, to inflict dangerously high levels of electrical shock on other human beings, have been used to explain the mass participation by Germans in the genocide of the Jews. Debates over focus on the individual are part of the politics of scholarship; the biomedical (individual-centered) approach has been increasingly countered by cultural psychiatry and related viewpoints in the social sciences such as psychiatric anthropology and cultural psychology. Reflecting postmodernist perspectives, these positions reverse cause and effect and allow the pathogenic individual to be seen as a product of a dysfunctional society—that is, subjected to generalized brutality, powerlessness, marginalization, and inequality.

> Thus, mental health is not only about biology and psychology, but also about education, economics, social structure, religion, and politics. There can be no mental health where there is powerlessness, because powerlessness breeds despair. There can be no mental health where there is poverty, because poverty breeds hopelessness. There can be no mental health where there is inequality, because inequality breeds anger and resentment. There can be no mental health where there is racism, because racism breeds low self-esteem and self-denigration; and lastly, there can be no mental health where there is cultural disintegration and destruction, because cultural disintegration and destruction breed confusion and conflict. (Marsella and Yamada 2000,10)

Despite this emphasis on social relationships as the origin of psychological dysfunction, the postmodernists continue to resist characterizing a society as pathological.

There are, of course, practical reasons to avoid making the nation the primary unit of analysis. Empirical laboratory research would be impossible with a subject so large as a nation, and sovereignty issues further complicate matters: what, after all, would be the international community's responsibilities toward a "sick state"? Broad explanations might be satisfying, but by making categorical generalizations about an entire nation, we risk over-simplification and attributions of collective guilt (the idea that an entire people can be held responsible for current and past national atrocities). A few psychologists have explored the issues of cultural pathology and parted ways with ethnographers who allege that societal practices almost always have adaptive value within a society. For example, Robert Edgerton (1992), in his book, *Sick Societies,* argues that all societies have some maladaptive practices and that some populations have become seriously disordered as a result of pathogenic values and paranoid constructions of reality. In 1969, Lewis Coser wrote an article entitled "The Visibility of Evil." His premise was that any society requires for its operation the performance of certain roles that are rarely admitted by that society's members (examples might be police brutality or elitist educational policies). While "good citizens" may be convinced that these roles are "necessary," they nevertheless try to shield themselves from knowledge about the events that occur. Genocide and ethnocide may be extreme manifestations of this phenomenon where the unsettling behavior also is defended by denying the essential humanity of a victim group. Because external observers are neither shielded from the actions nor convinced of the pathology of the victim group, they helplessly construe the actions as evil run rampant.

At this point, it is useful to turn to the field of ethics, the "systematic examination of the relations of human beings to each other"—ideas about how one treats one's fellow man, values, and beliefs about how life should be lived (Berlin 1991,1). From this perspective, the battles over ideas that shaped the last century can be viewed as attempts to define what and who is human, and then to set rules as to how human beings should live in society—and who must be excluded from it altogether (Bartov 2000). Libraries became battlegrounds between humanists, for whom the destruction of books was the destruction of human potential—that which advances and uplifts individuals and society—and extremists, for whom a specific instance of destruction was instrumental, a "liberating, redemptive act" for humanity (Bartov 2000, 30). According to Omer Bartov (2000), the outside world's disbelief that such acts of wanton destruction and ruthless plunder could be perceived as glorious is a reflection of humanistic sentiments, and exposes the limits of the humanists' moral universe and imaginations. Cultural psychologists and scholars of genocide have just begun to sift through the tangled web of individual accountability versus group pathology—and the absolution this shared dysfunction implies.

While issues of evil, barbarism, and pathology raised by the destruction of books and libraries have been constructively informed by new ideas from cultural psychology, the key to comparative analysis lies in a more comprehensive theoretical framework, one that links genocide and political violence. In this framework, destruction is viewed as resulting from responses to disruptive social conditions, including a frantic embrace of ideas that resonate with local values and offer the illusion of salvation. These ideas form the basis for utopian visions whose accomplishment justifies any action. This framework is broad enough to accommodate insights from many disciplines and multicausal explanations such as the idea that destruction to a particular culture may occur because a society becomes quasi-psychotic, *and* because the evil residing in human nature has resulted in a reversion to barbarism, *and* because of a combination of social disruption, ideology, and extremist leadership. Such a broad framework sustains the goal of this book, which is to open the door to various methods of analysis. What this study explicitly rejects is simplistic explanations of the systemic destruction of books and libraries as merely (or even primarily) the expression of barbarism and evil, in order to open discussion of some fundamental questions. Why are books and libraries deliberately destroyed? What is the connection between libricide and political violence? What is the impact of libricide on individuals and society? How are ideas used to justify the destruction of books? What sociocultural conditions favor such destruction? And, as a seminal issue, on what basis are books and libraries valued? It is with this last question that I begin, for only through a deepened understanding of the cultural needs that books and libraries fulfill can we begin to understand the motivation behind their destruction and the high cultural stakes involved.

REFERENCES

Andreopoulos, George J. 1994. "Introduction: The Calculus of Genocide." In *Genocide: Conceptual and Historical Dimensions*, ed. George J. Andreopoulos. Philadelphia: University of Pennsylvania Press,1–28.

Anzulovic, Branimir. 1999. *Heavenly Serbia: From Myth to Genocide.* New York: New York University Press.

Bakarsic, Kemal. 1994. "The Libraries of Sarajevo and the Book That Saved Our Lives." *The New Combat* (autumn):13–15.

Balic, Smail. 1993. "Culture Under Fire." In *Why Bosnia? Writings on the Balkan War*, eds. Rabia Ali and Lawrence Lifschultz. Stony Creek, Connecticut: Pamphleteer's Press, 75–83.

Bartov, Omer. 2000. *Mirrors of Destruction: War, Genocide, and Modern Identity.* Oxford: Oxford University Press.

Beardsley, Monroe C. 1976. "Reflections on Genocide and Ethnocide." In *Genocide in Paraguay,* ed. Richard Arens. Philadelphia: Temple University Press, 85–101.

Berlin, Isaiah. 1991. *The Crooked Timber of Humanity: Chapters in the History of Ideas,* ed. Henry Hardy. New York: Alfred A. Knopf.

Besterman, Theodore. 1946. "International Library Rehabilitation and Planning." *Journal of Documentation* 2 (1):174–180.

Chalk, Frank, and Kurt Jonassohn. 1990. *The History and Sociology of Genocide: Analyses and Case Studies.* New Haven, Connecticut: Yale University Press.

Coser, Lewis. 1969. "The Invisibility of Evil." *Journal of Social Issues* 25 (1):101–109.

Edgerton, Robert B. 1992. *Sick Societies: Challenging the Myth of Primitive Harmony*. New York: The Free Press.

Fein, Helen. 1984. "Scenarios of Genocide: Models of Genocide and Critical Responses." In *Toward the Understanding and Prevention of Genocide*, ed. Israel Charny. Boulder, Colorado: Westview Press, 3–31.

Fulford, Robert. 1993. "The Future of Memory: Cultural Institutions in Times of Radical Change." *Queen's Quarterly* 100 (4):785–796.

Horowitz, Irving. 1976. *Genocide: State Power and Mass Murder.* New Brunswick, New Jersey: Transaction.

Jackson, E.M., and Kenneth McLeish. 1993. *Key Ideas in Human Thought.* New York: Facts On File.

Kuper, Leo. 1981. *Genocide: Its Political Use in the Twentieth Century.* New Haven, Connecticut: Yale University Press.

Lesley, Van. 1994. "Abandoned in a Field: Librarians Save a Rare Bible." *American Libraries* 25 (6):582.

Maas, Peter. 1996. *Love Thy Neighbor: A Story of War.* New York: Alfred A. Knopf.

MacLeish, Archibald. 1942. "Toward an Intellectual Offensive." *ALA Bulletin* 36 (6):423–428.

Maier, Charles S. 1988. *The Unmasterable Past: History, Holocaust, and German National Identity.* Cambridge, Massachusetts: Yale University Press.

Marsella, Anthony J., and Ann Marie Yamada. 2000. "Culture and Mental Health: An Introduction and Overview of Foundations, Concepts, and Issues." In *The Handbook of Multicultural Mental Health: Assessment and Treatment of Diverse Populations*, eds. I. Cuellar and F. Paniagua. New York: Academic Press, 3–24.

Milgram, Stanley. 1974. *Obedience to Authority: An Experimental View.* New York: Harper and Row.

Oluwakuyide, Akinola. 1972. "Nigerian Libraries After the War." *Wilson Library Bulletin* 46 (10): 881–2, 947.

Pfaff, William. 1993. *The Wrath of Nations: Civilization and the Furies of Nationalism.* New York: Simon and Schuster.

Staub, Ervin. 1989. *Roots of Evil: The Origins of Genocide and Other Group Violence.* Cambridge: Cambridge University Press.

Stern, Guy. 1989. *Nazi Book Burning and the American Response.* Distinguished Lecture to the Friends of the Wayne State University Libraries, November 1, 1989. Detroit, Michigan: Wayne State University.

Stipcevic, Aleksandar. 1993. "Instead of an Introduction." In *Wounded Libraries in Croatia*, eds. Tatjana Aparac-Gazivoda and Dragutin Katalenac. Zagreb, Croatia: Croatian Library Association, 5–8.

Stubbings, Hilda Uren. 1993. *Blitzkrieg and Books: British and European Libraries As Casualties of World War II.* Bloomington, Indiana: Rubena Press.

Thiem, Jon. 1979. "The Great Library of Alexandria Burnt: Towards the History of a Symbol." *Journal of the History of Ideas* 40 (4):507–526.

Ting, Lee-hsia Hsu. 1983. "Library Services in the People's Republic of China: A Historical Overview." *Library Quarterly* 53 (2):134–160.

Tuchman, Barbara W. 1980. *The Book*. A Lecture Presented at the Library of Congress. Washington, D.C.: Library of Congress.

Wallerstein, Immanuel, and John Frank Stephens. 1978. *Libraries and Our Civilizations: A Report Prepared for the Governor of the State of New York*. Binghamton, New York: Fernand Braudel Center for the Study of Economies, Historical Systems, and Civilizations, State University of New York.

Wheeler, Gordon. 1993. "Translator's Introduction." In *The Collective Silence: German Identity and the Legacy of Shame*, eds. Barbara Heimannsberg and Christopher J. Schmidt. San Francisco: Jossey-Bass, xv–xxvii.

Chapter 2

THE EVOLUTION AND
FUNCTIONS OF LIBRARIES

"Library demolition is a sort of malign tribute to the power of
libraries."

(Line 1994, 6)

As societies grow in complexity, they increasingly depend on systems of
knowledge that serve to connect various types of behavior, apply lessons
from the past to future enterprises, and organize the indispensable activities of modern living. Written language fosters memory and makes these
memories retrievable in a body of literature whose value has partly to do
with the advantage it gives each generation over the last. When shared
and diffused, recorded memory allows a people to learn not just traditional
ways of life passed down by their own families and tribes, as the early
peoples did, but the traditions of many cultures and many eras (Fulford
1993). This enlarged experience makes possible the increased cultural
complexity of modern times. As long as a civilization exists, the preservation of experience, of social intelligence or "knowledge," is a derived
necessity. It must be passed down from one generation to another so that
a basic scaffolding of culture is always in place. With increased contact
and exchange, the instinct to keep one's culture intact is supplemented by
a drive to possess and adapt attractive elements of other cultures. At a
minimum, existing knowledge must be preserved because it constitutes
the substance of that which is specific to a civilization and that which
maintains not only identity, but cultural vitality. The erosion of knowledge

is a sure sign of cultural decline, as when Rome began to neglect its libraries in the last days of the empire. It is not surprising that in modern times, literate people, whether versed in history or informed by collective memory, have come to associate the destruction of books and libraries with barbarianism and a return to the Dark Ages.

The need to preserve the achievements of our time and our culture is a deeply human trait, an expression of the desire to transcend mortality. The book preserves information and knowledge in an easily produced, accessible form. The library organizes records of human activities into an institution (i.e. a component of culture) that is, to varying degrees, permanent and independent (Malinowski 1931). Books and libraries have come to serve many functions, both material and symbolic, and likewise embody certain values. It is worth remembering that while the formats of the materials housed in libraries have converged, the social and political functions that books and libraries serve have remained varied and controversial. It is the contests over these functions that frequently result in violence aimed at print materials.

THE ORIGINS OF LIBRARIES

Our knowledge of the earliest texts comes to us in historical fragments—eerie paintings on the walls of caves, tombs, and palaces; pieces of clay tablets and steles and assorted rubble. Driven by a basic need to preserve and communicate knowledge, early groups conveyed information first through pictures and symbols, then through increasingly abstract pictographs and ideographs, and eventually through alphabets. By the time alphabets appeared, the tradition of storing records was well established. The need for records that could be transmitted in a standardized form occurred with the advent of sophisticated commercial transactions and the formal government and education systems that characterize cities. In fact, historians have extrapolated that formal libraries began with the rise of cities. Cities, inevitable and indispensable when an economy becomes complex, sustain the level of surplus wealth that is necessary to support a civilization (Shapiro 1957).

Ever since written language evolved and information could be preserved and transmitted through time and space, experiments with media and storage have resulted in convergence of form (Pinch and Bijker 1987). Papyrus scrolls gave way to the vellum codex, which, in turn, yielded to the paper book. The artifact, "book," and the institution, "library," are social constructions emerging over centuries. Their formats and organizational structures ultimately display a fundamental uniformity, bowing as they must to the instrumental imperatives of culture. As useful forms evolved, they were diffused widely. The evolution of urban societies gave rise to needs that supplied impetus to the development of books and libraries; books (especially since the advent of the printing press) and libraries, in turn, have accelerated urbanization and exerted tremendous influence upon the progress of literacy and modern culture (Hua 1996).

Some of the earliest known libraries were Egyptian and date back to approximately 3000 B.C. By that time a written language had evolved and trained scribes were keeping records in archives. Temple and palace libraries developed as the sophistication of religious and governmental documents increased and a secular literature evolved. While we have only remnants of evidence as to Egyptian library history, in Mesopotamia (the land of the Sumerians and Assyrians) clay tablet collections have revealed a virtually continuous story of library development beginning in approximately 3000 B.C. (Harris 1995). The Sumerians are believed to be the first literate people, their earliest texts appearing around 3200 B.C. (Reichmann 1980). They developed archives of governmental, legal, and business records and preserved texts and treatises of religion, astrology, medicine, mathematics, literature, and even the beginnings of what we would call "history" (Krzys 1975). While we cannot be sure how well organized the Sumerian libraries were, we know that Assyrian libraries (which came later) were large and arranged by subject matter, with texts available through a primitive form of catalog. King Ashurbanipal (ca. 668–627 B.C.) was in possession of more than 30,000 clay tablets, which were made available to scholars; modern historians estimate that these tablets contained some 10,000 individual works, including many copies and translations of works from other cultures (Harris 1995). More than a half-million tablets have been preserved in the world's collections and estimates place original production at as much as ten times this number (Reichman 1980).

Ancient libraries typically existed to support the government officials, religious elites, and rulers who claimed legitimacy on religious grounds. The connection between written texts and religion has continued throughout history. For example, the Hebrews carried their national library in the mobile Ark of the Covenant (Krzys 1975); the Christian and Muslim religions both remain heavily dependent on written texts. Throughout history, texts and libraries have played an important role in preserving religious and dynastic records and in supporting the activities involved in running an empire. This role expanded as collections became support structures for scholarship and other intellectual activities of advanced civilizations.

Our ability to construct a history of libraries in classical Greece (between the sixth century B.C. and the third century A.D.) is hindered by the lack of physical remains. However, we can extrapolate from the individual accounts of scholars with libraries that perhaps early academic libraries existed and that the official collections of definitive copies of Greek plays may have served as the first rudimentary public libraries. Judging by the vast number of written works produced by the Greeks (only ten percent of which survives today), historians tend to assume that libraries were omnipresent. The greatest Greek library was, of course, the Alexandrian Library in Egypt, founded around 300 B.C. and later destroyed sequentially with perhaps the last section burning in 642 A.D. Staffed by outstanding librarians and scholars, the collection must have included most of the literature of that period; and, of course, its collections and scholars profoundly affected the scholarship of the time and after— the origins of liberal critical scholarship lie here (Vallance 2000). Its founders were visionaries of "the prototype of the great national, or universal, libraries of modern times" (Harris 1995, 47).

As empires rose and fell, the circumstances surrounding the destruction of libraries typically followed one of three major patterns. Some libraries were lost almost incidentally as part of the generalized ravaging of captured cities, palaces, and temples. Their destruction occurred as part of a ritual in which the enemy's cities were destroyed in the heat of battle, or as a price exacted for losing the war; such destruction reinforced the power and control of the victor. As texts came to be seen as valuable pieces of property, a second pattern emerged: In war, libraries and books became "loot" and were carried away at the prerogative of the victor. The removal of whole libraries demonstrated dominance in a new and different way from destroying them —the conquered people were humiliated, while the prestige and cultural patrimony of the conquering society was further enhanced. A third pattern evolved under religious or ideological mandates that labeled certain materials offensive and called for censorship through violent purging, or selective destruction. For example, among the different explanations for the ultimate demise of the great library at Alexandria is the hypothesis that alternate purging by religious groups (Christians and Muslims) was frequent, and that the destruction occurred not in a single catastrophic incident, but over time. All three patterns still figure into the destruction of books and libraries in the twentieth century.

The destruction of the Alexandrian Library has reverberated throughout Western civilization, becoming a symbol of either tragic loss or productive purging. Some view the loss of the historical and scientific records and collective memory as a disaster. For others, it was a costly triumph for the progress of mankind: the destruction of so encompassing a collection ultimately provided impetus for an even more creative future. For those in the first camp (perhaps the majority), this event exemplified the effect of time on the intellectual legacy of the past, and marked a grievous loss to the cumulative authority of classical learning (Thiem 1979). Allusions to the destruction of the Alexandrian Library frequently accompany modern accounts of attacks against books and libraries.

The great libraries of the classical world were destroyed by fire, disaster, war, internal conflicts, and eventually by barbarian raids. During the decline of the Roman Empire, libraries, many of which had been founded on collections looted in war, decayed and disappeared due to neglect. The historian Ammianus Marcellinus once complained, "The libraries are closing forever, like tombs" (Bingham et al. 1993, 259). Fortunately, during the height of the Roman Empire, the wealthy had built private libraries for personal use or prestige and Roman villa libraries may be credited with saving the classic Roman literature that survived the fall of Rome in A.D. 476 (Harris 1995).

The fall of Rome marked the beginning of a period of hard times for Western culture and its written expression. It has been said that the fate of libraries reflects the fate of culture in general, and certainly this was true during the early Middle Ages, when culture and libraries alike languished. Classical learning was kept alive during this time by the Arabs and by a string of European monasteries, where the preservation and copying of ancient texts became a part of religious practice: Monks in the Benedictine order, for example, copied texts as a practice of faith. Despite the depredations of the Vikings and the Magyars, scripture survived in Ireland, the Rhineland, and Northern Italy, and classical manuscripts were preserved, copied, and embellished to become works of art. In the East, although advanced centers of Greek learning had fallen into Muslim hands, a significant amount of classical literature was preserved and translated into Arabic. In the twelfth and thirteenth centuries, the learning of the Arab world, along with that of Byzantine, was passed to the West through war and trade.

Throughout the Middle Ages (from the late fifth century to the fourteenth century), church and mosque alike preserved the cultural products of antiquity while strictly controlling their use and dissemination and specifying their educational, research, and aesthetic roles (Wallerstein and Stephens 1978). In Europe, religious control over information began to erode in the 1300s with the Renaissance's revival of art, classical literature, and learning, and with the subsequent rise of humanism. During the Renaissance, Italian noblemen amassed large private collections and preserved

almost every important manuscript surviving at the time. In cities such as
Paris and Oxford, where the modern university began to evolve, acquisition of texts by university libraries supported the synthesis of Christian
and classical learning and culture. The first national collections emerged,
and the printing press (first developed in the mid-1400s) brought a secularization of knowledge that laid the social and cultural foundations for
modernity.

An increased access to books and texts and the subsequent spread of
literacy was responsible for exposing the corruption of religious leaders,
and ultimately led to the Protestant Reformation. The possibility of a new
relationship between man and God based on direct access to scripture
revolutionized ideas about the abilities and rights of the individual (first
expressed by humanism) and eventually played a part in revolutionary
activity and the evolution of democracy. With the advent of the printing
press came an increased use of vernacular languages (a change from the
dominance of Latin in the intellectual world); along with the development
of regional literatures came a consciousness that would eventually be expressed as nationalism. From the 1600s on, literacy promoted industrialization and the rise of a middle class, which in turn promoted literacy and
libraries in the circular pattern described earlier: libraries enhance cultural
development, and cultural growth fosters libraries. The extent to which
libraries were developed in the various European nations depended on the
economic resources available, the extent of literacy, the political stability
of the country, and the government's commitment to libraries (Harris
1995).

The fate of libraries has always been uncertain during times of political
instability. War almost inevitably causes the destruction of libraries; books
and print materials have been regularly carried off as loot just as often as
they have been caught in the line of fire. Napoleon was particularly fond
of confiscating precious books and libraries. Invading armies worldwide
have caused great damage, but some of the most extreme destruction came
from internal purging in times of religious and civil strife. In sixteenth-
century Britain, during the Protestant Reformation, extensive plundering
and dissolution of the cloister and monastery libraries occurred. It is estimated that only 2 percent of the 300,000 volumes in more than 800
monastery libraries survived the reformers (Billings 1990). Bibliophiles
quail at such daunting figures, while those who believe that book destruction can be positive point out that the reform activities weren't entirely
antagonistic to the cause of libraries. As a result of forced dissolution,
private and religious collections often became the property of the state
and, ultimately, more accessible to the general public. During the French

Revolution, for instance, revolutionaries seized the collections of Jesuits, monasteries, cathedral and church schools, and noblemen. Eight million confiscated books were declared national property and redistributed to form a network of municipal libraries centering around the *Bibliothèque Nationale* in Paris (Krzys and Litton 1983). Throughout history, major collections have undergone cycles of purging, diffusion, and redistribution, with both positive and negative results. Unfortunately, many books have failed to survive these cycles.

Theorists have posited that after its primitive beginnings, a culture proceeds naturally to develop political organization, artistic expression, and technology until decay sets in and the culture returns to a more primitive state. Books and libraries, according to this theory, are products of a culture during its stages of technological development. The remnants of texts that survive periods of cultural decay form the nucleus for subsequent advancement. This pattern was apparent in pre-modern China and in ancient civilizations in the West, where history seemed to be cyclic in the manner described in the Bible, "The thing that hath been, it is that which shall be; and that which is done is that which shall be done: and there is no new thing under the sun." Library history in the 2000 years of feudal culture in China is largely a story of the rise and fall of dynasties, each cycle accompanied by the removal and loss of books. Because bringing libraries into full participation in political life was important in all the dynasties (Hua 1996), a new collection system eventually emerged and traditional texts were resurrected. In many cases, the destructive inclination and action of particular emperors was countered by private Chinese book collectors who hid texts that might otherwise have vanished in periodic imperial purges, and who also undertook many of the social responsibilities of cultural exchange and the spread of information. Although power and collections in the Western world were less centralized, making literary heritage less vulnerable to the dictates of a single autocrat, collections nevertheless underwent cycles of destruction, diffusion, and reconstruction. An example, mentioned above, was the dispersal of elite-oriented libraries during the French Revolution and the subsequent reorganization of surviving books in public libraries.

As with the destruction of the Alexandrian library, these cycles can be viewed as either damaging or liberating to societies. The view that the cyclic destruction of libraries is inevitable has been made unacceptable by modern ideas regarding novelty in history, an improved lot for mankind, the perfectibility of the human race, and the existence of "progress" (Boorstin 1998). Those who believe that libraries sustain the human race find the destruction of libraries particularly repugnant because it negates notions of progress. In addition, it raises issues of cultural security for those aware of the threat posed by modern weapons. How much loss can a current culture sustain while remaining capable of regenerating? These concerns are nonexistent for radical revolutionaries whose political goals demand a clean slate, a cultural ground zero. Under Pol Pot's regime, the Cambodian government showed no compunction in destroying books and libraries—along with all people who could read. When books and libraries survive the ravages of war and political ideology, it is usually either through the cumulative efforts of individuals who love them or communities that value the functions that they fulfill.

A WEB OF ROLES AND RESPONSIBILITIES

The contents of books and libraries reflect the social and cultural needs of their societies; and the similarities between their forms across culture and time reflects the tendency of human minds, in certain stages of their development, to create similar institutions, social patterns, and civilizations (Krzys 1975). In the twentieth century, libraries with specialized services and functions have proliferated. Social and technological demands have made specialization necessary. At the same time, there is a mandate for individual libraries to participate in web-like systems of information production, storage, and dissemination. As a result, any library exists first within a local and national cultural system that includes authors, publishers, booksellers, scholars, and readers, and then, frequently, as a component in systems that link local communities and institutions into regional, national, and international networks. While the destruction of any individual library is a blow to its patrons, the destruction of national systems is increasingly of concern because of each system's impact on broader information systems, which are pervasively interwoven into all aspects of global society and culture. Awareness is growing—unfortunately rather slowly—that destruction of national library systems impacts the information structures of cultures and civilizations worldwide. Globalization and the need to network through electronic communication systems drive the mandate for traditional images of a geographically and politically fragmented world to give way to an awareness of cultural survival as a shared concern.

In modern information-processing systems, libraries are links that provide information essential to long-term survival of the species. Our social and environmental problems are increasingly complex and global—environmental degradation, questions of human rights, and peace—and libraries serve a crucial role at the interface between the human organism and the physical and social environment (Chapman and Dolukhanov 1993). Because information systems are essentially institutionalized pathways along which the "brain" of the world functions, the implications of library destruction are of global import. Yet the nodes of this brain are nations, and the individual nation is still the predominant determinant of the destruction or survival of books and libraries. While most of the important problems of contemporary civilization can be solved only through the agency of international mindsets, *all* of our sociopolitical structures are arranged to accommodate the sovereign nation. The fates of libraries and cultural heritage are interwoven in this dilemma, a subject that will be revisited in the last chapter of this book.

We turn now to an examination of the functions—both cultural and universal—of libraries in the twentieth century. By the end of the 1800s, the library had survived at least three millennia of experimentation and adaptation. It had evolved into an institution that met critical societal needs. Among its many responsibilities were preserving the information that forms the basis for government, the economy, property rights, and national and ethnic identity; rationalizing and supporting social, political, and religious systems, creeds, world views, and ideologies; disseminating information and underpinning education, intellectual development, and social progress; and supporting advanced or "high" culture.

In the literature on libraries, there is a plethora of descriptive material that spells out the specific structures, missions, collections, and operations that have been formulated to meet these needs. For the non-librarian, a short list of the major types of libraries and their missions is provided below:

PUBLIC LIBRARIES: Children's libraries and local, regional, or national libraries catering to the general public's reading and informational needs—includes mobile and alternative libraries (including workplace collections)

SCHOOL LIBRARIES: Libraries attached to schools that support reading enrichment and instruction

ACADEMIC LIBRARIES, RESEARCH INSTITUTES, INFORMATION CENTERS: Libraries that support higher education, instruction, research, problem-solving, and the generation of new knowledge

SPECIAL LIBRARIES: Archival collections, museum libraries, rare book collections, special focus collections; religious collections; business, law, and other organizationally maintained libraries

GOVERNMENT LIBRARIES: National libraries, legislative and judicial libraries, national databases, military libraries, libraries for government agencies, municipal records

PERSONAL LIBRARIES: Libraries in homes that support the recreational
or informational needs of individuals and families; libraries support an individual's scholarly activities

While this list implies that any given library must have a single specific
mission that aligns with these categories, the opposite is often more true.
There is an increasing interdependency between libraries that makes the
mission of any one library location a complex thing. Modern libraries tend
to be linked in networks or cooperative schemes that may be informal, as
when school librarians cooperate with collegial public librarians, or formal, as when a national library provides other institutions with contracted
services such as staff training, joint cataloguing, materials exchange, mi-
crofilming, bibliographical support, and database construction. The modern library must be thought of as a unit within complex systems. Within
these systems, even those libraries that fall within the same category vary
widely in mission and patronage—and, thus, in the degree to which they
emphasize traditional library functions: preserving, organizing, and disseminating knowledge. For example, a public library may acquire popular
or general informational materials and focus on their dissemination as part
of a broad mission of supporting a literate population. A university library
may build comprehensive and/or specialized collections that service students and faculty; however, its influence on research and technological
development may extend far out into society. A rare-books library may
focus primarily on preservation and, to a limited degree, on support of
scholarly activities.

While interdependency and variations within like missions are common, so are libraries that serve multiple functions (i.e. whose collections
and mission encompass more than one of the categories described above).
For example, a university library might include a general collection for
undergraduates, research collections for faculty and graduate students, as
well as a rare-books collection, a law library, musical archives, an extensive map collection, and a business collection that serves the local community. It may be a depository for government publications; it may
support a quasi-independent astronomy library for an affiliated research
unit. Or, while a public library mainly provides general materials for the
ordinary person, it might also contain a unique collection of local and
specialized materials that are of interest to the scholar, or it might provide
computer access or instruction that allows patrons to tap into external
databases. While libraries collectively shelter much of society's recorded
memory, most libraries are quite idiosyncratic and hold bits and pieces of
the whole heritage. Thus, a particular inquiry might involve painstaking

research in a combination of locations: in a public library, church library, university library, national library, or carefully selected personal libraries. The value of any one piece of information often depends on comparison, verification, or contextualization with other pieces. The destruction of libraries, particularly those containing unique or rare materials, has a devastating effect on scholarship and on knowledge. Our social intelligence, too, is torn as our ability to learn from the past is significantly compromised.

LIBRARIES, HISTORY, AND COLLECTIVE MEMORY

It is part of every culture to save things from the past. This practice expresses a belief that knowledge of the past can benefit us. If knowledge of our society and ourselves is advanced through studying the past, one might argue that the value of history is that it teaches us—by the study of what man has done—what man *is*. Like every human being, every civilization lives part of its emotional life in the past, and the creation and recreation of that past through institutionalized memories is one of the central and permanent tasks of civilization (Fulford 1993). As institutions that support culture through collections (others include museums and galleries), libraries provide artifacts and concrete testimony that allow insight into the intellectual and spiritual world of our predecessors and, thus, aid our understanding of the events of history (Feather 1986).

Sometimes, libraries are the primary bulwarks against cultural extinction. In the 1980s, a young student, Aaron Lansky, realized that trash heaps and dumpsters of the Eastern United States were claiming thousands of Yiddish books each year—a delayed aftereffect of the Holocaust. In Europe between the World Wars, despite a trend toward assimilation and a tendency for the young to abandon the language, eleven million people spoke Yiddish as their primary language, and publishers released a thousand new Yiddish titles per year. By 1945 one out of every two of those speakers was dead and the "[Yiddish] culture was literally ripped out of its roots in Europe" (Basbanes 1995, 389). Many survivors resettled in the United States, and thirty years later, as the remaining Yiddish speakers died, their books were consigned to scrap heaps. Lansky, with rare prescience, began gathering the books; in the beginning, he rummaged through dumpsters and rode a bicycle, then a moped, and, finally, drove a van around collecting donations. His campaign gained momentum through private and institutional support and has resulted in the National Yiddish Book Center, which held a million books by 1990. Lansky's mission has been to preserve all remaining Yiddish texts and, thus, preserve records of the way of life that they document—when surveying the center's collection, he is well aware that "[t]he life and the vitality and the culture of a thousand years is on those shelves" (Basbanes 1995, 394).

As the custodians of cultural heritage, "collected memory," librarians are concerned with the acquisition of materials, their systematic organization (including translation, authentication, and classification—the assignment of context), their storage and preservation, and their use. "The aim of librarianship, at whatever intellectual level it may operate, is to maximize the social utility of graphic records. . . . [L]ibrarianship is the management of knowledge" (Shera 1965, 16). Preserving historical knowledge is therefore a premise on which services and roles are based.

But of course, exactly what constitutes "history" is a complicated matter. Standard dictionaries define history as the branch of knowledge dealing with past events or their sum. A historian might describe it as a continuous, systematic narrative of past events relating to a particular people, country, period, person, etc., usually written as a chronological record. History can be the record of past events and times (especially in connection with the human race), or a record of current events that seem likely to shape the course of the future. Through these records, "stories" or myths are developed that give meaning to the past, explain the present, and provide guidance for the future; these stories involve principles that help cultures organize their institutions, develop ideals, and find authority for their actions (Postman 1992). While the construction and study of these stories may seem like an objective enterprise given their grounding in factual records, history can be highly subjective. And while libraries provide the evidence (i.e., graphic records) that leads to theories explaining the historical problems researchers are working on, the library's records can also be interpreted to support an extremist's attempts to reconstruct history and foster myths of a glorious past, present victimization, and transcendent future.

In other words, the stories and myths that are shared by a group of people, often referred to as "collective memory," have quite a different meaning and purpose in the field of librarianship than at the hands of political ideologues. While libraries can be co-opted to serve as witnesses and custodians to a particular politicized collective memory, libraries simultaneously express local cultural values *and* represent the achievement of civilizations far beyond their own borders. They are meeting places where various traditions, civilizations, ideas, and opinions mingle and mix (Aparac-Gazivoda and Katalenac 1993).

In incidences of cultural violence, a tension between history and collective memory is often expressed. This is because collective memory has been refashioned by political ideologues to further their ideological and personal agendas. The ideologue sees, in the collective aspect of memory, both power and an opportunity for manipulation. In the former Yugoslavia, Slobodan Milosevic, and in fact the entire leadership of Serbia, reinforced an inflammatory collective memory by emphasizing selective historic events and promoting social stereotypes as historical fact, as the truth behind the familiar traditions, myths, and customs that made up the Serbs' "spirit" or "psyche" (Gedi and Elan 1996). In this process, scholars, libraries, and the historical record were co-opted in order to validate ethnocentric myths and spread them across generations (Zhang and Schwartz 1997). Those who wouldn't buy in were pushed out of the national discourse.

A myth generated by collective memories has an affective, magical quality; it remains in a permanent state of evolution and only accommodates those facts that suit it. Political regimes that require such myths to support their ideologies and political programs frequently have intellectuals substantiate or validate the collective memories they have cultivated. Twentieth-century examples include the Nazi intellectuals who supported the imperatives of a German master race, and members of the Serbian Academy of Arts and Sciences who provided the rationale for Serbia's territorial aggression and ethnic cleansing. Both the Nazi and Serbian leadership manipulated their countries by misusing collective memories.

A hindrance to the politicization of scholarship, the physicality of written records displays a stubborn quality of witness and anchors legitimate methods of historical research. In fact, history, as a form of modern memory, is dependent on archival records: "It relies entirely on the materiality of the trace" (Nora 1989, 13). In the best-case scenario, libraries serve a history that calls for analysis and criticism, that is for everyone and belongs to no one (Gedi and Elam 1996). Thus, while an extremist regime in a country with significant library development can misuse libraries to promote an expedient collective memory, most libraries in developed countries serve as a counteracting force to radicalism. This counterweight is missing in underdeveloped nations, where the paucity of books and libraries leaves societies little with which to counteract the political manipulation of scholarship. Philip Gourevitch (1998, 648) writes that in contemporary Rwanda, within a context of "post-genocidal sobriety," some historians are taking seriously the political uses to which their writings have been put, and some readers are questioning the certainty with which racial claims have been advanced. Still a predominantly oral society, Rwanda's traditions are malleable. Stories of this fiercely hierarchical society's past are told (i.e., dictated) by those in power in the two factions.

With there being few written records about the relationship between Hutus and Tutsis, the pre-colonial roots of that relationship are largely unknowable, and much of what is passed as historical fact has to be considered tentative, if not outright fictional. The lack of libraries and written records increases the probability that constructions of Rwanda's history by one group may be prejudicial to the other.

Without written records, traditional societies that lose contact with their cultural past may have to undergo a rather painful reconstruction in order to have a basis for national identity, especially when the extinction of a print culture made them vulnerable to colonialism in the past. Timbuktu, a West African civilization that peaked during a sixteenth-century intellectual and literary revival and then declined, provides an example of a country whose libraries are said to have once included almost the whole of Arabian literature (Krzys and Litton 1983). Black Islamic libraries, mosque-schools, and centers of higher learning flourished during the revival but were devastated by invaders. To this day, Timbuktu's people have not regained the cultural ground that was lost (Wallerstein and Stephens 1978).

Linked with this is contemporary Black Americans' compilation of evidence of the historical accomplishments of their people. Arthur Alfonso Schomburg, whose documents and texts formed the basis for New York Public Library's Black History collection, was a pioneer in understanding and addressing the connection between racial self-esteem and a written heritage. Schomburg knew that the "Negro has been a man without a history because he has been considered a man without a worthy culture" (as quoted in Basbanes 1995, 398). Until his death in 1938, Schomburg acted upon a belief that a written history was essential in repairing the social damage inflicted by slavery. A similar mechanism applies to the need for written collections that support Women's Studies programs.

The importance of written records is perhaps best understood by religious groups (Wallerstein and Stephens 1978) like the Jews, who have experienced 2000 years of persecution, dispersion, and renewal. Since the early days when texts were hidden in tombs or caves, Jews believed that the survival of Judaism depended on the conscious preservation of religious laws and scholarship, with each generation passing on a sense of continuity with the past as well as an assignment for the future. Other people understand the Jews' message about the importance of survival and memory. A Muslim trying to stay alive in Bosnia in the 1990s compared the fate of his people to that of the Jews, stating: "It is not a question of who will survive but that someone must survive. In order to kill a people, you must kill memory, you must destroy everything that belongs to that people" (Maas 1996, 238).

Of course, Judaism is not the only religion based on scripture in text form. Wherever they ruled, Muslims carried collections of religious literature and established library systems within mosques and schools. Written materials were crucial in the intense early stages of Christianity and, in fact, the written word has been the core and impetus of the Christian religion throughout the ages. Books acquired symbolic importance among all major religious groups, sometimes referred to as the "people of the book." Even among those of lapsed faith, the symbolic significance of the book is powerful. The case can be made that from the earliest days, the basic concepts of religion (Christian, Judaic, and Muslim alike), and the behavioral inferences drawn from them, were transmitted, and therefore sustained, by the written word (Feather 1986).

The destruction of books and libraries is a mechanism by which a regime and its followers, who are influenced by the emotional appeal of a distorted collective memory, seek to legitimize their domination of competing minorities or press claims to territory and resources. While emphasizing those written records that support their claims, extremists also may seek to destroy any records that could compromise their position. For example, the Serbs have tried to erase all evidence of the centuries-old Muslim and Croatian occupation of contested lands. They have done this through the destruction of churches, monasteries, mosques, schools, and any institution holding printed documentation, including birth records, land titles, and historical materials. Similarly, the Nazis sought the total eradication of the Jews and destroyed thousands of texts—but in a quirk of fate, preserved many of their confiscated libraries for use in institutes devoted to the solution of the "Jewish problem." The Nazis' preservation of the Jews' texts (while taking their lives) is perhaps a backhanded tribute not only to books as significant repositories, but also to the worthiness of this cultural group as a subject of study.

We will now explore the dynamic relationships that exist between libraries and basic belief systems, libraries and national identity, and libraries and societal advancement. These relationships result in libraries becoming critical targets when any one of these elements of society comes under attack.

LIBRARIES AND BELIEF SYSTEMS

Books and libraries organize knowledge, facilitate decision-making, and support structured religious or political perceptions of ideas about the natural and the social world. Because libraries provide access to various worldviews and beliefs, they have broad functional roles in supporting or attacking major belief systems. Services and collections in Western libraries tend to support democracy, humanism, and individual rights. The government generally provides libraries in countries where an extremist ideology prevails with a mission, services to fulfill, and parameters for collections, all of which are presented as addressing collective rights. Those rights are defined in terms of ideological objectives: the achievement of nationalist, Communist, or religious utopias.

Contemporary Western libraries are based on one of the essential principles of the Enlightenment: that the growth of human knowledge implies an increased ability to behave rationally, to predict events, and to control blind natural and social forces (Markovic 1974). In broad theoretical terms, libraries are committed to the power and authority of truth, free intelligence, and the ultimate authority of the mind in human living (MacLeish 1942). Western libraries are committed to a morality that values the individual (Stuart 1995) and accords individuals the right to be presented with alternatives upon which to make informed choices (Poole 1996). Intellectual freedom—the inalienable right to think, write, and read—is a root concept of Western libraries.

These principles are institutionalized in public libraries, which, while providing for recreational reading, also provide free access to information important to an enlightened democratic citizenry (Harris 1995). For example, in the United States, the American Library Association's "Library Bill of Rights" obliges librarians to provide in their collections a balanced and unbiased picture of issues for independent decision-making. Actual institutional performance within frameworks of humanism and democracy vary, but as social theorist Herbert Schiller (1989, 69) states, free and equal access serves as a democratic bulwark, and the library "represents and puts into at least limited practice the democratic aspirations of the nation."

Under highly nationalistic or revolutionary regimes, libraries are also valued as institutions that legitimize the governing power by supporting social cohesion and inculcating "correct" beliefs and values (Hobsbawm 1983). However, in these cases the dissemination of information is controlled, books must be ideologically correct, and services are primarily geared toward achieving ideological objectives. Literacy efforts are often intense, and people are encouraged to engage with questions that address the very foundations of social order; but again, the goal of these educational efforts is not autonomous decision-making but the predominance of government ideology and the formation of a society that conforms to the government's ideals. For example, Communist Russia's libraries propagated Marxist-Leninist philosophy and disseminated Communist Party news and propaganda in an effort to create better socialists (Harris 1995). In Nazi Germany, libraries were purged of offending materials (especially those promoting humanism and democracy), and then well stocked with materials expressing National Socialist and racist perspectives. In both regimes, the focus of libraries was on the state's utopian goals and not the intellectual or personal development of the individual.

Michael Harris (1986), a prominent library historian, has posited that libraries are part of an ensemble of institutions dedicated to the creation, transmission, and reproduction of hegemonic ideology—that is, the guiding doctrine. The validity of his position is most apparent in situations where a particular ideology or belief system has become a controlling political program, and governmental support of that program approaches totalitarian extremes. Harris's theory challenges the apolitical conception of the library that dominates the profession and, by stripping it of ethical and political innocence, offers one way of understanding why books and libraries become casualties of political and social violence. In fact, as modern history has reminded us, libraries are highly political battlefields for differing perspectives on what Condorcet called "the instruction that every man is free to receive from books in silence and solitude" (as quoted in Boorstin 1998, 220). One might ask, does truth reside in multitudes of freely chosen and diverse books that, as Condorcet believed, make it impossible "to bolt every door, to seal every crevice" through which truth might escape (as quoted in Boorstin 1998, 220)? Or, does truth reside in carefully selected collections that avoid "pernicious falsities" and focus on a particularly compelling social and utopian doctrine? In countries where "truth" is believed to reside only in controlled texts and collections, autonomous libraries and free reading are threats to social well-being and political security, and, as a result, are subjected to intellectual purging.

In any political environment, libraries help in socializing people to prevailing sociocultural ideas by providing access to information that corroborates particular world views (Meyrowitz 1985) and promotes cultural truisms, the assumptions that ground major social and political practices and policies (Gaskell and Fraser 1990). But while supporting the status quo, libraries at the same time nurture new ideas; the contents of books and libraries have always directly influenced transcendent intellectuals—Darwin, Freud, Marx, and Locke, to name a few well-known examples—who reshape the world through new paradigms. Libraries also, subsequently, provide a means for transmitting new and revolutionary ideas to the general public (Feather 1986). In summary, libraries support official beliefs and ideologies, while at the same time bringing about sociocultural change by nurturing and transmitting new understandings. It is the latter's potential for presenting alternatives that extremists fear.

No discussion of the connection between libraries and basic beliefs is complete without giving attention to the ability of libraries to support the growth and development of the individual. The concept of self-realization is abstract and serves as a general and neutral theoretical framework that can be filled with very different images of man (Markovic 1974). In politically extremist ideologies, which channel the individual's development towards the goals of a utopian society, a "new man" replaces his personal desires and aspirations with collective visions of a transformed society. Humanistic thought, on the other hand, poses claims about the legitimacy and rights of the individual that contradict the very notion there is any "self," much less "realization," when an extremist ideology is in place. For the humanists, the search for knowledge is at the heart of the human condition, and this search begins within. Humanists believe that their goals are supported by the very nature of the medium of print, which stresses individualized learning, competition, and personal autonomy. However, reading's ability to enhance and give shape to one's internal reality (Meyrowitz 1985) implies that *what* one is allowed to read has a profound effect on whether the individual's constructed reality is ultimately shaded toward extremism or humanism.

At the core of humanist thought is a value for the dignity of the individual and the learning process by which we acquire information, gain self-confidence, and realize our potential. Education that is based on humanism supports processes in which books supplement the teacher and libraries support the essential goal of higher education, which is the development of reason, understanding, and initiative. Both books and libraries extend the inevitably limited horizon of a single human experience (Rostow 1981). It is because institutions like libraries support humanist values that they are often among the first casualties in ideologically based warfare or internal revolution. For the ideologue, the individual and all cultural institutions are merely means to an end.

LIBRARIES AND NATIONALISM

The relationship between libraries and national identity is symbiotic, for the roots of nationalism lie in the evolution of written language and the existence of a viable nation stimulates library development. With the advent of "writing" came the ability to codify culture and its rules and, then, to transmit this package to the next generation through formal education. With these developments, it also became possible, conceptually speaking, to be a "nationalist" (Gellner 1997). The invention of the printing press and the proliferation of written materials in vernacular languages, first in Western Europe and then worldwide, were precursors to modern cultural cohesion and identification. Multilingualism (the ability to access information in other languages), print capitalism (which encouraged the dissemination of books across regions), and of course commerce in general and imperialism, were responsible for spreading modern Western culture, including models of nationalism, nation-ness, and the nation-state (Anderson 1991). Emerging as a result was the desire to be a nation—i.e., have a common language, culture, history, and ancestry, and such subjective elements as a national consciousness and the will to remain together (Seymour, Couture, and Nielsen 1996). With a common cultural base and texts to transmit this commonality and foster homogeneity within a single high culture, people were able to imagine themselves as a distinct group; when the image was reinforced by political control of a specific geographical area, the group became a nation (Gellner 1997).

Because identification with a nation is so subjective, governments use language, culture, and tradition to consolidate their population's nationalism and to create a distinctive public culture (Seymour, Couture, and Nielsen 1996). Government-sponsored information systems (including libraries) and a uniform education system are two powerful means by which people become enculturated (and politicized). Benedict Anderson (1991), famous for his characterization of the nation as "an imagined community," has pointed out that the progress of schools and universities parallels that of nationalism, just as the schools (and especially the universities) become nationalism's most conscious champions. One could argue that libraries, by virtue of their association with the progress of schools and universities and their role in fostering nationalism, also serve as a measure of nationalism.

On the road to nationalism, it is essential to map an area, develop the vernacular into a national language, collect and record folk stories, and systematically compile a history that both testifies to the group's distinctiveness and promotes its claims to a specific region. Benedict Anderson (1991) pointed out that it was the libraries of nineteenth-century Europe that nourished the lexicographers, grammarians, philologists, and *litterateurs* who laid the foundations of national identity. With printed texts, including monolingual and bilingual dictionaries, conviction spread that languages were the "personal property" of quite specific groups who, when imagined as communities, were entitled to their autonomous place in a fraternity of equals as a nation among nations (Anderson 1991). Frequently the leaders of burgeoning nationalist movements have been persons whose professions consisted largely of the handling of language: writers, teachers, pastors, and lawyers. They used oral lore, libraries, and texts to study folklore and epic poetry, to compile lexicographic references, and to standardize literary languages. Through their work, folklore became the basis for mythological constructions essential for identification with a people and their nation.

First in Europe and then elsewhere, governments and ardent nationalists promoted systematic historiographical campaigns to research and create national histories and place the nation within a serial and continuous historical tradition. Establishing a historical and indigenous claim to an area or demonstrating patterns of continuous occupation were important sources of political legitimacy. Since the knowledge of one's own history (whether fabricated or not) contributed to ethnic and, thus, national identity, "history" was conscientiously transmitted through classrooms, books, and libraries. It and the national language (English, for example) became core curricula in expanding educational systems in the 1800s. The formation and dissemination of a unified foundation for national identity contributed to a cult of continuity—"the confident assumption of knowing to whom and what we owe our existence"—that was based on the importance of the idea of origins, "an already profane version of the mythological narrative, but one that contributed to giving meaning and a sense of the sacred to a society engaged in a nationwide process of secularization" (Nora 1989, 16). Ethnic belongingness became an important source of self-respect and personal authenticity (Eriksen 1993). Having replaced traditional forms of identity such as religion, caste, and estate, nationalism (and, in particular, ethnocentric nationalism) became a powerful construct for defining a person's position in his or her social world. Of the multitude of ways in which we define ourselves in modern times, national identity is the one with the widest circumference—yet it is also the one believed to define a person's very essence and guide his or her actions (Greenfeld 1992); thus, the import of the statements, "I am a German" or "I am a Serb."

In Third World countries, the relative absence of written records, libraries, and effective schools complicates the construction of cultural identity, and, thus, of a culturally unified nation state. For example, if the Somalis could develop a graphic knowledge base about themselves—their history, geography, ecology, traditional law and culture, resources, and everything about their affairs (Abdulla 1996)—this base might provide a foundation for a unified culture that could counteract the dominance of clan rule. Somalia is an example of the fragility of colonial nations that fail to achieve a healthy base for their nationalism. Collections of cultural materials in the native language did not reach a mass public that would support a common culture, a unified people, and a national consciousness.

The nation is a political state whose legitimacy depends on its claim to represent a community that is defined by its culture; but in Somalia, identity is defined by clans. In viable nations, group identity is facilitated by an official public culture—a recognized national language, a history, cultural traditions, and publicly accepted rituals (Poole 1996). Library collections (including archival) that are selected and organized with reference to local cultural conditions provide institutional support for public culture (Butler 1944). In turn, they often are supported by the public and by governments because of their connection with national pride (Cveljo 1998).

Post-colonial states, including those newly independent remnants of the former USSR, face an ongoing battle in retrieving their written heritage, especially archival, for use as the foundation of a strong state. Within empires, cultural materials are centralized, and the processes of developing or solidifying identity around a constituent nation exist in tension (often explosive in nature) with official doctrines that define identity ideologically as international and based on class or race, while, at the same time, favoring identification with the dominant state. Thus cultural materials are expected to support the imperatives of empire and identification with the dominant state: the British Empire and Anglicization, Communism and Sinicization or Russification, National Socialism and Germanification, and so on. With independence and freedom from occupation, the newly independent nation must repossess a substantive written heritage and create a history that can serve as a fount for nationalism and cultural unification. As posed by an expert in Ukraine's post-Soviet era efforts to rebuild national collections, Patricia Kennedy Grimsted (2001, 1):"The question of whether *any* nation 'has a history' cannot be fully answered without turning to its archives, because it is precisely a nation's archives that are simultaneously the concrete record and the abstract reflection of its historical development."

However, while libraries support national identity, they also support a whole range of identity *constructs*—from ethnicity and religion to regional or local culture to awareness of the ways in which one culture intersects with others. Libraries nurture the routine creation and sustenance of the reflexive activities of the individual, in which one understands oneself in terms of biography and history. Without libraries, without the continuity expressed in continuous narratives speaking to the progress of the human race and the ethnic group or nation, it is easy to become anxious and lose one's way on both individual and collective levels (Giddens 1990). The fostering of thoughtful and informed individuals has a cumulative effect in "balancing" a civilized community and nation.

On the other hand, power-seeking individuals and regimes may invoke powerful collective memories (and stifle others) in order to support extreme forms of nationalism, obfuscate issues, diffuse opposition, and capitalize on instability and chaos. The legitimacy of claims to dominance and land are advanced through manipulation or destruction of written records. When the driving force behind conflict is nationalism, the destruction of libraries occurs because they contain texts that validate or invalidate claims to power, and because of their roles in the construction of the nation and in supporting an informed and stable sociocultural environment. Violent destruction that seems wanton and inexplicable is actually often highly instrumental. Governments are seeking to diminish their enemies, to impede their enemies' social and cultural development, and to negate their enemies' ability to function within global systems.

LIBRARIES AND SOCIETAL DEVELOPMENT

In addition to preserving memory and bolstering sociocultural beliefs, libraries sustain and extend the intellectual achievement of a society. Through information dissemination and support of research and intellectual advancement, libraries support educational institutions and advance educational levels, science, technology, and modernization, thereby enriching the individual and society. Libraries are essential to educational processes that prepare man for civilized living; they preserve civilization by enabling each successive generation to maintain and operate its infrastructure, organizations, and scholarship (Butler 1944). Their dual purpose in preserving the accumulated wisdom of the past and gathering information in the present supports cultural synthesis and the generation of new knowledge ("The World's Great Libraries . . ." 1989).

Modern industrial nations have been called "information societies" because their populations depend on complex systems that feed on and produce a constant stream of information. Such systems require an educated populace, not the least of which are those equipped to translate data into meaningful information and finally into knowledge (Zuboff 1988). It is the complex nature of print media that allows for the development of extended analyses that are crucial for the expansion of knowledge, which is central to material progress, social change, and intellectual growth. Research, whether theoretical or practical, requires two things: an awareness of the state of existing knowledge and a relatively unfettered flow of knowledge. The medium of print makes this possible. And further, libraries extend the benefit of print by expanding collections to support higher and higher levels of specialization.

In major research libraries, comprehensive collections accommodate all disciplines and allow for borrowing within and across fields. Interdisciplinarity has emerged as crucial in working to improve major problems like ecological degradation, social injustice, and peace. In addition, libraries support humanistic research that is based on long tradition and the study of diverse, unique, and obscure materials, which can include manuscripts, parchment codices, and archival documents (Wallerstein and Stephens 1978). Library materials provide impetus for intellectual movements whose effects are felt far outside the circles of those directly concerned (Feather 1986). They help societies to escape from provincialism of time, from only knowing their own moment in history (Fulford 1993), and to adjust to a modern, industrialized world of capitalism and the rise of organizations and operations that depend on the separation of time and space (Giddens 1991).

Even the simplest animal societies, subject to stimuli and response patterns, have complex information systems. In the human world, language is the primary means for elevating human activity beyond the immediacy of the experience of animals; printed language serves as a time machine and spreads the effects of modernity worldwide. Modernity stems from the shift from agrarian cultures, in which literacy and access to information is a privilege of the elite, to urban and industrialized cultures, in which education is pervasive and high culture is accessible to all (Gellner 1997). In modern societies, everyone must have the capacity to articulate or comprehend information that is separated from the original context of time and place; this requires prolonged schooling and access to written materials. In closed societies, progress toward modernity is arrested. For example, the shortage of books in repressive and backward Romania was so critical that, after the overthrow of Communism in 1989, the pastor of one church asked first for books. "Clothes and food are short term and quickly finished," he wrote, "but the books are our passport to Western education to bring us up to date with a world we have been cut off from for 30 odd years. The books are our future" (Wood 1990, 918). In the newly opened Romania, many of the medical supplies received from Western countries were so modern that the doctors had no idea how to use them. In Somalia, the lack of statistical and economic data, information on practical and cultural matters, domestic literature, and a publishing industry all have contributed to economic and social collapse and cultural stagnancy (Samatar 1994). In 1990, Iraq's attacks on private and public institutions such as schools and libraries were integral to their plan for dismantling Kuwait's modern technological society (Cassidy 1990).

Specific fields of study are especially dependent on print media and collections. The most obvious is science, which could be described as a special way of employing human intelligence (Postman 1992) that involves a continuous process of trial and error, acceptance and rejection, discovery and rediscovery, refinement and redefinition (Shera 1965). Breakthroughs in scientific knowledge are the foundation of technological advancement, which, in turn, is a continuing process of invention, development, innovation, transfer, growth, competition, and consolidation. Libraries provide the cumulative and up-to-date information necessary for both processes. Ever since the days of ancient Egypt when the Ptolemies expected scholars at Alexandria to make practical applications, libraries have helped scientists and technologists to exchange information necessary for the collective, cumulative efforts in problem-solving that produce technological innovation (Pinch and Bijker 1987). The support of technology is just one of many ways in which libraries come in contact with administrators of government, industry, and commercial enterprises that cannot function without a constant stream of knowledge.

A society's cultural development is often linked to the level of its library development. The barbarism, illiteracy, and regression that characterized Roman culture after the fall of Rome contrasts sharply with the cultural richness of earlier societies like the Greeks, or even Roman culture itself at its peak. In stagnant cultures, the means by which the material, technical, scientific, literary, artistic, and moral patrimony of a society are generated, maintained, and transmitted are arrested. During such times, literature, poetry, philosophy, and science—the higher achievements of civilizations—decrease in quantity and quality (Wallerstein and Stephens 1978). The intellectual capital, so to speak, is nonexistent or inaccessible.

Comparison with thriving cultures shows that a living, developing community is inseparable from its records: it is through the written record that a culture achieves awareness of the totality of its physical, psychological, and intellectual environment (Shera 1965). Libraries are crucial to societies that value human learning that is additive (as in the case of scientific and technological advances), regenerative (referring to psychosocial progress, i.e. that which each generation learns), and transformative (that which fuels spiritual and moral progress) (Tehranian 1990). Libraries have important roles in the complex systems that manage social intelligence. They are analogous to the cells and neural pathways of the brain which, when destroyed, cause the brain to deteriorate. A society, if it is to avoid decay, must make constant provision for not only the preservation of existing knowledge, but also the acquisition and assimilation of new knowledge (Shera 1965).

The cultural advancement that is necessary for continuous progress ultimately implies a worldwide system of social intelligence in which knowledge is acquired, preserved, and made accessible. The system begins with local libraries, which provide recreational and informational materials and collect items of local interest. These libraries network with other institutions such as school, mobile, city, and university libraries. Urban and university libraries cooperate with special libraries like those maintained by the military, religious, or archival institutions. Guidance and coordination is provided by national libraries or by a designated university library, which collects and organizes the entire contemporary bibliographical output of a country. These preeminent libraries facilitate interlibrary cooperation and networking, which may ultimately transcend national boundaries. They provide access to international journal information through electronic databases. National librarians work through organizations such as the International Federation of Library Associations and Institutions and UNESCO to standardize documentation and formats that will ultimately allow for the sharing of the graphic heritage of all nations and cultures.

Libraries participate in the superstructure of international communications by being part of the expert systems by which those with technical and professional expertise organize large areas of the material and social environment (Giddens 1990). Libraries support information-transfer networks, which are supportive systems, channels of communication and information-sharing and -dispersal that provide links between users, electronic or bibliographical databases, and computers or library access. Their missions are increasingly regional, and ultimately global, as technology helps order the world.

Theorists struggle with whether distinct civilizations, defined either by geography or culture, still dominate the sociopolitical world or whether the forces of globalization are producing a single world civilization united by world systems. From the latter position, books and libraries must be seen as key institutions in that global system for they hold the knowledge that substantiates individual, national, and cultural identity. Their holdings can also demonstrate the force of common values (of human rights or democracy, for instance) and the effect of diffusion and convergence on cultural progress. Effective use of libraries also allows for the adaptation of the social intelligence necessary to deal with global problems.

Regardless of the political significance of regional boundaries, the fact remains that when a local library is destroyed, the local or national system in which it functions is damaged. If enough libraries are destroyed, the national system will also be destroyed, and its role in the maintenance of national strength disappears. Its effect upon regional and global information dissemination is also compromised. For example, in 1990 Iraq's devastation of Kuwait's library and information infrastructure not only hindered the capabilities of Kuwait's national information system, but also interfered with fledgling plans to network Arab libraries and, thus, facilitate the exchange of regional information and the provision of Arabic materials worldwide. Tribal and nationalist interests often find it advantageous to damage international information systems because the cooperative relationships these systems foster might extend to efforts to curb their aggression. "If there is an antithesis to networking, it is in all likelihood nationalism" (Fulton 1992, 40).

Destruction of an important library or an entire library system may involve a desire to diminish the prestige and vitality of the enemy—particularly when the motivation is nationalistic, imperialistic, or racist. The conscious or unconscious impetus is to destroy the enemy's intellectual and literary independence, diminish its cultural identity, and destroy books and libraries—witnesses to the cultural sophistication of the group or nation. This brings our discussion to the function of libraries in enriching the society's culture. As we have discussed in this chapter, the presence of libraries within a literate modern society demonstrates the achievement of a certain level of cultural advancement. Libraries are one of several institutional sites charged with the responsibility of "creating" a high culture, and their role in producing, extending, and refining the cultural heritage is considered essential by the intellectual elite (Harris 1986). Libraries are a concrete marker of those societies that have been through the "modern" experience (Pfaff 1993).

It is because libraries are clues to the existence of a high culture that national libraries, in particular, are assigned aesthetic functions. Indeed, within their walls, art and culture are linked, often to the point of synonymy. The building often expresses excellence in architectural design and construction and houses monuments and art that project a cultivated image; a magnificent library is an essential civic monument to the cultural sophistication of a nation (Harris 1995). Beautiful antique manuscripts and rare books are displayed as *objets d'art* and as evidence of a sophisticated past and/or a prosperous present. Libraries often serve as sites for literary and musical recitals, art exhibitions, and performing-arts events, and their link with the arts makes explicit that libraries are connected with cultural advancement (Wallerstein and Stephens 1978). A grand and distinguished library reflects on the society as a whole.

When a library is destroyed, not only is heritage lost, but also the group identifying with the library suffers a blow to its pride. When the historic building and rich collections of the National Library of Bosnia were burned in 1992, it was a major trauma for the beleaguered citizens of Bosnia, and of Sarajevo, in particular. Founded in 1945, the library was housed in an Austro-Hungarian era building that was itself a symbol of the city and "the pride of all Sarajevans" (Zeco 1996, 285). A library is both a repository and an arena; it exists as connective tissue between the present and future (Rostow 1981). Therefore, whatever the defining identity of the group, whether it is a nation, a race, or a religious or political group, the destruction of its libraries impedes the cultural development of the group as a whole, diminishes quality of life, and damages the self-esteem of group members. It also compromises, on many levels, the group's future.

REFERENCES

Abdulla, Ali. D. 1996. "Somalia's Reconstruction: An Opportunity to Create a Responsive Information Infrastructure." *International Information and Library Review* 28 (1):39–57.

Anderson, Benedict. 1991. *Imagined Communities: Reflections on the Origin and the Spread of Nationalism.* (Revised Edition). New York: Verso.

Aparac-Gazivoda, Tatjana, and Dragutin Katalenac, eds. 1993. *Wounded Libraries in Croatia.* Zagreb, Croatia: Croatian Library Association.

Basbanes, Nicholas A. 1995. *A Gentle Madness: Bibliophiles, Bibliomanes, and the Eternal Passion for Books.* New York: Henry Holt.

Billings, Harold. 1990. "Magic and Hypersystems: A New Orderliness for Libraries." *Library Journal* 115 (6):46–52.

Bingham, Rebecca T., Pauline A. Cochrane, David Kaser, Peggy Sullivan, Roderick G. Schwartz, and Robert Wedgeworth. 1993. "Library." In *World Book Encyclopedia,* Vol. 12, 234–262.

Boorstin, Daniel. J. 1998. *The Seekers: The Story of Man's Continuing Quest to Understand His World.* New York: Random House.

Butler, Pierce. 1944. *Scholarship and Civilization.* Chicago: University of Chicago Graduate Library School.

Cassidy, John. 1990. "Back to Year Zero: Saddam Eradicates Kuwait But Bush Must Hold Fire." *The Sunday Times,* 7 October, sec. 1A, p. 3.

Chapman, John, and Pavel Dolukhanov. 1993. "Cultural Transformations and Interactions in Eastern Europe: Theory and Terminology." In *Cultural Transformation and Interactions in Eastern Europe,* eds. John Chapman and Pavel Dolukhanov. Brookfield, Vermont: Avebury.

Cveljo, Katherine. 1998. "Wounded Libraries in Croatia: Destruction and Heroic Recovery Efforts." *International Leads* 12 (4):1, 4.

Eriksen, Thomas Hylland. 1993. *Ethnicity and Nationalism: Anthropological Perspectives.* London: Pluto Press.

Feather, John P. 1986. "The Book in History and the History of the Book." *The Journal of Library History, Philosophy and Comparative Librarianship* 21 (1):12–26.

Fulford, Robert. 1993. "The Future of Memory: Cultural Institutions in Times of Radical Change." *Queen's Quarterly* 100 (4):785–796.

Fulton, Gloria. 1992. "Nationalism and Networking in Yugoslavia." *Computers in Libraries* 12 (9):40–43.

Gaskell, George, and Colin Fraser. 1990. "The Social Psychological Study of Widespread Beliefs." In *The Social Psychological Study of Widespread Beliefs*, eds. George Gaskell and Colin Fraser. Oxford: Clarendon Press

Gedi, Noa, and Yigal Elam. 1996. "Collective Memory—What Is It?" *History and Memory* 8 (1):30–50.

Gellner, Ernest. 1997. *Nationalism.* New York: New York University Press.

Giddens, Anthony. 1990. *Consequences of Modernity.* Stanford, California: University Press.

Giddens, Anthony. 1991. *Modernity and Self-Identity: Self and Society in the Late Modern Age.* Stanford: Stanford University Press.

Gourevitch, Philip. 1998. *We Wish To Inform You That Tomorrow We Will Be Killed With Our Families: Stories From Rwanda.* New York: Farrar Straus and Giroux.

Greenfeld, Liah. 1992. *Nationalism: Five Roads to Modernity.* Cambridge, Massachusetts: Harvard University Press.

Grimsted, Patricia Kennedy. 2001. *Trophies of War and Empire: The Archival Heritage of Ukraine, World War II, and the International Politics of Restitution.* Cambridge, Massachusetts: Harvard University Press.

Harris, Michael. H. 1995. *History of Libraries in the Western World.* Metuchen, New Jersey: Scarecrow Press.

Harris, Michael H. 1986. "State, Class, and Cultural Reproduction: Toward a Theory of Library Service in the United States." In *Advances in Librarianship*, ed. Wesley Simonton. Vol. 14. London: Academic Press.

Hobsbawm, Eric. 1983. "Introduction: Inventing Traditions." In *The Invention of Tradition*, eds. Eric Hobsbawm and Terence Ranger. Cambridge: Cambridge University Press.

Hua, Xie Zhuo. 1996. "Libraries and the Development of Culture in China." *Libraries and Culture* 31 (3/4): 533–539.

Krzys, Richard. 1975. "Library Historiography." In *Encyclopedia of Library and Information Science*, eds. Allen Kent, Harold Lancour, Jay E. Daily, and William Z. Nasri. Vol. 15. New York: Marcel Dekker.

Krzys, Richard, and Gaston Litton. 1983. *World Librarianship: A Comparative Study.* New York: Marcel Dekker.

Line, Maurice B. 1994. "The New Tribalism: Its Implications for Libraries All Over the World." *LOGOS* 5 (1):6–12.

Maas, Peter. 1996. *Love Thy Neighbor: A Story of War.* New York: Alfred A Knopf.

MacLeish, Archibald. 1942. "Toward an Intellectual Offensive." *ALA Bulletin* 36 (6):423–428.

Malinowski, Bronislaw. 1931. "Culture." In *Encyclopaedia of the Social Sciences*, ed. Edwin Seligman. Vol. 4. New York: Macmillan.

Markovic, Mihailo. 1974. "Violence and Human Self-Realization." In *Violence and Aggression in the History of Ideas*, eds. Philip P. Wiener and John Fisher. New Brunswick, New Jersey: Rutgers University Press.

Meyrowitz, Joshua. 1985. *No Sense of Place: The Impact of Electronic Media on Social Behavior.* New York: Oxford University Press.

Nora, Pierre. 1989. "Between Memory and History: Les Lieux de Memoire." *Representations* 26 (spring): 7–25.

Pfaff, William. 1993. *The Wrath of Nations: Civilization and the Furies of Nationalism.* New York: Simon and Schuster.

Pinch, Trevor J., and Wiebe E. Bijker. 1987. "The Social Construction of Facts and Artifacts: or How the Sociology of Science and the Sociology of Technology Might Benefit Each Other." In *The Social Construction of Technological Systems: New Directions in the Sociology and History of Technology*, eds. Wiebe E. Bijker, Thomas P. Hughes, and Trevor Pinch. Cambridge, Massachusetts: MIT Press.

Poole, Ross. 1996. "National Identity, Multiculturalism, and Aboriginal Rights: An Australian Perspective." In *Rethinking Nationalism*, eds. Jocelyne Couture, Kai Nielsen, and Michel Seymour. Calgary, Canada: University of Calgary Press.

Postman, Neil. 1992. *Technopoly: The Surrender of Culture to Technology.* New York: Vintage Books.

Reichmann, Felix. 1980. *The Sources of Western Literacy: The Middle Eastern Civilizations.* Westport, Connecticut: Greenwood Press.

Rostow, Elspeth. 1981. "The Diary of the Human Race: Libraries in a Troubled Age." *Journal of Library History* 16 (1):8–15.

Samatar, Ahmed I. 1994. "The Curse of Allah: Civic Disembowelment and the Collapse of the State in Somalia." In *The Somali Challenge: From Catastrophe to Renewal?*, ed. Ahmed I. Samatar. Boulder, Colorado: Lynne Reiner.

Schiller, Herbert I. 1989. *Culture Inc.: The Corporate Takeover of Public Expression.* New York: Oxford University Press.

Seymour, Michel, Jocelyne Couture, and Kai Nielsen. 1996. "Introduction: Questioning the Ethnic/Civic Dichotomy." In *Rethinking Nationalism*, eds. Jocelyne Couture, Kai Nielsen, and Michel Seymour. Calgary, Canada: University of Calgary Press.

Shapiro, Harry L. 1957. *Aspects of Culture.* (Reprinted 1970 by arrangement with Rutgers University Press: Essay Index Reprint Series). Freeport, New York: Books for Libraries Press.

Shera, Jesse. 1965. *Libraries and the Organization of Knowledge.* Hamden, Connecticut: Archon Books.

Stuart, Mary. 1995. "Creating Culture: The Rossica Collection of the Imperial Public Library and the Construction of National Identity." *Libraries and Culture* 30 (1):1–23.

Tehranian, Majid. 1990. *Technologies of Power: Information Machines and Democratic Prospects.* Norwood, New Jersey: Ablex Publishing.

Thiem, Jon. 1979. "The Great Library of Alexandria Burnt: Towards the History of a Symbol." *Journal of the History of Ideas* 40 (4):507–526.

Tuchman, Barbara W. 1980. *The Book.* A Lecture presented at the Library of Congress. Washington, D.C.: Library of Congress.

Vallance, John. 2000. "Doctor in the Library: The Strange Tales of Apollonius the Bookworm and Other Stories." In *The Library of Alexandria: Centre of Learning in the Ancient World*, ed. Roy MacLeod. London: Tauris.

Wallerstein, Immanuel, and John Frank Stephens. June 1978. *Libraries and Our Civilizations.* A Report Prepared for the Governor of the State of New York.

Wood, Sally. 1990. "Books for Romania: The Scottish Appeal." *Library Association Record* 92 (12):917–919.

"The World's Great Libraries: Arks from the Deluge." 1989. *The Economist* 313 (7634–5):41–47.

Zeco, Munevera. 1996. "The National and University Library of Bosnia and Herzegovina During the Current War." *Library Quarterly* 66 (3):294–301.

Zhang, Tong, and Barry Schwartz. 1997. "Confucius and the Cultural Revolution: A Study in the Collective Memory." *International Journal of Politics, Culture and Society* 11 (2):189–212.

Zuboff, Shoshana. 1988. *In the Age of the Smart Machine: The Future of Work and Power.* New York: Basic Books.

Chapter 3

A THEORETICAL FRAMEWORK FOR LIBRICIDE

"As good almost kill a man as kill a good book; who kills a man kills a reasonable creature, God's image; but he who destroys a good book kills reason itself."

(Milton's *Aeropagitica* of 1644)

Because libraries express the humanist and democratic values that have come to characterize modern society and internationalism, violence directed at them is also an attack on these ideals, serving instead a world view in which the individual being exists solely to serve the collective mission of the state. Dignity, worth, and rights (including the right to choice, individual advancement, and survival) are not personal property because these qualities are a threat to the kind of regime that enforces orthodoxy through highly authoritarian and totalitarian controls. The destruction of books and libraries attacks not only individual selfhood but also culture as the foundation of group identity. Hence, violence to culture is a phenomenon that often shadows political violence; ethnocide shadows genocide. As the nineteenth-century poet Heinrich Heine wrote: "Whenever they burn books, they will also, in the end, burn human beings." The fact that the majority of this century's textual and human casualties have resulted from conflicts over political and ideological differences suggests that these two controversial elements of human society, politics and ideology, form a theoretical framework in which to understand libricide.

This chapter sets forth the argument that the large-scale destruction of books and libraries during the twentieth century has arisen from a combination of turbulent social environment, authoritarian or totalitarian leadership, and radical ideologies and policies. Disintegrative conditions on a national scale create an environment in which violence flourishes. The stressed and disoriented population turns to leaders who promise relief through a new political and social structure, based on transformational ideas. These ideas, which may be reactionary (nationalistic, imperialistic, militaristic, racist, or religious) and/or revolutionary (Communist), justify, and even glorify, the use of violence to achieve goals such as national fulfillment or achievement of a utopian world. As regimes consolidate control, often becoming totalitarian, they tend to cast libraries and books in a suspicious light, as either inherently seditious or the tool of the enemy or a scapegoat for a nation, an ethnic group or class of people that thwarts their policies. Looting, co-option, censorship, neglect, and violent destruction of books and libraries are therefore sanctioned practices.

The theoretical framework posited in this chapter focuses on behavioral patterns stemming from interrelationships between psychosocial forces and political context, and, thus, draws from theories in the fields of political science, psychology, sociology, and history. Because psychosocial environment is so crucial in understanding violence to culture, this chapter devotes significant space to a discussion of the psychological and sociological issues surrounding libricide. While examples of systematic destruction by specific regimes are used by way of illustration, detailed case studies are reserved for later chapters in which the theory is applied. It is a rational framework that attempts to explain seemingly irrational behavior, the violent destruction of books and libraries, as goal-oriented, officially sanctioned policy.

CAUSES FOR DESTRUCTION

One might argue that the destruction of libraries is over determined because of the interplay of many contributing forces. Indeed, the overlay of influencing factors and chaotic conditions often makes it difficult to determine whether acts of destruction are accidental or intentional. While it may be possible to attribute an isolated incidence of the destruction of books and libraries to the realm of the unintentional, systemic destruction must be considered intentional and relatively coordinated. Destruction can be internal (within a nation and ranging from quiet deeds of censorship to aggressive acts of vandalism, terrorism, civil unrest, civil war, or genocide) or external (a function of war or conquest). While small-scale destruction may occur during civilian unrest, major internal destruction occurs when a change in ruling regime initiates censorship and purging. This may escalate into the annihilation of the materials of a particular despised group, often a religious, racial, or political group. In extreme cases, revolutionaries who view libraries as remnants of a pernicious social or political system carry out massive destruction. Indeed, by the twentieth century, libraries throughout the world had come to be associated with intellectuals, education, scholarship, colonialism, history, tradition, and ideals of democracy and humanism, and the destruction of books and libraries was a means by which revolutionaries could express anti-intellectual, anti-humanist, anti-historical, and anti-Western attitudes. Some of the most violent destruction has occurred because of communism. This ideology, given form by totalitarian regimes, requires libraries to serve the revolution (as in Russia), serve or get out of the way of the revolution (as in China), or become irrelevant (as in Cambodia, where the literate population was eliminated). According to mainstream Communist doctrines, all cultural institutions must foster the goals of a new society and new man as defined by the leadership.

A different dynamic occurs in the *external* destruction of libraries. Nationalism, expressed through imperialistic, militaristic, and/or racist policies, provides the predominating impetus for destruction by the political right, although the left also may express tendencies of virulent nationalism. Thus, nationalists such as the Nazis and Serbs, as well as Communists whose socialist doctrines have been compromised by imperialist impulses (as in Tibet, for instance), have destroyed libraries. During war, sins of omission may occur in which books and libraries become casualties when bombs go astray or when troops occupy library buildings and indulge in random acts of vandalism or trophy collection. However, sins of commission, including widespread destruction of books and libraries, usually have a motivation that is often masked by claims of accidental destruction. At the less culpable end (but still of concern) is the violence to culture, such as that which occurs during strategic bombings, which is justified as part of modern warfare—unfortunate, but not intentional. Further along a scale of intentionality is the deliberate destruction of written materials and libraries because of their function as repositories of materials that legitimatize existing power structures and serve as national symbols that express prestige and culture. Justified as a wartime prerogative, military attacks often target such symbols. Regimes seize books as loot and dismantle information infrastructures as a way of neutralizing their enemies and preparing for long-term occupation or outright annexation. An example is Iraq's devastation of Kuwait's libraries in 1990.

Extremist regimes often seek to obliterate the identity and sovereignty of a defeated opponent and assume control of all its resources. Destroying the enemy's intellectual and cultural institutions is a means of breaking the will to resist, eliminating competition, and neutralizing the threat that the other nation's creeds and values may pose to one's own. Thus, the Iraqis destroyed Kuwaiti libraries as part of a plan to reduce the country to a neutralized colony, subject to the will of Iraqi nationalists—a pattern reminiscent of the Nazis' destruction of Poland. The Chinese destroyed Tibet's libraries because these institutions supported a separate Tibetan identity based on Buddhism, a creed antithetical to socialist transformation. The Serbs destroyed Muslim libraries because of the perceived imperatives of ethnic cleansing. When the goal of battle is the obliteration of a culture (as opposed to simply unseating a regime), the conquest of territories and their populations is accompanied by the destruction of libraries and any other institutions supporting memory or legitimizing past identities (Chapman 1994). Such conquests result in the devaluation of entire peoples and cultures.

The deliberate destruction of libraries and other cultural resources as a strategy of twentieth-century war began with the Germans' annihilation of the centuries-old university library at Louvain, Belgium, in World War I. During a six-day rampage of burnings, hostage takings, looting, and executions, troops destroyed the medieval city and a library holding 230,000 volumes, including a collection of 750 medieval manuscripts and more than a thousand incunabula (books printed before 1501). According to historian Barbara Tuchman (1962), the burning of Louvain was not just a punishment for alleged Belgian resistance but also a warning to enemies of Germany, a demonstration to the world of Germany's strength. Indeed, the burning of the library shocked the world—an indication of the innocence of the times.

Germans were forced to provide reparations, and these, along with a large-scale postwar international effort, led to the rebuilding of the library. During World War II, the Germans burned the Louvain Library again. In fact, under the Nazis, the Germans accelerated use of the destruction of cultural institutions as a weapon of modern warfare and extended their use of deliberate terror through policies of *Kriegsbrauch,* which stipulated that "[W]ar cannot be conducted merely against the combatants of an enemy state but must seek to destroy the total material and intellectual (*geistig*) resources of the enemy" (Tuchman 1962, 321). Destruction became more organized than in the past, and violence to cultural materials and institutions became a central part of the overall plan of dominance

(Borin 1993). The purpose was to break the population's will. There were numerous examples, but this one gives a flavor of the Nazis' attitude. In 1943, in retaliation for the shooting of a soldier, German troops methodically soaked each room of the Royal Society Library in Naples with gasoline and ignited them by throwing in hand grenades. Why? Perhaps the best explanation is that the Nazis knew the Neapolitan people placed great importance on the library (Stubbings 1993). Approximately 200,000 books and manuscripts were destroyed, including some of the finest treasures of Italian history. Nazi Germany was overt and explicit in its use of violence to culture as a weapon of war, as was Imperialist Japan. While some of their destruction may be attributed to the virulent nature of total war (which accounts for the questionable scale of collateral damage in the Allied carpet bombings of German and Japanese cities), Germany and Japan's initiatives during World War II (1939–1945) justify designation as libricide and closely parallel other cases: Iraq's devastation of Kuwait's libraries (1990–91), China's ethnocide in Tibet, and the "ethnic cleansing" of libraries in a disintegrating Yugoslavia (1991–1999).

Libricides are engineered by extremist leaders who wield unlimited power within their states, promote radical ideas, and justify violence (internal and external) as necessary to achieving ideological goals. The conditions conducive to the rise of libricidal regimes are the result of processes arising from group psychological tendencies that are rooted in cultural predispositions and activated, in part, by difficult life conditions or "hard times." The psychological and cultural origins of mass killings (i.e. political violence) lie in responses to the social disintegration brought on by war and/or upheaval from rapid urbanization, secularization, and economic depression (Staub 1989). This same constellation of factors is also involved in violence to culture, an end product of a process set in motion by frustration and an "underlying malaise in society that in various ways blocks the paths to personal or collective fulfillment of basic human needs" (Lumsden 1983, 4). When individuals perceive security, well-being, self-concept, world view, and even life itself as threatened, and when cultural and social conditions create demands exceeding a people's resources to cope, expressions of anger, resentment, and despair occur (Marsella and Yamada 2000). Traditional socio-cultural and political patterns are discredited, and people turn to alternate visions—nationalism or communism, for instance—that promise identity, hope, and control over events. In post-World War I Europe, the large and vague expectations on the part of millions of unemployed and uprooted peasants, war veterans, frontline heroes, and dissatisfied students created a breeding ground for intense nationalism and fascism, which promised novelty as well as shelter, food, and jobs and proffered the security of group identity, guidance, and structure (Einaudi 1968). At the same time, communism posed an alternate vision of an end to oppressive economic structures and the promise of an egalitarian and just society. In general, both reactionary ideologies and communism offered the vision of a radically new and better world in which the individual and his or her group or society could reach full potential.

Political ideologies are particularly seductive in that they justify action in response to the victimization, frustration, and impotence brought on by hard times. Still further, by identifying scapegoats, ideologies provide a channel for aggression stemming from feelings of vulnerability. Identifying an "enemy" has beneficial psychological effects in times of chaos when there is no overt aggressor (Staub 1989). Any threat to well-being, safety, and survival can be construed as the enemy, as when neighboring states or distant powers are seen as "thwarting" nationalist destiny; when races "contaminate" bloodlines and prevent dominance by a master race; or a class of society "sabotages" revolution. Because any entity with this kind of potential has an institutionalized cultural framework that usually includes books and libraries, these material artifacts and institutions become targets.

Libricide involves regime-sponsored activities that express the full scope of the pattern discussed above. A slide toward extremism may trigger an initial stage of libricide, which involves the homogenization of national discourse and censorship of public libraries. It also involves influential leaders identifying an enemy and calling for campaigns to negate subversive influences. However, this process can be arrested. In the 1950s, an escalation of anti-communism in the United States under the guidance of Senator Joseph McCarthy resulted in the targeting of intellectuals and media figures and censorship of libraries. McCarthy's campaigns played on predispositions within the population toward anti-intellectualism, anti-liberalism, and virulent anti-communism. While the American people eventually rejected this movement, contemplation of McCarthyism does inhibit complacency concerning the immunity of democratic societies to ideological extremism.

But what is an "ideology" and what else does one do besides identify the enemy?

IDEOLOGIES

Although ideology is often defined broadly as any body of doctrine or thought, it is used in many different ways. While sometimes used as a synonym for creeds and outlooks, ideology often was defined by twentieth-century historians and political scientists as a *political* belief system that seeks the total reconstruction of society, differing from creeds and outlooks in its greater explicitness, systematization, comprehensiveness, and urgency, as well as in the high intensity of concentration focused upon it (Shils 1931). To these scholars, ideology refers to an extremist sociopolitical program or philosophy constructed around a transforming idea, and that is the sense in which the term is applied in this book. Under this usage of the term, political regimes use ideologies to organize beliefs and attitudes into a common, public, and broadly agreed set of rules that help regulate and control behavior in social and political contexts (Taylor 1991). Rather than originating among the people whose behavior is being governed by the ideology, these rules are shaped and imposed by an authoritarian or (ultimately) totalitarian elite. An ideology is a theory that is like a map; it explains complex social phenomena, makes behavioral expectations concrete, and simplifies sociopolitical behavior. Ideological precepts are explicit and rigid (Taylor 1991), and they replace traditional value systems, such as those based on religious principles.

In an ideology-based political climate, both individual and cultural behavior must conform to a comprehensive pattern of moral and cognitive beliefs. In the eyes of political extremists, for example, reading and research are political acts, their purpose to further ideological goals, rather than inherently valuable activities that enrich the individual and advance the knowledge base of the human community. In fact, citizens under an extremist regime need not—indeed must not—have recourse to ideas that fall outside the ideological system of thought. Regimes espousing such ideologies do not regard "the disciplined pursuit of truth—by scientific procedures and in the mood characteristic of modern science—as part of its obligations" (Shils 1931, 73). The concepts of autonomous spheres of activity, an autonomous tradition of disciplined intellectual pursuits, and even of an individual's independent cognitive powers and strivings are alien to the orthodoxy demanded by the ideological orientation.

Despite the appearance of strength in the unity of ideas, fear is the real source of power. Ideologues fear books. They fear letting information reach the people, and they also fear unfettered scholarship and learning. Since ideologies thrive on intellectual closure, books and libraries fall under tremendous suspicion as entities that support both traditional systems and intellectual expansion, and have the potential to influence individual perception and to sow dissent. Libraries and books can be antithetical to ideological vision. Throughout history, extremist rulers have declared the necessity of destroying books and libraries. In 640 A.D., after the Arabic conquest of Egypt, Omar the Caliph is said to have instructed his commander, "If these writings of the Greeks agree with the book of God, they are useless and need not be preserved; if they disagree, they are pernicious and ought to be destroyed"—whereupon the manuscripts of the Alexandrian Library were used as fuel to heat the 4,000 baths of the city (as quoted in Thiem 1979, 509–10).

In the hands of extremist elites, ideology becomes an abstract solution requiring universal application; they mobilize elements of irrationality in human conduct (Pfaff 1993). For example, book burning becomes celebratory and invigorating; beating up an elder from a despised group demonstrates virility. Millenarianism—the rejection of an evil contemporary world (a demonized world of Jews, Muslims, imperialists, counterrevolutionaries, or any other maligned group)—is based on the expectation that only complete and radical change will produce a world without deficiencies, a transformed world of political or social perfection, a utopia. People are exhorted to reject the past, and within an environment of passionate and total commitment to millenarian missions, traditional cultural items become expendable. Under the influence of Nazism, Joseph Goebbels, the German Minister of Propaganda, joyously lauded book burning:

> Therefore, you [students] have done well in the middle of this night to throw into the flames these unspiritual relics of the past. It is a strong, great, and symbolic performance, a performance which should document for all the world: here the spiritual foundations of the November [Weimar] Republic sink to the ground. But out of these ruins there will arise the phoenix of a new spirit. . . . The past lies in the flames . . . today under this sky and with these flames we take a new oath: The Reich and the Nation and our Leader, Adolf Hitler—*Heil! Heil! Heil!*. (Snyder 1981, 121–2)

For an ideology to gain political backing, a critical mass of citizens must ultimately embrace it. The first step often is its forced imposition. The state through its official structures employs methods of dominance that reinforce the government's ideals. Dueling ideologies result in a dire fate for cultural materials (and populations) in contested areas. In 1940 Russian troops occupied the Baltic states of Estonia, Latvia and Lithuania and "cleansed" the bookstores and libraries, burning unacceptable titles and proscribing 4,000 books and pamphlets as part of the process of transforming the cultural environment to align with Communist tenets. In 1941 the Nazis conquered these states, purged Communist materials, and aligned printed materials and cultural institutions within the tenets of Nazism. They, in turn, were driven out in 1944–45. "Succeeding regimes brought not only an appalling waste of human lives, but also rapidly alternating prohibitions of books, purging of libraries and the rewriting of history and textbooks" (UNESCO 1996, 4).

Ideologies can reflect politics of the right or the left. To varying degrees, destructive and aggressive regimes may express multiple ideological tendencies. Because of the political structure of modern nations, nationalism is the organizing force behind most political regimes. When a state becomes aggressively nationalistic and adopts nationalism as an all-encompassing ideological program, it also may adopt imperialistic, militaristic, and racist rationales and practices. Nazi Germany and pre-World War II Japan come to mind. Even a revolutionary state like China, which is driven by communism, may be influenced by nationalism and its attendant tendencies (as in its relations with Tibet). However, even among these coexisting ideologies and policies, one typically dominates and provides the principal rationale for violence and libricide. In internal conflicts in the twentieth century, communism was the main player; in international conflicts, it was most often nationalism.

Nationalism

From its roots in Europe, nationalism has grown to become the dominating political ideal of modern times. It is linked with popular sovereignty; consent of the governed; secularism; diminishing loyalties along religious, tribal, clannish, and feudal lines; and the spread of urbanization, industrialization, and improved communications (Kohn 1968). Nationalism is the identification of a people with a state formed around a specific geographical location. The identity of this "imagined community" (Anderson 1991) is forged within communal bonds of primordial identities shaped by common language, ethnicity, or religion. Loyalty once linked to these seminal identities is channeled, and nationalism derives its charismatic appeal from a combination of political legitimacy and emotional power, i.e. the power sensed from "belonging," from being assigned an esteemed identity. However, nationalism has the potential for a polarization based on clear rules for inclusion and exclusion. In the hands of extremists, nationalism may be pitched at a virulent level, co-opted to rationalize violent policies, and developed as the ideological foundation for fanatic behavior.

There has been much academic agonizing and confusion over the relative efficacy of nationalism because its role in contemporary politics and world affairs has been, alternately, an integrative and a deconstructive force. Few scholars question the importance of nationalism as the foundation of modern political and organizational structure, but some have spoken out on its potential for toxicity. Benedict Anderson (1991) refers to nationalism as the "pathology of modern developmental history." As early as 1849, John Stuart Mill wrote that nationalism makes men indifferent to the rights and interests of "any portion of the human species save that which is called by the same name, and speaks the same language, as themselves . . . the sentiment of nationality so far outweighs the love of liberty, that the people are willing to abet their rulers in crushing the liberty and independence of any people not of their race and language" (as quoted in Kohn 1968, 67). On the other hand, some scholars emphasize that nationalism can be a positive force, as when it served as the fundamental political force mobilizing resistance to Nazism. It was "Churchill's indomitable Englishness, his ability to mobilize the British people by means of a soaring rhetoric of patriotism and evocation of history; the appeal of De Gaulle to a 'certain idea' of France 'as dedicated to an exalted and exceptional destiny'; the patriotism of Dutch, Belgians, Norwegians, Czechs, Poles, and the others prepared to fight on in 1940 and 1941, when victory was impossible to foresee" that halted Hitler (Pfaff 1993, 77).

These examples from scholarly literature on nationalism reflect the two common uses of "nationalism": to denote doctrines of excessive patriotism that seek to advance one nation's interests at the expense of others; and to refer to a less expansionist patriotism, a devotion and loyalty to one's own nation. Another way to interpret the range of usage is that it marks the difference between "open-society nationalism," a pluralistic political society that stresses the self-determination of the individual and a nation of fellow citizens irrespective of race or ethnic descent, and "closed-society nationalism," which stresses the nation's native character, common origins (race, blood), rootedness in ancestral soil, and ethnic purity. The inspiration for closed-society nationalism is tribal and territorial, and it is informed by biological or historical determinism (Kohn 1968). Open-society nationalism becomes closed when it assumes an extreme nature and takes on the characteristics of an ideology.

Hans Kohn (1968) described nationalism as a political creed that inspires the supreme loyalty of the majority of people to the nation-state, and which serves as the indispensable framework for all social, cultural, and economic activities. Kohn (1968) believes that nationalism is manifested differently because it is conditioned by the social structure, the intellectual traditions and cultural history, and the geographic location of the society in which nationalism finds itself. What is striking, however, is the basic similarity of the trigger pattern that often occurs and is instrumental in shifting nationalism from benign creed to toxic ideology: nationalism, expressed as an ideology, thrives on conditions of social

disruption, which fosters grievances and an increased receptivity to ideological commitment and authoritarian leaders who offer transformative
solutions.

In this book, nationalism concerns us as an ideology: an encompassing,
belief-driven sociopolitical program that provides systematic rules and
seeks the ultimate transformation of society. As an ideology, nationalism
"expresses the inflamed desire of the insufficiently regarded to count for
something among the cultures of the world" (Berlin 1991, 261). Leaders
like Hitler, Milosevic, and Saddam Hussein exploit the real grievances of
their people and invoke the great myths of national destiny and national
persecution in order to marshal support for aggressive actions leading to
an allegedly glorious future. The victimization felt by a critical mass of
the population paves the way for creating scapegoats and identifying "enemies." The enemy is anyone that interferes in the realization of the idealized nation by refusing to recognize its claims, by occupying what is
regarded as national territory, and by blocking the expression of its national character or the use of its language (Pfaff 1993). Because of the
function of libraries as material and symbolic preservers of memory and
national and cultural identity, libraries provide stubborn witness against
nationalistic claims; they may be annihilated if perceived to block goals
of national grandeur and power.

Militarism and Imperialism

Nationalism is often supported by militarism and a quasi-ideological
policy, imperialism. Militarism is a way of thinking that places war and
the preparation for war as the central instrument of foreign policy and the
highest form of public service (Burns 1933). When the state and society
accords primacy to the armed forces, militarism is expressed as both a
policy orientation and as a hierarchical power relationship. In a militaristic
society, the armed forces (often, through a leader that constitutes himself
as supreme commander of both military and civil affairs) unilaterally determine the nature of basic institutions, the choice of leaders, the allocation
of resources, and the rights and duties of citizens (Radway 1968). Militarism can overshadow creeds by providing rule-governed default mechanisms as when a nation mobilizes for war, or it can link with ideology
in totalitarian societies where the military and state apparatuses are fused.
Militarism accommodates very well to extreme ideologies, because the
very term "military" implies an acceptance of organized force as a legitimate means for realizing social objectives (Lang 1968). Militarism exalts
an institutional structure—the military establishment—and its function—

the application of violence (Radway 1966). Extreme militarists often view violence as an expression of virility in which "[b]loodshed is a cleansing and sanctifying thing, and the nation which regards it as the final horror has lost its manhood" (as quoted in Blackey 1982, 412). Militarism is shadowed by imperialism. Imperialism adds a set of values (including national self-interest and manifest destiny) that rationalize and justify war to the extent that war becomes imperative (Carlton 1990). Imperialism, which is not as comprehensive as nationalism, militarism, or communism, is perhaps better thought of as a *policy*. Imperialism aims at "creating, organizing, and maintaining an empire; that is, a state of vast size composed of various more or less distinct national units and subject to a single centralized will" (Bonn 1968, 605).

Imperialism and militarism have a symbiotic relationship. By supporting expansion, national wealth, and foreign conquest, imperialism seeks glory, wealth, and dominion. The aggression of the imperialistic nation arises from attitudes characteristic of militarism—what is alien, foreign, or outside the frontier is barbarian. Perversely, whether or not the outside entity is overtly threatening, it is construed as something that must be "defended" against. Rigidly disciplinarian and hierarchical, militarism requires citizens and soldiers alike to have a fanatical personal loyalty to a leader and to surrender all individuality. War is an instrument for enforcing the will of either a god or an idolized leader, or for prompting the biological and social determinism of natural selection and the survival of the fittest. Imperialism, while a creed of superiority and strength, is founded on the belief that a nation's power is of a divine origin that obligates its carriers to make use of it. For example, Japan's pursuit of empire was executed under the mantle of an Emperor whose authority was greater than any god's. The military, motivated by visions of Japan's transformation into a divinely sanctioned empire, believed that the war—even the violence—would ultimately benefit not only Japan but its victims as well. China, for example, would become a better China because of Japan's aggression (Chang 1997).

Militarists identify the enemy as deserving destruction. A prototypical militaristic regime, Japan's quest for empire in the 1930s and 1940s resulted in the murder of almost six million men, women, and children; during their occupation of China, Korea, Indonesia, Burma, Indochina, and elsewhere in Asia, the odds in these regions of being killed by a Japanese militarist in any given year was about 1 percent (Rummel 1992). The destruction toll for books and libraries paralleled this in ferocity. For example, the Japanese destroyed every library in the Philippines. Throughout history, militarism and imperialism frequently have been implicated in the destruction of books and libraries. When they weren't burned or scattered to the elements after a military loss, libraries were triumphantly carried home as prizes of war. Julius Caesar and Napoleon are particularly well known for enriching their nation's patrimony through loot from despoiled libraries. In this century, the Germans systematized, as they did mass murder, the tendency of belligerents to neutralize the aesthetic and cultural arm of the enemy by destroying or stealing material resources. According to the logic of nationalism and militarism, if culture gives an aura of prestige to an enemy city, country, or regime, conquering that culture must include the removal of this aura (Detling 1993). This is how a nation motivated by a millenarian vision ascends the cultural ladder and achieves the destiny and dominance promised by its leaders.

In World War I, it was out-of-control militarism and thwarted imperialism that ushered in the era of total war. Germany's military enthusiastically carried out the terror that nineteenth-century theorist Karl von Clausewitz and subsequent military strategists had posed as necessary to expediting war. According to modern theories of war, the need for war to be short, sharp, and decisive presupposes that civilians cannot be excluded as targets of offensive missions; when the war becomes oppressive enough, terrorized populations will pressure their leaders to surrender (Tuchman 1962). During World War I, the Germans (and the Allies) experimented with tactics in which the lives of civilians and the nation's resources were fair tender; both sides would perfect their techniques in World War II, never acknowledging that the use of terror often was counterproductive and stiffened resistance. One of the lures of war has always been the promise of material gains. Militaristic and imperialistic regimes ignore the possibility that gains may be ephemeral and are often outweighed by the costs that retaliation and prolonged battle can bring. In pursuit of a transformed society, the militaristic or imperialistic government steps easily from mere political goals into the realm of outright fanaticism, and total war leads to total devastation.

Racism

Nationalism, militarism, and imperialism together form a lethal trinity, rendered even more toxic when their tendencies toward prejudice reach ideological proportions that encompass racist policies. The belief or doctrine that inherent racial differences determine cultural and individual achievement, racism is essentially an ethos of paranoia that equates "otherness" with "enemy." Racism takes on ideological characteristics when extremist leaders seek to promote the superiority of their own race through

official programs that deny simple rights to other races. Racism, like other
ideological expressions, thrives when a society is disintegrating, when
desperate populations will embrace what seems a simple, clear-cut solutions to their plight, and a scapegoat provides a channel for their aggression. Tapping into a basic human fear of strangers, racist ideology can
rapidly turn a majority against a subsection of the national populace simply because the goals of the nation are presented as dependent on race-
linked attributes, and all individuals without those attributes are seen as
standing in the way of progress.

Exactly what defines a race of people, of course, is a variable thing. In
the field of anthropology, a race is a group of people with common physical and genetic characteristics. A more common use of the word refers to
a group of people related by common descent or heredity. It can also refer
to any people united by history, language, or cultural traits. Racist identification of an enemy can be based on any one or any combination of
these definitions, a flexibility that only adds to confusion in pinpointing
the doctrine's error. Blurred distinctions between race and ethnicity add
another level of confusion. It has been argued that "race" should be reserved for those showing similar *physical* characteristics, and "ethnicity"
for those with similar *cultural* characteristics (Carlton 1990). Race, some
have argued, has to do with the categorization of people, while ethnicity
has to do with a group's ethno-cultural identity (i.e. the extent to which
an individual endorses and expresses the cultural traditions, practices, and
lifestyle of a particular group) (Marsella and Yamada 2000). Another word
that is frequently thrown into the pot is "ethnocentric," which is defined
as "regarding one's own race or ethnic group as of supreme importance."
Racism, especially ideologically justified racism, is the exponentially enhanced expression of ethnocentrism.

Germany's National Socialist doctrine, also called Nazism, stands as a
prominent, infamous example of racist ideology. The well-known statistician of democide (murder by government), R.J. Rummel (1992, 84) argued that the destruction wrought by the Nazis' vision of a supreme Aryan
nation was every bit as potent as Soviet and Chinese Marxism—their
"view of the Good Society, a particular interpretation of facts, and a program for moving toward this utopia [was] no less absolutist, no less ty-
rannical, no less murderous" than the Communist regimes'. The genocide
of the Jews—like other genocides, essentially an exercise in community
building (Gourevitch 1998)—was the result of an embedded inclination
toward authoritarianism, careful ideological indoctrination, and one of the
most meticulously administered states in history. Nazis constructed an
image of the Jews as the "specter of an absolute menace" (Gourevitch

1998, 95) and held Jewish blood responsible for contaminating and weakening the nation, causing the loss of World War I and postwar depression and decline. According to the Nazis—a group that included many scholars and intellectuals—full realization of the preordained dominance of the Aryan race was dependent on extinguishing Judaism. Absolute, unapologetic commitment to racism was evident in policies that placed racial cleansing higher in priority than essential wartime activities. Boxcars carrying Jews to the concentration camps, for instance, were given priority over the transport of military supplies and troops, even in critical stages of the war. Behaviors aimed at the extinction of the Jewish population did not stop until Nazi Germany expired in the ruins of Berlin. In a concentrated effort to distinguish between "us and them," the Nazis also moved beyond anti-Semitism to devise programs to deal with all "inferior" ethnic groups, beginning with the Poles. First executing Polish intellectuals and teachers, dismantling education systems, and destroying libraries, German officials attempted to work the remaining peasantry to death. In what has been termed "a forgotten holocaust," Nazis killed three million non-Jewish Poles along with three million Polish Jews—22 percent of Poland's total population (Lukas 1986).

The Nazi program against the Jews neatly illustrates what genocide is: A coordinated plan of actions aimed at complete destruction of a group. Genocide is characterized by a totality of intention (Carlton 1990), the reason that it often extends beyond the taking of lives to the dismantling of the group's cultural artifacts and institutions. In Germany and Poland, synagogues were demolished and Jewish books and libraries were methodically destroyed or confiscated for use in institutes devoted to addressing the "Jewish problem." These institutes and any scholarship, whether "scientific" or "historical," that demonstrated the superiority of the Aryan race received generous funding. Such practices are common in ideology-driven systems: All social and cultural institutions eventually become instruments of ideological promotion, and prejudice becomes intellectualized as fact (Carlton 1990). Genocide demands the total co-option or extinction of evidence of a despised group's existence or cultural achievement that could contradict the perpetrators' rationalizations for discrimination or annihilation.

The fact that a racist regime may place more credence on ethnicity than the minority itself does suggests the subjectivity of various classifications, as does the fluctuating degree to which individuals identify with an ethnocentric group or hold their identity as significant. Once a group is attacked because of its ethnicity, the group's awareness of its own ethnic identity intensifies. An example is the Serbian ethnic cleansing of Bosnia during the 1990s, which caused many secular Bosnians to adopt radical Muslim beliefs in reaction to the attack. In themselves, racial groupings are neither absolutes nor purely intellectual categories: but they can be called into play when the assignment of identity confers advantage in competition over scarce social or geopolitical goods (Eriksen 1993). Racism can be an effective ideology in nationalist wars when the goal is to conquer, cleanse, and take all (Maas 1996); it certainly served Japan's attempts to dominate Asia earlier in the century and, similarly, has propelled the Serbian quest to bring about a Greater Serbia.

When racism accompanies extreme nationalistic tendencies, identity becomes all-important and leaders often exhibit a single-minded, even fanatic, concentration on demonizing and demolishing the alien group. Because cultural artifacts and institutions express identity so concretely, it becomes necessary to extinguish the group's cultural expression and expunge from disputed territories any evidence of the group. For example, in Liberia, Burundi, and Rwanda, continuing racist acts of terrorism, ethnic cleansing, and related archival cleansing have almost completely destroyed all repositories and archives (UNESCO 1996).

Throughout the 1990s, as the nation of Yugoslavia disintegrated into separate republics and enclaves, various areas were cleared of offending ethnic groups. In the most egregious instances, Serbs killed, raped, and drove Muslims and Croats from their villages; often, the price of survival was the signing over of deeds to farms, houses, and cars. In addition, official documents including diplomas, car registration papers, and birth certificates were confiscated and destroyed; individuals and families were left with no proof of identity and no possessions. Municipal, historical, and cultural records were expunged, and archives and libraries were burned to the ground along with churches, mosques, museums, and historical monuments. Over the long term, destruction of monuments and institutions may do even more to "disinfect" the area than even the destruction of houses and shops, which can be rebuilt. To materially and psychologically diminish people's dignity, happiness, and ability to fulfill basic needs, to turn them into human flotsam, is a decisive step in the direction of the ultimate evil: the taking of human life. Ideologies that uproot entire groups and their traditions express a profound rejection of humanity and facilitate descent into a moral abyss.

Communism

It is important to note that *reactionary* ideologies and policies such as nationalism, imperialism, and militarism are not the sole agents of genocide. Communism, a revolutionary ideology, has been heavily implicated in genocidal practices, as Stalin's devastation of the *kulaks* (comparatively wealthy Soviet peasants) and Pol Pot's destruction of Cambodia's urban and educated population has too clearly demonstrated. Thus, the qualities that define a target group may be historical, biological, ethnic, or religious but also, as in the case of the Communists, political or socioeconomic. The goal of Communism was revolution, which has been defined as "political and/or social and/or economic and/or cultural upheaval which calls for a fundamental change in the existing order; it is relatively rapid and generally employs the use or threat of force" (Blackey and Paynton 1976, 8). Thus, the economic and political elite of the previous order and groups that might function as recalcitrant reactionary counter forces often become natural targets. The genocidal actions almost always extended to attacks on traditional cultural materials and institutions, and thus, on books and libraries. J.W. Fulbright once observed, "A true revolution is almost always violent and usually it is extremely violent. Its essence is the destruction of the social fabric and institutions of a society, and an attempt, not necessarily successful, to create a new society with a new social fabric and new institutions" (as quoted in Blackey 1982, 405).

Communist doctrines have their roots in events that responded to great social distress—in the French Revolution, which set the precedent of revolt against blatant economic and political inequality; and in the Marxist movement, which was an intellectual response to the brutal working conditions and social disintegration of industrialization. Marxism, a set of theories developed by German philosopher and economist Karl Marx in the 1800s, identified class struggle as the main agency of historical change and predicted the succession of capitalism by a socialist order, or classless society. After the Russian Revolution in 1917, Marxist doctrines were adapted to Russian conditions, most profoundly by Lenin, who created an administrative structure for radical socialism and contributed to a new ideological platform: Communism. His 1902 publication *What Is To Be Done?* is considered the seminal source of Communist organizational doctrine. Four ideas stand out: a fear of spontaneity as a guiding force in revolution; the belief that the working class needed the guidance of a politically conscious revolutionary vanguard; the idea that this vanguard should be a small party of carefully selected, disciplined professional revolutionaries operating under highly centralized direction; and the concept of a "political monopoly" in which there is no competition with the Party for access to the masses (Fainsod 1968). All opposition was suppressed. Leninism, the state ideology, rationalized the Russian government's progression from authoritarianism to totalitarianism. Lenin's successor, Stalin, took the dictatorship still further by repudiating egalitarian and utopian Marxism and establishing a dictatorship within the Party, based on his "discovery" that the state must grow stronger before it could wither away. Under his leadership, Russian Communism became a fanatical ideology that justified the destruction of all human or institutional opponents. With socialism as a facade for the pursuit of power, Stalin ordered the mass murder of millions, a significant percentage of the estimated 62 million citizens and foreigners killed by the Soviet Communist Party in the twentieth century (Rummel 1994).

Communist doctrines would ultimately provide an ideological base for the overthrow of oppressive power structures in many countries. Like other ideologies, communism sprang from and appealed to those struggling with disastrous economic and social conditions. The Communists strove to export their revolution by making people aware of the possibility of other realities, and then posing communism as the inevitable alternative to oppression. The enemies of their revolutions are typically the rich and powerful—including local political and religious elites and colonial powers with their Western worldviews. For revolutionaries, books represent, even embody the oppressor because they support skills, values, and the oppressive way of life of the bourgeoisie. Books are vanities that by perpetuating the past become a hindrance to present and future revolution, creativity, and progress (Thiem 1979). Since libraries supported tradition and existing power structures, they were the embodiment of cultural systems that assigned lower-status groups to varying degrees of cultural invisibility (Harris 1986). Within revolutionary parameters, the triumph of the proletariat required the elimination of bourgeois tendencies and a clean break from the past and so the effects of Communism on libraries were highly destructive.

For Marx (1963), "[t]he tradition of all the dead generations weighs like a nightmare on the brain of the living" (Marx 1963:15). According to Jon Thiem (1979), utopians (including Communist revolutionaries such as Marx) harbor no doubts about their methods of selecting books for destruction or about the permanent implications of irrevocable destruction. Their worldview is the only acceptable worldview and denying later generations the right of choosing what they would read is conscionable because the new order will remain forever. "For the modern utopian the destruction of the learning of the past, or its radical revision and reduction, represents the cessation of historical process and constitutes a basic precondition for happiness and justice" (Thiem 1979, 519). For revolutionary regimes, history begins with the revolution.

Russia carried censorship to extremes. Beginning in 1917, Russian libraries were governed by a "policy of permanent purge" in which recurring censorship initiatives occurred in accordance with current Party dictates (Korsch 1983, 2). The purges had two major aspects: ideological protection of the masses and serial denigration of political opponents. By the middle of 1918, the shelves of old established libraries were almost denuded as books were sent to the paper mills or locked away. By 1924 booklists guided the expunging of problematic materials, particularly in the areas of philosophy, psychology, ethics, religion, social sciences, natural sciences, history of literature, history, geography, *belles-lettres,* and children's books. In what Gorky called "intellectual vampirism," the works of Plato, Kant, Tolstoy, Dostoevsky, and others were removed. Insight into Party policy may be garnered from the comments of Lenin's wife, Krupskaia, one of the censors: It was desirable to purge the books of philosophers because they promoted harmful ideas and also because their presence was senseless— "a man of the masses will not read Kant"; other books were pernicious because they dealt with God, or monarchist rubbish, or subjects that "had long outlived their time" (as quoted in Korsch 1983, 12). Krupskaia posed her actions as protecting the interests of the mass readers and shielding them from the destructive influence of undesirable works, and under her guidance, purges proceeded willy-nilly, as fearful librarians purged obediently, but blindly, and local political figures demonstrated their adherence to what they perceived as a political mandate. Krupskaia commented on the zeal:

> The librarian is afraid to lend the book out, "to be on the safe side." In the Northern Caucasus, they look at it this way: to give or not to give Krzhizhanovskii's book. Better not to give it; there will be trouble. . . . Not only librarians purge libraries[,] . . . everybody comes. A Komsomol member comes and says: "What's going on here? It's a disgrace, we're organizing a purge." A member of the village council comes: "The book is suspicious. Organize a purge." Everybody and his brother organizes purges. (as quoted in Korsch 1983, 13)

The situation became even more chaotic under Stalin when book purging paralleled the mass purges of political enemies. According to Soviet specialist Boris Korsch (1983, 27), "People were purged and everything related to them had to disappear, including every word they had ever written. Their books, articles and speeches became 'unbooks,' 'unarticles,' and 'unspeeches,' just as they had become 'unpersons.'" By his death in 1953, the censorship of works by out-of-favor political figures had become Party policy and Stalin's own works were targeted. Book purges became a necessary procedure by which the current leader would "undo" his predecessor.

The Soviets developed a model of "socialist librarianship" that would subsequently be exported and implemented as part of ongoing cultural revolutions within states aspiring to socialist transformation (Sroka 2000). It involved centralized, state control of all libraries and standardized policies of access and collection development. Highly censored collections were available to the public; problematic materials were withdrawn and restricted to authorized users. Librarians were enlisted as censors and charged with purifying collections of bourgeois and reactionary materials and promoting "socialist realism"—the officially sanctioned model of culture, the only acceptable mode of artistic expression. All librarians were affected, including archivists. Archivists imbued with the traditional functions of archeography—"the scholarly work of identifying, collecting, describing, and publishing manuscripts and other history sources"—were replaced by politically correct individuals who could guarantee a "positive archival development" that would advance Russification and support Soviet propaganda (Grimsted 2001, 3, 7). For example, librarians and archivists were charged with concealing World War II trophy materials seized from Germany, including eleven million books and huge numbers of archival documents (many that had been looted by the Nazis from occupied territories), while at the same time, supporting the inflated official statistics about Nazi destruction and plunder that were used to support Soviet claims of victimization (Grimsted 2001). All librarians were expected to place social activism and service to the closed Soviet system above service and traditional norms of librarianship; they were shock troops, soldiers of the cultural revolution. A detailed description of the effects of such a model, as implemented by the Chinese, can be found in Chapter Seven.

In China, censorship also was affected by Party policy and factional politics. The Communists were highly focused on an inherent tension within socialist revolutions between residues of traditional thinking and the current revolutionary thought; radicals are constantly on guard against reactionary thinking and slippage towards capitalism. In China in the mid-1960s, years after the initial revolution, Mao Tse-tung, ostensibly in reaction to a degenerating commitment to Communist tenets, led a revolution of revitalization against the "four olds"—old ideas, old cultures, old customs, and old habits. A principle target was, of course, China's intellectual and cultural structure, including books and libraries. Cultural violence and hysteria prevailed for almost a decade.

The focus of Mao's "cultural revolution" on attaining an agrarian Communist society was influential in the Khmer Rouge's takeover of Cambodia in 1975. The leadership carried Mao's doctrines to their logical conclusions: in a few days, the cities were emptied and the people driven into the countryside; the urban, governing, military, and educated classes and religious leaders were exterminated as quickly as possible. Over the next four years, 30 percent of the population was killed. While there was wholesale destruction of religious shrines, temples, and schools and, thus, of religious texts, it wasn't necessary to destroy all the books and libraries. When possessing reading skills is punishable by death, printed materials become irrelevant. Ultimately unsuccessful, Cambodia's revolution was a bizarre demonstration of the power of an extremist leadership to create not a new utopia, but a living hell.

EXTREMIST LEADERSHIP

Populations most likely to turn to ideological solutions are those with inclinations toward authoritarian power structures and with established patterns of submission and conformity, punitive rejection of other groups, and a tendency to see the world in black and white (Taylor 1991). When power falls to authoritarian regimes, control is imposed in an extremely hierarchical manner by a small group of leaders who are not constitutionally accountable and who demand obedience from the population. Ideologies flourish under authoritarian regimes because they provide a philosophical basis for acquiescence and abandonment of self, referred to by Erich Fromm (1941) as "an escape from freedom." Under conditions of acute social stress, the freedom to claim privacy, to struggle with justice, injustice, and difficult life conditions, and to express ideas in a social context (Taylor 1991) is exchanged for the certainty and simplicity of ideology. Anxiety over basic needs and securities is exchanged for a closed intellectual system based on simple suppositions that explain all existence and rationalize fate (Buchheim 1968). If conditions of social fragmentation and individual isolation become severe enough, and a leadership emerges that can use deteriorating circumstances to launch a new order, authoritarianism may intensify into totalitarianism, which is the ultimate mode in crisis and identity resolution (Tehranian 1990).

In a totalitarian system, there is finally no separateness and no autonomous spheres—but also no authentic group life. Every facet of life is understood in terms of politics. The governing party demands total conformity and assumes an unchallengeable power to bind an entire people to its vision. Books are feared as an alternative voice—a voice not necessarily of dissent but of difference (Tuchman 1980). In a narrowing of thought and social life, every part of society must be brought under the dominion of ultimately right principles (Shils 1931). There can be no challenges to the ideological liturgy. The prevailing mindset is fanaticism, which Maxwell Taylor (1991, x) defines as "behaviour which is excessive and inappropriately enthusiastic and/or inappropriately concerned with something, implying a focused and highly personalised interpretation of the world. In a political sense, [fanaticism is] behaviour which is strongly influenced and controlled by ideology, where the influence of ideology is such that it excludes or attenuates other social, political, or personal forces that might be expected to control and influence behaviour."

A crucial element in the attraction of ideologies that are institutionalized by totalitarian regimes is a willingness among the population to abandon autonomy, individuality, and social responsibility to a system of thought *and* to a charismatic leader. This leader—often an individual who possesses strong intellectual and imaginative powers—shapes a powerful, expansive, and simplified vision of the world by fleshing out a positive alternative to existing patterns of a society and its culture. The leader demonstrates an intellectual capacity to articulate this vision as part of the cosmic order (Shils 1931), and progressively removes constitutional restraints as he pushes the nation toward his vision. The fewer restraints on power within government and the more encompassing the leader's grip over all domains of citizens' lives, the more likely it is that government will act even on the leader's darkest whims and impulses (Chang 1997).

Strong identification with a leader often occurs in non-extremist forms of government, but there is a difference in quality and intensity. Just as an ideology can assume the characteristics of a messianic religion, the ideologue-leader can acquire the infallibility of a god. With an illusion of personal connection and partnership with cosmic deities through their leader, the ideology is more compelling than if the object of veneration were merely an abstraction (Buchheim 1968). Worship of Stalin spread despite (or perhaps perversely *because of*) his instituting a reign of terror fueled by paranoia, ambition, vanity, and envy. Turning on even his own comrades, he killed one million Party members between 1936 and 1939 and altogether three-quarters of Russia's governing class (Curtis 1979). During China's Cultural Revolution, the Chinese people—in the name of love for Mao and under his direction—killed and maimed thousands and destroyed large numbers of books and cultural institutions including libraries. In Germany, centuries of cultural progress were lost when, under Hitler, the people participated—actively or as witnesses—in the genocide of millions.

When deified cult leaders and persuasive ideologies numb intellectual processes (not the least of which is doubt), citizens become agents of authority and suspend critical evaluation of the morality of an action. Both the leader and those followers who carry out acts of extreme violence share a psychological process that begins within a fanaticism and progresses to antisocial behavior and, then, to an incapacity for empathy (Staub 1989). Neither human beings nor those cultural ideals (such as religious beliefs or humanism) or artifacts that were once held most dear are accorded value.

CONCLUSIONS

A theoretical framework for libricide, the violent destruction of books and libraries, has been presented above. Instability, social change, and hard times lead to the assumption of power by leaders who promise to alleviate current woes, transform society, and create a new and better world. Their comprehensive program resonates with local socio-cultural predispositions and offers simple, but compelling principles that address all aspects of behavior. As the regime consolidates its power, ideology becomes a rationale for totalitarianism; ideological orthodoxy crowds out all dissent and difference, and conformity is imposed, if necessary, through violence. Because books and libraries preserve memory, provide witness, store evidence of the validity of a multitude of perspectives, facilitate intellectual freedom, and support group identity, they are carefully controlled, sanitized, and even extensively purged. When texts are too closely associated with an enemy, a group that stands in the way of transformation or cannot or will not further ideological goals, they are attacked along with the renegade group. When human voice is extinguished, texts as the disembodied material expression of that voice are also destroyed. And that, in short, is the dynamics of libricide.

The next five chapters consist of case studies, analytical accounts of prominent twentieth-century libricides. Each is an attempt to explain libricide in a particular environment and each addresses these questions:

1. What predisposing sociocultural, economic, and political conditions existed to make an ideology and specific regime acceptable to a population?

2. How did the regime use ideology as a basis for authoritarian or totalitarian policies and programs?

3. What was the role of leaders, particularly radicals or cult figures, in libricide?

4. What was the fate of intellectuals, scholarship, and history under a particular regime?

5. On what basis was a victim group targeted and what was the ultimate fate of group members?

6. What was the regime's perception of the function of books and libraries and why were they targeted along with the groups associated with them. How and to what extent was libricide accomplished? Whose interests were served? How was it rationalized ideologically?

I believe the details of the case studies support my thesis that an extremist ideology, when promulgated fanatically by leaders with unbounded political power, poses a significant threat to the preservation of the world's written heritage. It is the prerogative of the reader to determine whether the evidence presented is sufficiently compelling as to elicit agreement.

REFERENCES

Anderson, Benedict. 1991. *Imagined Communities: Reflections on the Origin and the Spread of Nationalism.* (Revised Edition). New York: Verso.

Berlin, Isaiah. 1991. *The Crooked Timber of Humanity: Chapters in the History of Ideas,* ed. Henry Hardy. New York: Knopf.

Blackey, Robert, and Clifford T. Paynton. 1976. *Revolution and the Revolutionary Ideal.* Cambridge, Massachusetts: Schenkman.

Blackey, Robert, ed. 1982. *Revolutions and Revolutionists: A Comprehensive Guide to the Literature.* Santa Barbara, California: ABC-Clio.

Bonn, Moritz Julius. 1968. "Imperialism." In *International Encyclopedia of the Social Sciences,* ed. David L. Sills. Vol. 7. New York: The Macmillan Company and The Free Press, 605–613.

Borin, Jacqueline. 1993. "Embers of the Soul: The Destruction of Jewish Books and Libraries in Poland during World War II." *Libraries and Culture* 28 (4):445–460.

Buchheim, Hans. 1968. *Totalitarian Rule: Its Nature and Characteristics,* trans. Ruth Hein. Middletown, Connecticut: Wesleyan University Press.

Burns, C. Delisle. 1933. "Militarism." In *Encyclopedia of the Social Sciences,* eds. Edwin R. A. Seligman and Alvin Johnson. Vol. 10. New York: Macmillan Company, 446–451.

Carlton, Eric. 1990. *War and Ideology.* Savage, Maryland: Barnes & Noble Books.

Chang, Iris. 1997. *The Rape of Nanking: The Forgotten Holocaust of World War II.* New York: Basic Books.

Chapman, John. 1994. "Destruction of a Common Heritage: The Archaeology of War in Croatia, Bosnia and Hercegovina." *Antiquity* 68 (258):120–128.

Curtis, Michael. 1979. *Totalitarianism.* New Brunswick, New Jersey: Transaction Books.

Detling, Karen. 1993. "Eternal Silence: The Destruction of Cultural Property in Yugoslavia." *Maryland Journal of International Law and Trade* 17 (1):41–75.

Einaudi, Mario. 1968. "Fascism." In *International Encyclopedia of the Social Sciences*, ed. David L. Sills. Vol. 5. New York: The Macmillan Company and The Free Press, 334–341.

Eriksen, Thomas Hylland. 1993. *Ethnicity and Nationalism: Anthropological Perspectives.* London: Pluto Press.

Fainsod, Merle. 1968. "Communism: Soviet Communism." In *International Encyclopedia of the Social Sciences*, ed. David L. Sills. Vol. 3. New York: The Macmillan Company and The Free Press, 102–112.

Fromm, Erich. 1941. *Escape From Freedom.* New York: Holt, Rinehart & Winston.

Gourevitch, Philip. 1998. *We Wish To Inform You That Tomorrow We Will Be Killed With Our Families: Stories From Rwanda.* New York: Farrar Straus and Giroux.

Grimsted, Patricia Kennedy. 2001. *Trophies of War and Empire: The Archival Heritage of Ukraine, World War II, and the International Politics of Restitution.* Cambridge, Massachusetts: Harvard University Press.

Harris, Michael H. 1986. "State, Class, and Cultural Reproduction: Toward a Theory of Library Service in the United States." In *Advances in Librarianship*, ed. Wesley Simonton. Vol. 14. London: Academic Press, 211–252.

Kohn, Hans. 1968. "Nationalism." In *International Encyclopedia of the Social Sciences*, ed. David Sills, Vol. 11. New York: The Macmillan Company and The Free Press, 63–69.

Korsch, Boris. 1983. *The Permanent Purge of Soviet Libraries.* (Research Paper No. 50). Jerusalem: Hebrew University of Jerusalem: The Soviet and East European Research Center.

Lang, Kurt. 1968. "Military." In *International Encyclopedia of the Social Sciences*, ed. David L. Sills. Vol. 10. New York: The Macmillan Company and The Free Press, 305–312.

Lukas, Richard C. 1986. *The Forgotten Holocaust: The Poles Under German Occupation 1939–1944.* Lexington, Kentucky: University Press of Kentucky.

Lumsden, Malvern. 1983. "Sources of Violence in the International System." In *International Violence*, eds. Tunde Adeniran and Yonah Alexander. New York: Praeger, 3–19.

Maas, Peter. 1996. *Love Thy Neighbor: A Story of War.* New York: Alfred A Knopf.

Marsella, Anthony J., and Ann Marie Yamada. 2000. "Culture and Mental Health: An Introduction and Overview of Foundations, Concepts, and Issues." In *The Handbook of Multicultural Mental Health: Assessment and Treatment of Diverse Populations*, eds. I. Cuellar and F. Paniagua. New York: Academic Press, 3–24.

Marx, Karl. 1963. *The 18ᵗʰ Brumaire of Louis Bonaparte.* New York: International Publishers.

Pfaff, William. 1993. *The Wrath of Nations: Civilization and the Furies of Nationalism.* New York: Simon and Schuster.

Radway, Laurence I. 1968. "Militarism." In *International Encyclopedia of the Social Sciences*, ed. David L. Sills. Vol. 10. New York: The Macmillan Company and The Free Press, 300–305.

Rummel, R.J. 1994. *Death By Government.* New Brunswick, New Jersey: Transaction.

Rummel, R.J. 1992. *Democide: Nazi Genocide and Mass Murder.* New Brunswick: New Jersey.

Shils, Edward. 1931. "The Concept and Function of Ideology." In *Encyclopedia of the Social Sciences*, ed. Edwin Seligman. Vol. 7. New York: Macmillan, 66–74.

Snyder, Louis L. 1981. *Hitler's Third Reich: A Documentary History.* Chicago: Nelson-Hall.

Sroka, Marek. 2000. "'Soldiers of the Cultural Revolution': The Stalinization of Libraries and Librarianship in Poland, 1945–1953." *Library History* 16 (2):105–125.

Staub, Ervin. 1989. *Roots of Evil: the Origins of Genocide and Other Group Violence.* Cambridge: Cambridge University Press.

Stubbings, Hilda Uren. 1993. *Blitzkrieg and Books: British and European Libraries As Casualties of World War II.* Bloomington, Indiana: Rubena Press.

Taylor, Maxwell. 1991. *The Fanatics: A Behavioural Approach to Political Violence.* London: Brassey's.

Tehranian, Majid. 1990. *Technologies of Power: Information Machines and Democratic Prospects.* Norwood, New Jersey: Ablex.

Thiem, Jon. 1979. "The Great Library of Alexandria Burnt: Towards the History of a Symbol." *Journal of the History of Ideas* 40 (4):507–526.

Tuchman, Barbara W. 1962. *The Guns of August.* New York: Macmillan.

Tuchman, Barbara W. 1980. *The Book.* A lecture presented at the Library of Congress. Washington, D.C.: Library of Congress.

UNESCO Memory of the World Program. 1996. *Lost Memory: Libraries and Archives Destroyed in the Twentieth Century.* Paris: UNESCO.

Chapter 4

NAZI GERMANY:
Racism and Nationalism

"The history of the book, the object, is the dramatic history of ink, lead, and fire. In the thirties the smell of quality fuel hung over Germany. They were burning books."

(Ugresic 1998, 154)

Hitler's Germany may be the perfect case with which to explore the destruction of books and libraries in the twentieth century. With the exception of communism, every ideological element discussed in Chapter Three as contributing to cultural destruction was present. Nationalism, imperialism, militarism, racism, and totalitarianism all found well-established places in German society under Hitler's direction. These ideals converged around National Socialism—an ideology promising complete unity and a new utopia—in other words, profound relief from social conditions that had emerged after World War I. Despairing Germans, whose society had exhibited deeply nationalistic tendencies and an undercurrent of racism that had flowed since the nineteenth century, welcomed the ideas. Their acceptance created the historical phenomenon that caused World War II: a convulsive rejection of modernity and humanism. The rejection of the principles of Western civilization led ultimately to the misuse and destruction of that civilization's material expression, books and libraries.

In what was essentially a war of ideas, the Nazis murdered approximately 21 million men, women, and children. Further, they sought to expropriate or expunge their enemies' cultural heritage in outbreaks of violence justified by a Darwinian notion of Aryan races as superior and, therefore, destined to dominate and outlive all others. In seizing this destiny, they used the destruction of national and ethnic heritage as a weapon of war, as an instrument for cultural annihilation or diminishment, and as a tool for molding a Germanified future. They calibrated acts of censorship, looting, and ultimately, the destruction of books and libraries according to designations of relative racial and ethnic inferiority and superiority. The result was cultural loss proportional to the death toll.

THE RISE OF NAZI GERMANY

National Socialism (Nazism) emerged out of post-World War I trauma, severe social and economic disruption, and a pervasive condition that might be described as collective despair. The German people were disillusioned, frustrated, and filled with a sense that order and traditions had been profoundly disrupted. While other Europeans experienced much the same post-war emotional letdown, the Germans, in their bitterness, felt that the old gods of Kaiser, nation, and Germanic identity had not only been displaced but also somehow betrayed. An emotional vacuum of anger existed along with a cultural predisposition toward romanticism, hero worship, and feelings of cultural and biological superiority, paving the way for Hitler and his ideology. Hitler channeled the people's rage toward scapegoats. He provided an action plan to address immediate economic woes and promised a glorious future of national and ethnic supremacy. The energy with which Germans embraced their new quasi-religion was merely an escalation of similar enthusiasms and cultural patterns that reached back at least a hundred years.

In his 1961 study of the rise of Germanic ideology titled *The Politics of Cultural Despair,* Fritz Stern analyzes the lives and writings of three influential social critics of the late nineteenth century. This study provides the basis for his argument that the roots of Nazism were deeply embedded in German cultural consciousness. Paul de Lagarde, Julius Langbehn, and Moeller van den Bruck, Stern claims, wrote out of deep-seated political discontent. In their desire for a new faith, a new community of believers, and a world of fixed standards and certainty, they rejected liberalism and modernity, favoring instead a national religion that would bind all Germans together. Their writings resonated with the romanticism of professional Germanists, the ideology of philologists, and a superstitious faith in Nordic culture. Claiming that modern liberal society denied the spirit and tradition of their people, they called for national redemption and unity and propounded all manner of reforms—ruthless and idealistic, nationalistic and utopian. They exalted intuition and abjured reason; they longed for a new Caesar and a national heroism, justifying violence with notions of social Darwinism and outright racism. Along with the work of other intellectuals, theirs reinforced deeply rooted mechanisms of German thought and laid the foundation for what would become Hitler's National Socialism. In fact, it is possible to trace most of the ideological motifs of Nazism back to the ideas of the German romantics and these three notable disciples (Taylor 1985).

The work of Lagarde, Langbehn, and Moeller contributed to a politically exploitable climate of cultural pessimism and malaise that was widespread between 1890 and 1933. Germany, like much of the rest of the world, was undergoing a transformation from a traditional agrarian economy to a secular, urban society. After Germany's defeat in World War I, vague discontent over social disruption kindled into political violence as various factions battled in the streets. A humiliating peace treaty had profoundly threatened the people's pride in their country; many spoke of Germany as having been stabbed in the back by internal enemies, including Bolsheviks and Jews. By 1932, 7.5 million people were out of work and seventeen million—almost a third of the population—were dependent on government assistance. The economic burden of reparations, combined with a perceived breakdown of social mores (including sexual promiscuity and lack of respect for family life) caused great anxiety and depression, and a weak central government only made things worse (Staub 1989).

Group consciousness and social dialogue, which defines much of the individual's understanding of the world, was moving toward a manifestation of nationalism, in no small part because, as brought out in the last chapter, nationalism thrives where a people feels both victimized and thwarted. By 1933, the Germans—and, in particular, the professional classes—had rejected the Weimar Republic and democracy and embraced an ideology of radical German nationalism, a vision of a community based on racial purity and strength (Friedlander 1995). Hitler marshaled an ideology whose powerful emotional appeal rested firmly on making the nation the paramount object of loyalty. He capitalized on an ethnocentrism that, like anti-Semitism, had been long simmering in German culture and was brought to a boil by acute social and political conditions.

Indeed, the roots of German nationalism during the Nazi period can be found in the process by which the people came to identify with each other as a community bound together by the concept of a pure *volk* (people). In this closed society that stressed the nation's indigenous character, common blood, and rootedness in ancestral soil, the guiding ideal was an image from Germany's past. Nazi ideology took the ideas of the *volk* and "survival of the fittest" and added to them a specific imperialistic destiny that called for *lebensraum* (living room) and extension of the German Empire. Prussian military culture, which glorified force, dominance, and service to the state, added fuel to the desire to pursue Hitler's program, *Weltmacht oder Niedergang,* world-power or ruin. Traditional German notions of being a warrior people harkening back to the Teutonic Knights (erstwhile crusaders who sought to introduce Christianity and a German and Catholic culture into the Balkans) were but a short step from outright militarism.

The influence of nationalism and militarism extended far beyond the domains of government and military. Prominent German academics and intellectuals, including Roentgen (who discovered x-rays) and Reinhardt (the pioneer of the modern theater), so strongly supported nationalistic aims that in 1914 they issued the "Manifesto to the Civilized World," a declaration denying Germany's war guilt and proclaiming that it would have been national suicide not to have marched into neutral Belgium. Arguing it was Allied, not German, activity that violated international law, the Manifesto concluded: "Were it not for German militarism, German culture would have been wiped off the face of the earth. That culture, for its own protection, led to militarism since Germany, like no other country, was ravaged by invasion for centuries" (Nathan and Norden 1968, 3). In the post-war years, the authors of the Manifesto and other intellectuals, using rationales of self-defense and national entitlement, explained Germany's defeat in WWI not simply as an unfortunate loss (which would have implied the existence of a people superior to the Germans), but as the result of a Jewish-led conspiracy. This document is an important sign of how well-established the subjective postures of nationalism were even before Hitler's rise to power in the 1930s and the formal linking of nationalism with racism.

Though often using the rhetoric of nationalism, Nazism (or National Socialism) was an (ostensibly) internationalist ideology based on a theory that explained and justified everything in terms of race. Theories of evolution and biological determinism were used to justify racial hierarchies and a mandate for dominance. With Aryans being the "fittest" of all races in this scheme, evolution became the basis of state policy directed toward the fulfillment of a superior Aryan race. The creation of a superior German being and nation took precedence over all else. Nazism was fundamentally anti-intellectual and focused on will and force. Rejecting modernity, reason, the tenets of the Enlightenment, and humanism, Nazi ideology stressed the collective, loyalty to Hitler and the Reich, and obedience to ideological imperatives over individual moral responsibility.

The Nazi Party emerged from the chaos of the 1920s and early 1930s as the one group able to establish order and stability. Compatible with German national, cultural, and political roots, the Nazi program also had a distinct appeal to Germany's youth, whose need for vision and purpose was especially critical, and to veterans, who may have been suffering from posttraumatic stress disorder (PTSD), a debilitating condition characterized by restlessness, loss of meaning, lack of goals, anger, and loss of faith in the world and in authority (Staub 1989). Further adding to the appeal of Nazism was the regime's explanation of Germany's defeat in WWI as the result of the racial and biological decline of Nordic man, the creator and carrier of all culture (Buchheim 1968). According to the writings of Hitler, the decline of the Aryan race lowered on the earth "the dark veils of a time without culture," and anyone who undermines human culture by destroying its main cast (i.e. Aryans) commits the most execrable crime (Mosse 1966, 6). To prevent this crime from taking place, sources of cultural pollution had to be identified and eradicated both from within the German people and outside.

And so, while considering themselves the height of culture and civilization, the Nazis proceeded to commit some of the most horrendous crimes against humanity ever recorded in history. In the 1930s, the Nazis initiated systematic internal policies to eliminate degenerate elements. First came compulsory sterilization of the mentally ill, mentally retarded and chronic alcoholics. Having secured the future for the Aryan race, the next step was cleansing the present and erasing the past. A policy of euthanasia for handicapped babies and adults considered unworthy of life—the categories mentioned above, plus asocial or chronic criminals—was implemented. Hitler's signature alone resulted in the medical profession's "euthanasia" of more than 75,000 handicapped German babies and adults (Friedlander 1995). This series of policies was merely a prelude to Nazi genocide. Hitler's program of euthanasia paved the way for the development of killing techniques like the gas chamber and revealed the willingness of Germany's medical profession to adopt an ideological biomedical vision in which killing was a therapeutic imperative (Friedlander 1995). With wartime as a convenient cover for violence and the most basic of moral boundaries behind them, the Nazis were a short step away from extending the target of euthanasia policies to include anyone deemed unworthy of life, for any reason, by their leader.

Hitler has been the subject of an exhaustive body of literature examining everything from his background and motivations to his particular mystique as one of the most powerfully charismatic leaders of the century. He is characterized in a multitude of ways: as a mentally deranged yet skilled politician; as a case of a borderline personality disorder with a compulsive need for destruction; as a self-deluded prophet; as a destructive force inflamed by hatred of contemporary civilization and of a bourgeois society in which he had been a miserable failure; and as a cunning opportunist using both calculation and fanaticism to achieve his objectives (Curtis 1979). Hitler alone gave the Nazi ideology its form, adding appeal through riveting speeches and rhetoric. And to a large degree, his charisma was responsible for the fanatical support he received.

During huge public rallies, Hitler, with his vibrant oratory and decisive gestures, was able to mobilize the German masses by creating the impression that they had a personal relationship with him. Under his leadership, Nazism achieved cult status: the people's will was manifest in the will of Hitler, their *Fuhrer* or supreme leader; indeed, their very identity was consumed by his subjective totalitarianism, his self-proclaimed right to dominate them: "Hitler is Germany—Germany is Hitler" (Buchheim 1968, 19). Hitler became the supreme arbiter, operating above even the law. He redesigned society by issuing mandates for every component of life, from professional performance to art and to ethics and moral principles, all according to his ideological stance, National Socialism. Within the framework of a Greater German Reich, the German people were simply means to his ends (Pfaff 1993). His goals were revolutionary in that he sought to create a new kind of man by means of global expansion, racial conquest, and the science of the cleansing of humankind, or eugenics. With him, violence became an elevating and creative experience.

Some have suggested that the German people's desire for community and a sense of belonging and their willingness to relinquish moral responsibility actually drove them toward an "escape from freedom" (Fromm 1941). Others attribute their phenomenal support of Hitler to German traditions of authoritarianism; and still others argue that placing too great an emphasis on social norms of obedience have historically permitted individuals to escape responsibility for their actions. However one explains it, there is no doubt that Hitler had the German masses behind him, "those cheering, waving, adoring millions pictured in the newsreels as being always at the pitch of enthusiasm before their Fuhrer . . ." (Rosenfeld 1985, 16). A relieved Germany accepted Hitler's totalitarian system with relative ease. Almost as much as the political system was dictatorial (in that there were no formal mechanisms to check Hitler's power), it was consensual: The German public accepted the program and Hitler's authority as desirable and legitimate (Goldhagen 1997). What little dissent there was became an early casualty of the regime; rigid control was maintained by fear. Stagnant eddies of moral drift became powerful currents. In 1936, a beleaguered German Jew, Victor Klemperer (1998, 165), wrote in his diary:

> The majority of the people is content, a small group accepts Hitler as the lesser evil, no one really wants to get rid of him, all see in him the liberator in foreign affairs, fear Russian conditions, as a child fears the bogeyman, believe, insofar as they are not honestly carried away, that it is inopportune, in terms of Realpolitik, to be outraged at such details as the suppression of civil liberties, the persecution of the Jews, the falsification of all scholarly truths, the systematic destruction of all morality. And all are afraid for their livelihood, their life, all are such terrible cowards.

By 1937, multiple entries witness Klemperer's (1998, 229) growing belief that "Hitlerism is after all more deeply and firmly rooted in the nation and corresponds more to the German nature than I would like to admit," that the Party expresses the true opinion of the German people, and that Hitler really does embody the soul of the German people.

ANTI-SEMITISM AND THE DESTRUCTION OF THE JEWS

Debates over the extent of German anti-Semitism and its function as a motivating factor in the Holocaust have been ongoing and explosive. In 1997, Daniel Jonah Goldhagen's *Hitler's Willing Executioners: Ordinary Germans and the Holocaust* antagonized traditional scholars who fiercely attacked his "monocausal simplicity" in posing deep-seated eliminationist anti-Semitism as the motivational force behind the participation of millions of ordinary Germans in the genocide of the Jews (Eley 2000, 30). The book became a bestseller in Germany and the United States, its acceptance perhaps a backlash against abstract academic explanations of the Holocaust that focused on bureaucratic rule and fragmented decision-making and refused to confront the reality of mass murder head-on (Bartov 2000b). In terms of explaining Nazi *libricide* as well as genocide, anti-Semitism seems to have been part of a receptive undercurrent in German culture that was drawn out and given shape by the Nazis. Anti-Semitism was key to the racism and exclusivist identification with the *volk* that provided agency, the involvement of individual Germans, in cultural as well as human atrocities.

According to Goldhagen (1997), the history of anti-Semitism reaches back to the beginnings of Christianity. In Germany, the notion that a *Judenfrage* (Jewish problem) existed was apparent as early as the late 1700s.

It was expressed in literary and intellectual discourse and had wide support from political and cultural sectors. The concept of the *volk* (a pure and superior German race) had, in fact, emerged out of antagonism toward the Jews. German Jews, nevertheless, managed to achieve civil equality by 1871. This progress resulted from a shift in the designation of "Jew" from specifying race to merely indicating religion, which was considered to be a matter of choice, rather than biology. However, in the later part of the nineteenth century, pseudo-scientific and evolutionary theories were used to restore a racial interpretation, making the Jews' identity both immutable and—to a culture that clung to a perception of them as a depraved enemy—irredeemable.

The finality of the differentiation between religious and racial connotations allowed notions of the Jews as a malevolent and noxious people to flourish, and by the late nineteenth century, anti-Semitism was so widespread that it became a standard component of the political and social culture. Under the tutelage of the Nazis, the Jews were typified as a *Fremdkorper*—an alien body within Germany—and propaganda identified them with every social, political, and economic ill that had ever befallen the nation. For example, a children's book from 1938 entitled *The Poisoned Mushroom* provided an illustrated and explicit attack on the Jews, who, like mushrooms, may appear to be good, but can be fatal. "Without a Solution to the Jewish Problem, No Salvation of Humanity" announced the title of the book's last chapter (Goldhagen 1997). Public discussion of the need to eliminate them intensified during the 1930s. At first, forced emigration was favored; but later, when the onset of war made it possible, the idea of their annihilation appealed to hardened Nazis, for whom only extermination of the entire population of Jews could usher in the new age of harmony and prosperity promised by National Socialism (Taylor 1985).

With the chaos that followed World War I came conditions in which expression of anti-Semitism functioned as a social pressure valve. When the Nazi Party came to power, they fanned the flames of racism. The Party unleashed a barrage of propaganda that demonized the Jews and blamed them for all of Germany's misfortunes. Newspapers, posters, speeches, performances, and books stressed their toxic influence on the Aryan race and on humanity as a whole. Under Party commission, German scientists "proved" the superiority of the Aryan race and identified the dangers of bloodlines polluted by inferior races; in the less-than-scientific findings that were published, they characterized those races as diseased appendixes and called for their removal. The Jews represented the root of all evil, notwithstanding empirical evidence to the contrary or obvious examples of "good" Jews—for example, scientists and doctors who benefited German society, or a particular Jew with whom an individual German might have had a positive relationship. Hitler's characterization of the Jew in *Mein Kampf* included images of maggots in a rotting corpse, a plague worse than the black death, a germ carrier, a parasite, a vampire (Jackel 1972). The Party gave license to the people's passion against the Jews and unleashed a ferocity that previously had been curbed by the forms and values of civilized society.

From 1933 on, the Jews were systematically stripped of social, civil, and legal rights. Jewish citizens were dismissed from the Civil Service; they were disallowed labor protections; their businesses were boycotted and shut down. Many Germans profited from the Aryanization of businesses (the transfer of title to non-Jews) or from the removal of competition in the professions and, indeed, in all arenas. Mandatory wearing of the six-pointed Star of David, a symbol of Judaism, allowed officials to easily recognize Jews and, hence, to enforce regulations that cut them off from German culture. They were banned from public places, including libraries and theaters, and Jewish children were removed from the schools. The streets became dangerous for Jews, with incidents of assault and rape practically commonplace. Conditions became so desperate that in the decade preceding the war, and before Hitler's plan of action was fully in place, 60 percent of German Jews left the country. Those who remained faced systematic exclusion and degradation until the war began and Hitler felt comfortable enough to begin a formal extermination policy.

Throughout the 1930s, Party propaganda urged the German people to strike out, with any means available, at both the individual Jew and at Jewish cultural roots. Verbal and physical assault quickly progressed to legal and administrative ostracizing, all of which were forces behind the mass emigration throughout the decade. The Jews were reduced to being "socially dead," a phrase coined by Orlando Patterson (1982) to refer to those who have had all rights, power, and honor denied them by a secular excommunication that removed them from any legitimate social order. Ultimately, eradication measures progressed to forced deportation, neglect causing death, slave labor as a facade for murder, death marches, and outright genocide. But these measures were aimed at more than just the Jews' physical presence. Jewish cultural influence was purged from all institutions—Jewish books were burned as libraries were purified of Jewish content, and Jewish publications were forced to discontinue; even art collections and cultural performances were Germanified, i.e. the works of Jewish artists, composers, and dramatists were banned, and Jewish performers were not allowed to appear before the German public.

Goldhagen (1997) has pointed out that because the psychological effect of destroying a community's institutions is so similar to that of destroying its people, violence to culture is almost as satisfying to the aggressor. Certainly members of the Nazi Party and youth groups derived great satisfaction from the burning of Jewish synagogues and cultural artifacts. A nationwide orgy of violence, referred to as Kristallnacht, occurred in 1933 when the windows of 7,500 Jewish businesses were smashed and the streets of Germany were littered with glass. Hundreds of synagogues and schools were destroyed as well as Jewish artifacts and books, including 16,000 volumes in the Jewish community center in Frankfurt am Main (Hill 2001). Thirty thousand Jews were removed to concentration camps. While some Germans expressed criticism of the immense economic damage and unseemliness of the frenzied violence, few articulated any intimations of injustice—and certainly not the 100,000 Germans who gathered at a rally in Nuremberg to celebrate the infamous night (Goldhagen 1997). This crowd's enthusiasm foreshadowed the glee felt by Nazis involved in the 1941 burning of the Great Talmudic Library of the Jewish Theological Seminary in Lublin, Poland:

> For us it was a matter of special pride to destroy the Talmudic Academy which has been known as the greatest in Poland. . . . We threw out of the building the great Talmudic Library and carted it to market. There we set fire to the books. The fire lasted for twenty hours. The Jews of Lublin were assembled around and cried bitterly. Their cries almost silenced us. Then we summoned the military band, and the joyful shouts of the soldiers silenced the sounds of the Jewish cries. (as quoted in Shaffer 1946, 84)

With the invasion of Poland in 1939, the government moved beyond encouragement of violence to explicit and organized involvement. Genocide became a top-priority policy around which the whole administrative apparatus of the German state was organized. As German Jews were shipped east and Polish Jews were confined to ghettos, hundred of thousands of the books they left behind were burned; in cities such as Bedzin and Poznan, special German arson squads were assigned to burn Jewish synagogues and books (Borin 1993). In general, destroying Jewish books was no small task. In addition to synagogue libraries, each family had at least a few books; there was at least one library, often more, in every Jewish urban settlement. For Polish Jews, libraries had been the most important secular institution and the center of Jewish youth life (Shavit 1997). Warsaw, for example, had fifty Jewish libraries. Some collections were saved from immediate destruction and placed under the supervision of German professors and experts, who oversaw their disposal. They were apportioned to German libraries or special institutes assigned with the task of studying the Jewish problem. Thus, while many small personal collections and local libraries containing *pinkassim* (records of synagogues, burial societies, Rabinic courts, etc.) were destroyed during the deportations or subsequently pulped to alleviate German paper shortages, larger libraries, such as the Jewish Theological Seminary in Breslau, which had supported Jewish studies, a scholarly discipline since the 1900s, were confiscated for use by the Nazis.

Nazi scholars and ideologues, organized in various bureaucratic units, often fought over possession of important collections. The Reich Security Main Office (RSHA)—the headquarters of the Nazi Security Police, which included the Gestapo and the Security Service and functioned as the main institution organizing the Nazis' fight against the enemies of the regime— had a library section charged with supplying Jewish books for RSHA's pseudo-scholarly research institutes. These collections eventually totaled some two million books. Jewish scholars, academics, and businessmen were conscripted into forced labor on the collections, their work done under concentration-camp-like conditions (Schidorsky 1998). One of those who resisted conscription was the grandson of the founder of the famous Strashun library, who committed suicide rather than assist with the removal of the collection (Borin 1993). The Germans viewed the Jews' printed heritage as a tool for use in their eventual eradication, and they displayed no hesitation about forcing Jews to labor on this task—another example of the psychological degradation heaped upon Jews.

The other major group seeking Jewish books for their institutes was the National Socialist German Workers' Party (NSDAP). Books for its Institute for Research into the Jewish Question, headed by Alfred Rosenberg, a philosophical leader of the Nazi Party, were provided by the *Einsatzstab Reichsleiter Rosenberg fuer die Besetzten Gebiete* (ERR)—the Rosenberg Task Force for Occupied Territories. The ERR diligently followed in the wake of troops in Poland, confiscating an enormous amount of Judaica and Hebraica and transferring it to the institute in Frankfurt. Among other tasks, the institute was charged with documenting an overview of Jewish influence on the world for the last two hundred years. It was slated to serve as a nucleus for research and Aryan education. Another reason for competition over Jewish libraries was because of the Nazis' "strange craze" to establish museums commemorating their enemies; several services competed bitterly for the honor of establishing anti-Jewish museums and libraries (Arendt 1964, 37).

At the end of World War II, the Commission on European Jewish Cultural Reconstruction calculated that 469 Jewish collections (with more than 1,000 books each) existed in 1933 (Schidorsky 1998). Few of these libraries would survive the war intact. Few of the Jews would, either. At the Wannsee Conference in Berlin in 1942, German officials targeted 14 million Jews for extermination; it is estimated that they succeeded in killing approximately six million. In Poland, the Nazis killed 90 percent of the Jewish population and destroyed an estimated 70 percent of the Jewish books. Ironically, the decision to preserve books for the use of German scholars actually saved many books that otherwise might have been destroyed.

The destruction of Jewish books occurred first within Germany as an extension of programs of civic transformation in which Jews were forbidden to use the nation's libraries. The public and university libraries were purged of undesirable materials, this process posing as hygienic and sometimes culminating in public book burnings, quasi-purification ceremonies. But to paraphrase the nineteenth-century German philosopher Heinrich Heine, after the burning of books came the burning of men. The Jews' civil and social ostracism was followed by the absolute segregation of the ghetto. The fate of their written materials was interwoven with their fate as a race because the Nazi's Final Solution was to be complete when not only the outward manifestations of Judaism, its people, were expunged, but when the memory of that culture, held in its books and libraries, was in German hands and texts were ultimately relegated to serving as archaic documents of a lost culture.

THE FATE OF EUROPEAN LIBRARIES

Poland and Eastern Europe

Part of Germany's sense of manifest destiny was its entitlement to more *lebensraum,* territory for the country's expansion and consolidation of foreign land occupied by German minorities. These lands were to be Germanified, i.e. purged of alternate ethnic identification and subjected to cultural homogenization along German lines. Thus, after Germany's acquisition of the Czechoslovakian Sudetenland as a result of the Munich Conference of 1938, the Nazis were swift in implementing systems of cultural control. Valuable collections were carried off to Germany, including forty-eight monastic libraries and forty-two special museum and archival libraries. National treasures prized as sources of cultural achievement, such as the Slavata Bible and the Bohemian Crown Archives, also were confiscated. When they cemented control of Czechoslovakia, just as they would do in other annexed territories, the Germans expanded library systems for the German population while selectively clearing certain areas of libraries or significantly purging local collections. In libraries allowed to remain in operation, all local (Czechoslovakian) library books dealing with geography, biography, and history (which might contradict German claims and interpretations), any materials that were incongruent with German ideology, and many books by Czech authors were removed and destroyed. Many books were used as raw materials for paper mills that supported the German war effort. Overall, losses of books, manuscripts, and incunabula totaled approximately two million, or about half of Czechoslovakia's libraries and archives. Very little of this destruction occurred during bombings or shelling; it resulted from directives of the German authorities, representing "a clinical case of planned destruction of libraries" (Grzybowska 1954, 2) in which highly developed systems of public and scholarly libraries are themselves attacked as the enemy.

With increased *lebensraum* through annexation of the Sudetenland, Hitler's appetite for more land was whetted. Again with a rationale of uniting all German-speaking peoples within contiguous lands, he launched a full-scale *Blitzkrieg* invasion of Poland in the name of its German-speaking minority. While this invasion soon precipitated an international war, the Poles initially stood alone against the Germans and put up an amazing defense. Infuriated at their own losses, especially at the hands of those considered a subhuman race, the Germans responded with a reign of terror geared to devastating the Polish nation so badly that it would never again rise as a cultural entity.

Poland's fate, of course, was a matter of indifference to the Germans. Heinrich Himmler, the head of the SS, articulated his attitude toward inferior people thus: "Whether other nations live in prosperity or starve to death interests me only insofar as we need them as slaves for our Kultur . . ." (as quoted in Kamenetsky 1961, 103). Martin Bormann, a German administrator and policy-maker, expressed a similar sentiment: "The Slavs are to work for us. In so far as we don't need them, they may die" (as quoted in Kamenetsky 1961:103). These comments, among many made by German officers and officials, and ongoing German aggression make it clear that German racism was extended beyond the Jews to other ethnic groups deemed inferior—in this case the Slavs of Eastern Europe (the Poles and Soviet populations). In the case of Poles, their eventual extermination was a matter of official policy; for example, in the *Generalplan Ost* only 3 to 5 percent of the population was considered suitable material for Germanification (Gross 1979).

Immediately after invasion, Field Marshall Hermann Goering announced the confiscation of the entire property of the Polish state for the benefit of the German state, the Third Reich. The German government then decreed that all Polish book collections owned by private persons, corporations, and associations other than those of German nationality be surrendered to the authorities. Huge amounts of books were collected and sorted; again, valuable library and museum items were to be removed to Germany, along with all scientific books and periodicals. The library of the Polish Parliament, for example, was moved to Germany. However, after a series of wholesale removals, the Nazi administrators in Poland opposed this plan, arguing that administrators would need collections to gather information and to support new German educational institutions in Poland. Thus, many scientific books and university collections were preserved for use by German administrators and for Germanification, especially in the areas of Western Poland, where the Poles were to be replaced with German-speaking settlers (Dunin 1996). By 1941 four *Staatsbibliotheken* (state libraries) had been set up in Cracow, Warsaw, Lublin, and Lvov to serve as the "new bulwark[s] of German intellectual work in the outermost Southeast" (Sroka 1999, 7).

Private libraries (especially those of deportees) were looted, destroyed, and pulped in the hope that Polish intellect would starve and the cultured class would wither away (Stubbings 1993). School libraries—expendable under Nazi education policies—were used for barracks and their collections ruthlessly destroyed. As befitting a nation of peasants, Polish children were to be allowed only a few years of education, during which they would learn to write their names, count to 500, and learn obedience to their German masters; the ability to read would be irrelevant to their lives (Kamenetsky 1961). The Polish publishing industry, too, was halted. Almost all public libraries were destroyed, including Kalisz Public Library, whose books were used to fill a storm sewer (Dunin 1996).

To further strike at the roots of Polish culture and intellect, the Nazis committed mass murder of Poland's educated classes and those who might provide leadership for a resistance effort or cultural regeneration. According to Governor General Frank, "The Fuhrer told me: 'what we have now recognized in Poland to be the elite must be liquidated; we must watch out for the seeds that begin to sprout again, so as to stamp them out again in good time'" (as quoted in Lukas 1986, 8). In Bydgoszcz, it was part of daily routine to round up priests, judges and lawyers, professors and teachers, merchants and industrialists, and worker and peasant leaders and gun them down in the town square—in the end, some 10,000 in all. "In my area," declared one Nazi administrator, "whoever shows signs of intelligence will be shot" (as quoted in Rummel 1992, 80). At the University of Cracow, 167 Polish professors, assistants, and instructors who had been invited to attend a lecture on Nazification policies were imprisoned by the Secret Service; many died in captivity. Overall, Poland would lose 40 percent of her professors (Lukas 1986). "Two masters cannot exist side by side, and this is why all members of the Polish intelligentsia must be killed," Hitler explained (as quoted in Gross 1979,75), perhaps unwittingly revealing the extent to which an active, free mind threatened his ideology. The material destruction or confiscation of Poland's books and libraries, the dismembering of its educational system, and the annihilation of the educated and intellectual classes were calculated to speed the extinction of national and cultural identity, facilitate slavery, and serve as a stop-gap measure until general extinction was possible.

Western Europe

In his own country, Hitler had begun a process of cultural homogenization under the Nazi program after taking over the government in the 1930s. Nazis seized control of the German publishing industry, retrained librarians and booksellers, purged libraries of undesirable and ideologically incorrect materials, and directed the country's whole intellectual apparatus toward producing materials that promoted a Nazi vision. There were "black lists," (*Schwarze Listen*) for the purposes of book removals, and "white lists" to guide library acquisitions. The plan was to purify collections, maintain this purity by controlling publication, and expand access to "healthy" materials by building more libraries. It was akin to the processes of euthanasia and sterilization being performed in German hospitals (in which inferior specimens of the *volk* were eliminated or prevented from reproducing) and the official promotion of child bearing by German women. Like the doctors who participated in these programs, librarians were expected to function counter to the normal ideals of their profession. Librarians, who had been steeped in humanism, were recast as censors and propaganda agents, just as doctors had been transformed into killers rather than healers. Just as hospitals changed from places of care to laboratories for the cultivation of a genetically superior race (Lifton 1986), libraries converted from cultural institutions serving the individual to political tools serving the collective goals of the *volk*.

In philosophy the plan for Germanifying libraries was narrow, but it was broad in ambition: the model was to be imposed on all of Eastern and Western Europe. The annexed areas of Sudetenland and Poland served as trial runs. The full range of Hitler's policies included comparatively mild programs of control and restrictions as well as all-out extermination of Jewish, pacifist, or anti-German material, materials promoting nationalist and humanist world views, and, even, whole libraries. The army was given the task of securing collections as they advanced. For example, in the Soviet Union the Special Service Battalion of the German Ministry of Foreign Affairs was instructed to seize manuscripts, archives, and books immediately upon the capitulation of each town and city along the invasion route (Shaffer 1946). Civil authorities, aided by specialized administrative units, made long-range plans for the disposal of these materials. For example, the Rosenberg Task Force for Occupied Territories (ERR) was developed to seek out and confiscate the libraries, including archives of Jews, Slavs, freemasons, and communists. Nazi scholars could then study them for the purpose of understanding and combating their former owners, the enemies of the Reich. In addition, the ERR was one of several special bureaus established to incorporate the literary heritage and artistic treasures of vanquished countries into a massive system of German high *Kultur.* It was charged with seizing and transporting valuable books and *objects d'art* back to Germany. By the end of World War II, the Rosenberg Task Force collecting teams had visited an estimated 325 archival institutions, 402 museums, 531 institutes, and 957 libraries throughout Europe (Borin 1993).

In many cases, confiscations and purges had been planned well in advance according to policies for cultural domination. German librarians had prepared lists of desirable materials, which were to be secured for German use, and undesirable materials, which would be destroyed in the Germanification effort. Many of these lists were generated when librarians attended prewar international conferences or worked in foreign libraries during exchange visits and internships. German institutes and scholars were involved in planning for reshaping the European mentality into a German mode and the combating of forces of tradition and cultural intransigence within each occupied country (Carlton 1990). The control of books and libraries was seen as a key element.

In proceeding to unify Europe under the Nordic peoples, the Germans' use of violence to culture in each region was proportional to the racial value assigned each nation's people (Western Europeans being assigned greater value than Eastern Europeans) as well as the degree of resistance encountered. For example, many libraries in the northern part of France were destroyed in combat, but, in general, France was treated less harshly than Poland or Russia. The Germans' respect for Western European cultural treasures, based in no small part on the desire to possess them, did not, however, extend to a sense of loss when valuable items were destroyed in battle. These losses were blamed on the defenders' intransigence. Furthermore, in total war, the Nazis considered all resources of the enemy fair game; attacking material culture was a blow to the lifeblood of the enemy and part of war strategy. Therefore, Britain's resistance, despite the German's admiration for the British race, led to the devastating loss of twenty million books; fifty major libraries throughout the country were damaged or destroyed in bombing raids. In a 1940 aerial fire bombing, at least six million books were burned in London's Paternoster Row area, the wholesale bookseller's district (Butler 1945). Through air raids targeting cultural sites listed in the *Baedeker Tourist Guide to Britain,* the Germans made casualties of irreplaceable works such as the unique prints, drawings, and archival materials of Coventry, including the Gulson Library. The Guildhall in London, which housed the ancient Corporation Library, was burned to the ground and 25,000 volumes—many of them unique—were lost. These losses struck at the heart of British culture, violating both the sense of continuity and pride supported by historic records and the dynamic mood fostered by a modern publishing industry.

The occupation of Denmark and Norway was relatively peaceful and fell within recognized norms of modern military occupation. The cleansing of Scandinavian libraries was scheduled to occur over a period of time, suggesting that the Germans anticipated that in dealing with fellow Aryans, the process of Germanification need not be terribly dramatic. In Norway, there was some resistance to special German-sponsored bureaucracies, so the occupation was a little more aggressive. Disappointingly for the Germans who viewed the Netherlands as a "basically Germanic region" with a natural place within the Reich (Nicholas 1994), the Dutch proved stubbornly intransigent. Thus, the Germans intensified the purification of libraries in the Netherlands. Many libraries were either seized or rigorously purged of works by anti-Nazi authors, by Jews, by those who escaped abroad, and by Russian, British, or American writers who died before 1904; books about living members of the royal family were not allowed (Grzybowska 1954).

In Western Europe where racial composition legitimized nations' cultural heritages, the Nazis' emphasis was on Germanification, surveillance of libraries, blacklists (which were applied across the board—to institutions and private libraries alike), and purification. According to historian Lynn Nicholas (1994, 97), "There was no need for the conqueror to take away the national collections of these new 'provinces'; the Thousand-Year Reich now owned them." In some countries, the Germans placed particularly valuable collections under "safekeeping." In France, distinctions were made whereby German inspectors of libraries carefully "protected" institutions such as the *Bibliotheque Nationale* while pillaging, burning, and desecrating private collections, large and small, such as those belonging to Jews or refugees. The ERR seized 723 French collections comprising 1,767,108 volumes, including 12,743 rare books (Hill 2001). Hilda Stubbings (1993), a historian of World War II library destruction, has described the Germans as torn between wishing to destroy native French culture, pretending it to be decadent, and coveting its treasures— an apt characterization, given the provincial nature of many Nazi officials and a history of war with France. There was widespread purging of French textbooks and educational materials, especially in the fields of history, literature, and geography, particularly materials that presented Germans as aggressors or losers. However, in annexed Alsace-Lorraine, where the people were considered to be of the German race, *all* French books were removed and thousands were destroyed. To complete the Germanification effort, the remaining collections were supplemented by German books, as many as 70,000 in the case of the city of Mulhouse.

The Dutch, Belgians, French, and Scandinavians were basically permitted to maintain their own culture, but only in a position clearly subordinate to German culture; all other foreign cultural influences were marked for elimination. In Luxembourg, non-German reference materials (i.e. French or English) were confiscated and replaced by German encyclopedias. In fact, after 1940, there was an attempt to eliminate all English and French books from collections in the Netherlands, Belgium, and Luxembourg. It was an attempt to seal off occupied countries from the intellectual currents of democracy (Grzybowska 1954).

Exceptions to general policies of postponing the dismemberment of Western Europe's national collections occurred because of the Germans' desire to recover materials that "rightfully" belonged to Germany and might enhance their own cultural heritage and projected renaissance— these included manuscripts and documents with a German provenance. Hitler was particularly insistent that these be gathered in immediately. In accordance with the "principle of Germanic heritage," German experts arrived in occupied France with lists of cultural treasures to be confiscated from French libraries and museums (Hamon 1997, 63). When Italy turned against Germany, a German archival expert drew up a plan that called for the removal to Germany of all Italian archival material related to the history of the German Empire. "Reclamation" was the preliminary gambit in long-term postwar strategies calling for the truly massive transfer of cultural goods into new and grandiose German museums and libraries.

In all occupied countries, Jewish collections (public and private) were mercilessly looted and destroyed. According to Holocaust scholar Philip Friedman (1980), the Germans went after Jewish libraries that were connected with institutes of higher learning, rabbinical seminaries, educational and research institutes, synagogues, and youth organizations. The Germans laid claim to Jewish materials in municipal, state, and university collections. Special attention was paid to the personal libraries of rich Jews, especially scholars and bibliophiles. There was widespread spoliation of Jewish libraries in France and high numbers of confiscations in Holland, including the stock of Jewish-owned publishing houses. The Library of the International Society of Social History in Amsterdam, staffed by refugee Jewish scholars from Germany, was packed into 776 cases and removed (Friedman 1980). Catholic libraries were often treated in the same way—religion being the natural enemy of Nazism, and, indeed, any extremist ideology.

SCHOLARSHIP AND NAZISM

In his book *Hitler's Willing Executioners*, Goldhagen (1997, 440) quotes a poem by W.H. Auden in which he condemns those Germans who stood by and watched the atrocities committed against the Jews as having displayed "intellectual disgrace." A more literal form of intellectual disgrace was the active and enthusiastic participation of Germany's academics and scholars in promoting racism and, in the interests of ideological promotion, perverting science, scholarship, and reason. While they weren't the only scholars in history to fall into the trap of political ideology, their work was enabling to a regime that on every level contradicted the very premise of scholarship. The scholars knew that they were making a choice. The prominent professor Dr. Alfred Baeumler stated it thus: "Instead of the vague mixture of general concepts and values which used to be called the spirit of humanism or the idea of Western culture, National Socialism set up an organically founded *Weltanschaung* [worldview]" (as quoted in Weinreich 1999, 23); the world of German scholarship embraced this vision.

In fact, a tradition of distorted scholarship had evolved in Britain in the late nineteenth century. British researchers coined the term "eugenics" in 1881 to refer to a science of the improvement of the human race by better breeding. Their goal was to develop a biological argument for social Darwinism, or "survival of the fittest." Eugenics quickly spread around the world, and research findings in the field gained wide acceptance. It wasn't until well into the twentieth century that awareness developed of the ethical standards violated by eugenics research, in which, all too often, researchers' prejudices and political motives corrupted their premises and tainted their conclusions. What was being called "inquiry" (investigations like brain-measurement studies, for instance) was more sociopolitical in aim than scientific.

However, when scientists worldwide began to pull back from such research, the Germans further institutionalized the field. In Germany after the Weimar Republic, eugenics scholarship took the form of "race hygiene," a field of study emphasizing Aryan supremacy. As the professional classes embraced the racial ideology of radical Germanic nationalism, with its emphasis on racial purity and strength, the groundwork was laid for an ideology of human inequality that would eventually legitimatize Nazi objectives. Herbert Rothfeder's 1963 dissertation on Alfred Rosenberg describes a series of institutional measures designed to usher Party doctrines into the scholarly world and produce a complementary relationship between Nazi ideology and German science. By 1932, more than 40 courses on race hygiene were taught at German universities; research centers in that field were springing up and academic chairs and professorships were created. At the University of Munich, plans were made for an Institute for Aryan Intellectual History. Heinrich Himmler sought to establish a huge research complex with hundreds of scholars and archaeologists engaged in a systematic exploration of the Northern Indo-Germanic race and its achievements. In addition, Rosenberg's *Institut zur Erforschung der Judenfrage* tried to raise "the Jewish question" from propaganda to the level of pure scholarship with the aid of selective bibliographies and annotated book lists compiled by librarians. Researchers published papers that used extensive quotations from allegedly primary materials and employed copious footnotes, creating the appearance of meticulous scholarship. By 1943 the institute had 550,000 books plus large archival collections, mostly confiscated from deported Jews; when necessary these materials were distorted and taken out of context in order for the research to provide unequivocal corroboration of Nazi tenets, including the necessity for exterminating the Jews. The government provided generous support for vehicles for the dissemination of these pseudo-scholarly articles. The journal *Der Weltkampf* was one such vehicle. The institute was deemed critical in "teaching the spiritual basis and tactics of our ideological adversary" (Pugliese 1999, 245).

Many scientists became Nazi theorists, their work explicitly reinforcing the national ideology by providing a biological justification for policies that discriminated against the Jews (Friedlander 1995). As one might imagine, the careers of those scholars who produced government-approved findings flourished. On the other hand, Jews were progressively and then decisively excluded from academia. Non-Jewish dissenters (motivated by either professional ethics or political qualms) were ostracized and their careers extinguished by Nazi officials whose aggressive responses to objectivity or moderation left virtually no opportunity for critical analysis or alternate discourse. Taking Nazism to its most extreme conclusions, the scientific community gave intellectual credence to official policies of anti-Semitism and to the "final solution" to the *Judenfrage* (the Jewish question)—eradication of the Jews (Borin, 1993). Furthermore, medical doctors and scholars themselves engaged in acts of genocide by conducting terminal experiments on prisoners in concentration camps, the death of subjects being part of the experimental design. German scientists and professionals were accomplices in genocide by helping to develop technology like the gas chambers used for mass killing.

Race hygiene was merely one aspect of the loss of a defensible and productive intellectual environment in Nazi Germany. Even before 1914, academic learning took second place to the building of racial character. After the Nazis took control, education was only incidentally an intellectual process; ideas were largely limited to political conditioning (Stieg 1992). Content took second place to ideology in secondary-school textbooks that eulogized the destiny of the *volk* and condemned modernity as evidence of moral decay, while the spirit of the Teuton during the Dark Ages was upheld as a model for future generations (Taylor 1985). Under the Nazis, higher education suffered a serious decline as students turned instead to political activities, so engaged were they by the promise of a new Germany. Between 1933 and 1939, enrollment in universities and technical institutions declined by 50 percent (Ebenstein 1943). Students who did attend the university spent a large amount of time in party and youth activities (Klemperer 1998). In regard to the 1933 book burnings that electrified the world, it was students "who were manipulated to spearhead the book burnings by seizing books from the shelves of their own universities" (Stubbings 1993, 367). While designed to look like a spontaneous repudiation by an outraged youth, of all that was spiritually unhealthy, it was actually an organized, administratively dictated "funeral pyre of the intellect" (Stieg 1992, 91). University graduates were groomed for positions in the elite and deadly SS units. Indeed, "the leaders of the notorious *Einsatzgruppen,* the murder squads of the SS, as well as many of the most active and extreme members of the Reich Main Security Office—charged with organizing the Final Solution—were holders of doctorates from Germany's most prestigious universities" (Bartov 2000a, 184).

Either by active promotion or passive acquiescence, the educational and cultural establishment in Germany endorsed Nazi indoctrination, anti-Semitism, Aryan "science," abandonment of scientific objectivity, violence, and book burnings. As schools and libraries quickly incorporated new goals of ideological purity and totalitarian conformity, professionals who were unwilling to comply were ostracized, especially those guilty of "irresolute" or "insipid" intellectualism (Klemperer 1998, 86, 116). In a turnover four times as high as normal, no less than three-quarters of all librarians who directed scholarly libraries left their positions or were forced to resign during the five years following the establishment of the Nazi regime (Ebenstein 1943). Remaining librarians removed from the shelves of public institutions books written by Jews, Marxists, pacifists, and those who promoted humanistic or democratic views. Cultural institutions in general retreated from Enlightenment values: censorship replaced free access to materials, collectivism triumphed over individualism, and dogma overcame reason. It is difficult to say whether most teachers and librarians who worked under the Nazi regime merely bowed to the intense pressures and acquiesced grudgingly or were swept up in the ideological frenzy and fervently embraced Nazism and its practices. Certainly many prominent librarians appeared to participate whole-heartedly in the ideological purification of German collections and in perpetrating intellectual and cultural imperialism in occupied countries.

In the first half of the 1930s, libraries open to the public, many of which had been previously unregulated, were placed under the control of a newly created Federal and Prussian Ministry for Science, Formal Education, and Popular Enlightenment. They were weeded of all non-conformist material and restocked with Nazi materials. About 10 percent of German public library collections were placed on blacklists (UNESCO 1996); however, in an excess of rigor, some public libraries actually exceeded the censors' expectations. By 1938, Munich's public libraries had divested themselves of 76 percent of their 1934 collection (Stieg 1992). Librarians were guided by a running list of all those books which "endanger[ed] the National Socialist cultural will" (Ebenstein 1943, 129). Legislation that protected minors from obscene literature was revised as *all* citizens were now deemed in need of protection; the scope of dangerous literature was extended from obscenity to anything which a party official might find incompatible with Nazism (Ebenstein 1943). Academic library collections were left basically intact but access was limited to those who were sympathetic to Nazism. A notable decline in use of university libraries occurred: in 1932–33, 973,724 persons used the ten leading university libraries; in 1937–38, this figure dropped to 339,035, a decrease of about two-thirds (Ebenstein 1943).

Throughout the 1930s, the police and Nazis were raiding private homes and confiscating books (especially those on socialism), financial papers, personal correspondence, large personal libraries, and non-print valuables. Fear of the house searches led many Jews and leftists to burn their own papers and libraries, "preemptive book burning" (Hill 2001:17). Authors were a problematic group, especially "*dekadenten Zivilisations literaten-tums,* decadent literary people with the values of Western liberal civilization" (Hill 2001, 20). In April, 1933, the SA tore apart a Berlin apartment house owned by the *Schutzverband Deutscher Schriftsteller,* the largest association of German writers, and home to 500 writer-members; they destroyed suspicious materials and perpetrated gratuitous vandalism (Hill 2001). Terror was a goal rather than a by-product in efforts to extinguish materials that were "un-German"—anything expressing the "rationalism, materialism, cosmopolitanism, egalitarianism, parliamentarism, pacifism, tolerance, assimilationism, ecumenism, and modernism the Nazis detested" (Hill 2001, 11). Bookstores and lending libraries also were purged. Indeed, the Nazi Party held courses for librarians and owners of lending libraries to equip them with the "proper attitude" toward literature. The leading Nazi Party theorist, Alfred Rosenberg, was put in charge of intellectual training and education, scientific research, literature, and general cultural evaluation for the entire nation (Rothfeder 1963). In short, German culture, education, and scholarship existed to serve National Socialism.

In a celebratory speech on the night of the 1933 Berlin book burnings, Dr. Paul Goebbels, the Nazi propaganda director, triumphantly proclaimed, "The past is in flames!" (Snyder 1981, 122). Libraries were very important to German society, and Goebbels, as architect of a new society, was celebrating the book burning as symbolic of revolutionary purification and an impending cultural renaissance. With the advent of World War II, the plan was to destroy outright or subjugate all institutions of despised races and conquered nations so that no intellectual mechanisms existed that contradicted a Nazi worldview. Hitler's logic was based on the premise that German-Nazi *Kultur* was the highest point of civilization; the conclusion he sought was German domination of the world of letters as well as of every other aspect of world society.

ASSESSING THE DAMAGE

But, ultimately, the Allies triumphed and Hitler's fantasies met the same fate as the millions of lives and other precious things he had destroyed. German world domination was just another dashed illusion. But even inevitable defeat was met with a show of ferocity, and some of the most outrageous examples of libricide occurred towards the end of the war. The retreating Nazis were involved in a high incidence of direct, gratuitous damage to culture, venting their spleen on cultural artifacts and institutions. During their retreat from Italy, the Germans burned irreplaceable archives, including the 850 cases of the Neapolitan State Archives. In France, Nazi destruction often occurred in reprisal against activities by the Resistance members and the Allied troops. For example, in August 1944, in what has been described as a wanton act, German *Brandkomando* squads destroyed the collection of precious manuscripts and incunabula from the Municipal Library in Metz, which was stored in Saint-Quentin, even though (or perhaps, because) the town was already surrounded by the American Third Army (Grzybowska 1954). Retreating troops blew up the Municipal Library in Dieppe, and before abandoning Paris, German soldiers set fire to the Palais-Bourbon, the Library of the National Assembly, destroying 40,000 volumes (UNESCO 1996). The actual plan was for the wholesale destruction of historic Paris, but key German officers, recognizing the unique cultural contributions of the city, resisted Hitler's orders.

It was a different story in the Eastern regions, where libraries had been targeted all along. And one has only to compare the fate of Paris with that of Warsaw to calibrate a significant discrepancy in restraint. Hitler intended to make Warsaw a "second Carthage," and he almost succeeded in duplicating the Romans' annihilation of the city-state and its culture (Hoffman 1993, 9). In 1944, after an insurrection in Warsaw and during their retreat from Poland, *Brandkomando* squads deliberately torched Poland's most prestigious libraries, as if to leave nothing of cultural importance intact. As secretly outlined in contingency plans for defeat, the Nazis burned many of the illustrious collections they had gathered for "safekeeping." For example, they burned prints, manuscripts, and maps from the university library, the Zamoyski Library, the National Library, and Rapperswil Library—these had been stored in the library of the Krasinski estate. The National Library lost nearly all of its 700,000 volumes; the Central Military Library, containing 350,000 books concerning the history of Poland, was totally wrecked. One million books were lost from the university library in Warsaw, and many research and special libraries were destroyed (Bilinska 1946). On the eve of evacuation, the main stacks of the Warsaw Public Library were burned; the library had housed 300,000 books and functioned as the center of a national network of branch and children's libraries. After the war was over, estimates of the loss of books in Warsaw's public libraries stood at two-thirds. It could have been even worse: Employees hid some 125,000 library books.

Some scholars estimate that, altogether, Poland lost about 90 percent of its school and public-library collections during German occupation, 70 percent to 80 percent of its specialized and private collections, and about 55 percent of its scientific collections (Dunin 1996). According to another estimate, 15 million out of 22.5 million volumes in Polish libraries were destroyed (Sroka 1999). These are fairly moderate estimates based on extensive information about Poland that is available because of methodical records kept by the Nazis in annexed areas. Figures for the rest of Eastern Europe are much less exact, though also devastating. Estimates of the loss of Soviet books (mainly in the Ukraine, Belarus, and Russia) during Germany's invasion totaled one hundred million volumes (UNESCO 1996). Yugoslavia's cultural losses were similar to Poland's. The wholesale destruction of Slovenian institutions was particularly extensive: Libraries were torn down and their contents publicly burned.

Despite the phenomenal effort the Germans spent on their projects of genocide and subjugation, their reign of terror was finally halted. The fate suffered by Hitler's victims was probably the single most influential factor in clarifying to the world the necessity of a resolute and united response. The case of Poland, where his plan came so close to completion, stood as a frightening illustration of how far Hitler intended to take his ideological program. The Germans' treatment of the Jews proved that no moral boundaries were in place, and through their flagrant murdering of teachers, writers, and intellectuals and the pillaging of Polish libraries, it became evident that the real target of Nazism was the very foundation of Western culture and humanity itself. In light of this realization, the British, in particular, were able to withstand devastating human and cultural losses and still muster the strength to resist.

Hitler's ideological program, which had traumatized the rest of Europe, in turn brought ruin on Germany and its own treasured cultural heritage. By the end of the war, in an ironic turn of events, Germany had lost between one-third and one-half of its books, primarily in the course of Allied bombings and through Russian confiscations (an estimated eleven million books, including two Gutenberg Bibles, were removed to the Soviet Union as trophy collections, spoils of war). The libraries of German cities and universities swelled the toll of losses. In Berlin, the National Library lost about two million volumes, and the Library of the Reichstag was almost completely destroyed. In Frankfurt, the Municipal and University Library lost 550,000 volumes, 440,000 doctoral dissertations, and 750,000 patents. The *Staatsbibliothek* in Bremen lost about 150,000 volumes, including many rare and precious works (UNESCO 1996). The list goes on and on. That the loss of their own books and libraries cost the Germans dearly is a fact beyond question. However, unlike the atmosphere of national self-pity that prevailed after World War I, it appears that since

World War II the Germans have developed a more general empathy for the losses sustained by their enemies and a greater sense of personal and national responsibility. It can only be hoped that another legacy of the cultural destruction that occurred in World War II is the development of a heightened and *worldwide* sense of not only the value of human life but of the importance of books and libraries, and indeed all objects and traditions of cultural heritage, as communal and global, essential and precious.

This chapter ends with a comment on the ultimate irony of World War II libricide, the fact that the threat posed by the Germans' ideological extremism ultimately provoked a temporary escalation of the creed of democracy to extremist proportions. This occurred when the Allied nations, fearing for Western civilization, assumed the mantle of militarism and nationalism and defended their democratic way of life through the almost unprecedented violence of undifferentiated urban bombing, including the carpet bombing of Dresden. Rationalized as breaking the will of the Germans to continue the war, Dresden represented the "greatest Anglo-American moral disaster of the war against Germany" (Johnson 1991, 404). In one night, eight square miles sustained a firestorm that killed perhaps 135,000 civilians and destroyed a renowned center of European culture. Again in the Pacific, to oppose right-wing fanatics, in this case, Imperial Japan, the Americans saw the creation of massive damage as a necessary and justifiable defensive response to virulent expansionism. The Americans' firebombing of Japanese cities and the explosion of nuclear bombs over Nagasaki and Hiroshima again resulted in a heavy loss of life and destruction of unique cultural sites. Allied bombings, in both Europe and Asia, resulted in what could be typified as large-scale collateral destruction rather than libricide (as libricide is defined in this book), just as it represented mass murder rather than genocide (as internationally defined). Nevertheless, this collateral destruction of books and libraries, along with the intentional destruction by Axis extremists, demonstrates conclusively that the violent, mass destruction of books and libraries is a toxic by-product of ideological extremism and the intense militarism that is a feature of total war.

REFERENCES

Arendt, Hannah. 1964. *Eichmann in Jerusalem: A Report on the Banality of Evil.* New York: Viking Press.

Bartov, Omer. 2000a. *Mirrors of Destruction: War, Genocide, and Modern Identity.* Oxford: Oxford University Press.

Bartov, Omer. 2000b. "Reception and Perception: Goldhagen's Holocaust and the World." In *The "Goldhagen Effect": History, Memory, Nazism—Facing the German Past*, ed. Geoff Eley. Ann Arbor, Michigan: University of Michigan Press, 33–87.

Bilinska, Helena. 1946. "Poland Faces Intellectual Famine." *Library Journal* 71 (4): 1022–3, 1034.

Borin, Jacqueline. 1993. "Embers of the Soul: The Destruction of Jewish Books and Libraries in Poland During World War II." *Libraries & Culture* 28 (4): 445–460.

Buchheim, Hans. 1968. *Totalitarian Rule: Its Nature and Characteristics*, trans. Ruth Hein. Middletown, Connecticut: Wesleyan University Press.

Butler, Pierce. 1945. "War in Library History." In *Books and Libraries in Wartime*, ed. Pierce Butler. Chicago, Illinois: University of Chicago Press, 9–27.

Carlton, Eric. 1990. *War and Ideology*. Savage, Maryland: Barnes & Noble Books.

Curtis, Michael. 1979. *Totalitarianism*. New Brunswick, New Jersey: Transaction Books.

Dunin, Janusz. 1996. "The Tragic Fate of Polish Libraries After 1939." *Solanus* 10: 5–12.

Ebenstein, William. 1943. *The Nazi State*. New York: Farrar & Rinehart.

Eley, Geoff. 2000. "Ordinary Germans, Nazism, and Judeocide." In *The "Goldhagen Effect": History, Memory, Nazism—Facing the German Past*, ed. Geoff Eley. Ann Arbor, Michigan: University of Michigan Press, 1–31.

Friedlander, Henry. 1995. *The Origins of Nazi Genocide: From Euthanasia to the Final Solution*. Chapel Hill, North Carolina: The University of North Carolina Press.

Fromm, Erich. 1941. *Escape From Freedom*. New York: Holt, Rinehart & Winston.

Goldhagen, Daniel Jonah. 1997. *Hitler's Willing Executioners*. New York: Vintage Books.

Gross, Jan Tomasz. 1979. *Polish Society Under German Occupation: The Generalgouvernement, 1939–1944*. Princeton, New Jersey: Princeton University Press.

Grzybowska, Zofia. 1954. "A Study of the Destruction of European Libraries by Totalitarian Aggressors in World War II." (master's thesis, Catholic University of America, Washington, D.C.).

Hamon, Marie. 1997. "Spoliation and Recovery of Cultural Property in France, 1940–94." In *The Spoils of War: World War II and Its Aftermath: The Loss, Reappearance, and Recovery of Cultural Property*, ed. Elizabeth Simpson. New York: Harry N. Abrams, 63–66.

Hill, Leonidas E. 2001. "The Nazi Attack on 'Un-German' Literature, 1933–1945." In *The Holocaust and the Book*, ed. Jonathan Rose. Amherst: University of Massachusetts Press, 9–46.

Hoffman, Eva. 1993. *Exit into History: A Journey Through the New Eastern Europe*. New York: Penguin Books.

Jackel, Eberhard. 1972. *Hitler's Weltanschauung: A Blueprint for Power,* trans. Herbert Arnold. Middletown, Connecticut: Wesleyan University Press.

Johnson, Paul. 1991. *Modern Times: The World From the Twenties to the Nineties.* (Revised edition). New York: Harper Perennial.

Kamenetsky, Ihor. 1961. *Secret Nazi Plans for Eastern Europe: A Study of Lebensraum Policies.* New Haven, Connecticut: College and University Press.

Klemperer, Victor. 1998. *I Will Bear Witness: A Diary of the Nazi Years 1933–1941,* trans. Martin Chalmers. New York: Random House.

Lifton, Robert Jay. 1986. *The Nazi Doctors: Medical Killing and the Psychology of Genocide.* New York: Basic Books.

Lukas, Richard C. 1986. *The Forgotten Holocaust: The Poles Under German Occupation 1939–1944.* Lexington, Kentucky: University Press of Kentucky.

Mosse, George. L. 1966. *Nazi Culture: Intellectual, Cultural and Social Life in the Third Reich,* trans. Salvator Attansio and others. New York: Grosset and Dunlap.

Nathan, Otto, and Heinz Norden, eds. 1968. *Einstein on Peace.* New York: Schocken Books.

Nicholas, Lynn. 1994. *The Rape of Europa: The Fate of Europe's Treasures in the Third Reich and the Second World War.* New York: Vintage Books.

Patterson, Orlando. 1982. *Slavery and Social Death: A Comparative Study.* Cambridge, Massachusetts: Harvard University Press.

Pfaff, William. 1993. *The Wrath of Nations: Civilization and the Furies of Nationalism.* New York: Simon and Schuster.

Pugliese, Stanislao G. 1999. "Bloodless Torture: The Books of the Roman Ghetto Under the Nazi Occupation." *Libraries & Culture* 34 (3):211–253.

Rosenfeld, Alvin H. 1985. *Imagining Hitler.* Bloomington, Indiana: Indiana University Press.

Rothfeder, Herbert. 1963. "A Study of Alfred Rosenberg's Organization for National Socialist Ideology." (Ph.D. diss., University of Michigan, Ann Arbor, Michigan.)

Rummel, R.J. 1992. *Democide: Nazi Genocide and Mass Murder.* New Brunswick, New Jersey: Transaction Press.

Schidorsky, Dov. 1998. "Confiscation of Libraries and Assignments to Forced Labor: Two Documents of the Holocaust." *Libraries & Culture* 33 (4):347–387.

Shaffer, Kenneth R. 1946. "The Conquest of Books." *Library Journal* 71 (2):82–85.

Shavit, David. 1997. *Hunger for the Printed Word: Books and Libraries in the Jewish Ghettos of Nazi-Occupied Europe.* Jefferson, North Carolina: McFarland.

Snyder, Louis L. 1981. *Hitler's Third Reich: A Documentary History.* Chicago: Nelson-Hall.

Sroka, Marek. 1999. "The University of Cracow Library Under Nazi Occupation: 1939–1945." *Libraries & Culture* 34 (1):1–16.

Staub, Ervin. 1989. *Roots of Evil: The Origins of Genocide and Other Group Violence.* Cambridge: Cambridge University Press.

Stern, Fritz. 1961. *The Politics of Cultural Despair: A Study in the Rise of the Germanic Ideology.* Berkeley, California: University of California Press.

Stieg, Margaret F. 1992. *Public Libraries in Nazi Germany.* Tuscaloosa, Alabama: The University of Alabama Press.

Stubbings, Hilda Uren. 1993. *Blitzkrieg and Books: British and European Libraries As Casualties of World War II.* Bloomington, Indiana: Rubena Press.

Taylor, Simon. 1985. *Prelude to Genocide: Nazi Ideology and the Struggle for Power.* London: Gerald Duckworth.

Ugresic, Dubravka. 1998. *The Culture of Lies: Antipolitical Essays.* University Park, Pennsylvania: Pennsylvania State University Press.

UNESCO Memory of the World Program. 1996. *Lost Memory: Libraries and Archives Destroyed in the Twentieth Century.* Paris: UNESCO.

Weinreich, Max. 1999. *Hitler's Professors: The Part of Scholarship in Germany's Crimes Against the Jewish People.* New Haven, Connecticut: Yale University Press.

Chapter 5

GREATER SERBIA

"[T]he emperors of today have drawn conclusions from this
simple truth: [W]hatever does not exist on paper, does not exist
at all."

(Milosz 1990, 224)

Despite the fact that the Balkans had been a political fracture zone for
hundreds of years, the virulent implosion of post-Communist Yugoslavia
in the 1990s caught its Western neighbors by surprise. By the late 1980s,
an entire generation separated Europeans from World War II. For over
forty years (slowly at first and then gaining momentum), Western Europeans had conducted mental and emotional postmortems on the war with
the aid of documentation compiled by officials, independent presses, and
researchers. Historical documents and eyewitness accounts served as a
springboard for dialogue, education, and soul-searching as the results of
extreme nationalism were sifted through and (often painfully) processed.
While this process was far from perfect (the French, for example, have
had great difficulty in dealing with their collaborationist past), contemporary Germans had publicly denounced Nazi atrocities, and even made
it against the law to deny that the Holocaust occurred. Western Europeans
were bringing former enemies together in the European Union as new
generations demonstrated a consciousness of time as linear and the past
as instructive but removed.

In Eastern Europe, the Communists had used a different tactic to handle wartime divisions: They imposed top-down doctrines and policies that were designed to extinguish sociopolitical rivalries by administrative fiat. After World War II, the six Balkan nations—Slovenia, Croatia, Bosnia-Hercegovina (hereafter referred to as Bosnia), Serbia, Montenegro, and Macedonia—were forced into one entity, the federated state of Yugoslavia. Redefining the unit of loyalty as Yugoslavia rather than the individual constituent nations rationalized the intermixing of ethnic groups, particularly in Croatia and Bosnia where a history of ethnocentric conflict between the Croats, Serbs, and Muslims existed. The new ideology, Communism, which stressed internationalism over ethnic nationalism, appeared to resolve the Serbs' and Croats' claims to disputed lands. To the Communists, it did not matter whether one was a Serb living on Croatian lands or a Muslim living among Serbs. The Party reckoned with history only in terms of Marxist dialectics, the truth about past events was suppressed, and notions of independent national identities were replaced, by force if necessary, with the ideals of socialist brotherhood. Citizens of Balkan nations, denied the tools of critical thinking, access to information, and open debate, buried unresolved enmities, and a consciousness much like the Germans after World War I—composed of bitterness, victimization, exclusivist identification with an ethnic group, and the demonizing of its enemies—was forced underground.

After the death of Tito in 1980 and the disintegration of Communist domination later in the decade, federated Yugoslavia began to dissolve. Peaceful coexistence became problematic and when Serbia began to dominate the federation, Slovenia, Croatia, and then Bosnia declared independence. In response, Serbia waged war, ostensibly a civil war in the name of a united Yugoslavia, which was viewed by the other nations as nationalist aggression perpetrated in the interest of a Greater Serbia. Yugoslavs reemerged as nationalists, while two groups, the Serbs and Croats, revisited fascism. Ruptures occurred along national, religious, and ethnic lines as Serbs and Croats attacked each other and the Muslims. Questions of political and territorial legitimacy were addressed in the same way they had always been: Ethnic groups were attacked and driven from areas that were claimed as exclusive enclaves of either the Serbs or Croats. A modern concept of time was lacking—the "perpetual repetition of the same archetypes obliterates any distinction between yesterday, today, and tomorrow" (Debeljak 1994, 19). Memories, suppressed and left to fester since World War II, became an inspiration for violence; ethnic and national identity rationalized excesses of every kind.

The war that racked the former Yugoslavia in the 1990s has been called many things: a post-Communist implosion, a civil war, a tribal war, a religious war, a racist war, an expansionist war. It was a struggle for power, identity, historical entitlement, and the establishment of what each side perceived as the "truth." Serbs and Croats practiced ethnic cleansing, amplified to ethnocide proportions, as a final solution to competing land claims and a necessary step in preparing for homogeneous nations. While the two rival groups sought to revise history to deny that any other group had ever occupied their land, the Serbs, in particular, not only sought to wipe out evidence of the enemy's physical presence in an area, but also all personal and political claims and all testimony to their enemies' cultural achievements and legitimacy as a people.

This chapter begins with an overview of the evolution of Serbian nationalism, the role of intellectuals in fostering ethnocentrism, and the events that led to libricide. Following that is a description of Croatian nationalism and an account of the destruction of books and libraries in, first, the six-month fight between Croatia and Serbia in 1991 and, then, in the bitter struggles within Bosnia lasting from 1991 to 1995.

THE EVOLUTION OF SERBIAN NATIONALISM

The roots of the conflicts in the former Yugoslavia extend far back in Balkan history, a history shaped by conflicting religious and cultural systems, migrations, and foreign dominance. The border between the Byzantine and Roman churches ran through the Balkans, and the effect of this division lingered as the Serbs, proselytized by missionaries from the Orthodox Constantinople region, became distinguishable on the basis of religious affiliation from the Croats, who had come under the influence of the church in Rome (Sells 1996). Under pressure from the Turks, who controlled sections of the eastern Balkans from the 1400s to the early nineteenth century, some Slavs converted to the Islamic faith. The Serbs, who remained faithful to the Orthodox Church, thereafter stigmatized the converted Muslims as traitors against Serbdom and as an innately inferior group. Over time, despite an identical biological make-up and a common language, there emerged three distinct and competitive cultural groups, each with their own religion: the Serbs (Christian Orthodox), the Croats (Catholic) and the Muslims.

Religion became an issue of critical importance after the demise of the first Serbian kingdom. Under the Nemanjic dynasty, which ruled for two hundred years, Serbia emerged in the eleventh century as a major power.

Modern-day Serbs view medieval Serbia as a golden era, making doubly bitter their devastating loss in a battle with the Turks at Kosovo in 1389. After this loss, which the Serbs attributed to betrayal, the Serbs were forced to pay tribute to the sultans, and by 1459 their lands were entirely overrun and thereafter ruled by the Ottoman Empire. Independent existence remained beyond reach for almost 400 years. Epic folk poetry—possibly the most authentic expression of identity and history as perceived by the Serbs themselves—frequently revisits the loss at Kosovo as the definitive event in Serbian history. Kosovo marked the end of the golden age of monarchy, the beginning of cultural and political bondage and, to this day, fuels the Serbs' sense of victimization, entitlement, and hatred of the Muslims. With the loss of political autonomy, the Orthodox Church became the font of Serbian identity. This faith connected them to a glorious past and supported their sense of being a chosen people. "What made them Serbs then was religion"—i.e. their Orthodox affiliation as distinguished from the Muslim and Catholic faiths (Judah 1997, 43). Separate cultural identity was also reinforced by use of a Slavic script developed by two monks in the late eighth century. This Cyrillic script was "another badge of Serbdom, which complemented Orthodoxy and yet again set them apart from their Muslim and Catholic neighbours" (Judah 1997, 44).

For more than three centuries, the Ottomans and their Serbian subjects were on one side of a defensive line that stretched 1,000 miles and separated them from areas under the influence of the Austro-Hungarian Empire. The border became the site of friction between the two regions, producing a sociocultural version of the violence and upheaval that occur when two tectonic plates grate together to produce new geological formations (Allen 1996). The Croats, on the Austro-Hungarian side, adhered to Roman Catholicism and developed their own national myth, in which they were the outer wall and bulwark of Christianity. The Croats viewed themselves as Central European and highly cultured, in contrast to the Serbs, who were Byzantine, Balkan, and primitive (Judah 1997). This Croatian myth of superiority inevitably resurfaced in ongoing conflicts with the Serbs. By the twentieth century, "Balkanization" was accelerating: Cultural groups were fragmenting into myriad nations with mutually exclusive borders. The region came to be known as the shatter-belt of Europe, where the incompatibilities of ethnic groups and religious beliefs defined regional and interregional political structures (Chapman and Dolukhanov 1993).

Some of the instability stemmed from the intensely ethnocentric and nationalistic behavior that characterized Serbia before and after independence from the Turks was achieved in 1878 (Cigar 1995). Serbian nationalism was expressed in policies of ethnic exclusivity that sought to gather all Serbs into a single Orthodox state. Throughout history, as Serbia expanded, Muslims were forced out, converted, and killed, a continuation of hostilities dating back to the fourteenth century. In 1813, for instance, the Serbs recaptured Belgrade from the Turks and, during the next hundred years, leveled every mosque in the city but one (Cohen 1998). A nineteenth-century document, the *Nacertanije* (a draft plan for creating a unified Serbia), directed policies of exclusivist nationalism and displacement of competing ethnic groups. The definitive 1847 epic poem *The Mountain Wreath* (still required reading in modern Serbian schools) celebrated violence against Muslims and helped to foster a consciousness in which "ideas of national liberation became inextricably intertwined with the act of killing your neighbour and burning his village" (Judah 1997, 77). By the end of the 1800s, the nation of Serbia had nearly achieved the homogeneous population it sought.

During the Balkan Wars of 1912–1913, the issue of Muslim co-occupation—framed by the Serbs as a "problem," not unlike the later Nazi attitude toward Jews—reemerged when Serbia annexed two predominantly Islamic provinces from the Ottoman Empire: Kosovo and Sandzak. The Balkan Wars achieved the final removal of Ottoman Turks from the region and created the conditions for waves of massacres and forced migrations as Serbian and Croatian nationalists began a "map game that they have continued to this day: claiming for their modern states the boundaries of short-lived medieval ones, all of which overlapped in time" (Judah 1997, 63). In 1914, unrest in the Balkans, as epitomized by the assassination of the Austro-Hungarian Crown Prince Franz Ferdinand in Sarajevo, precipitated World War I. After the war, the victorious Allies created Yugoslavia (the kingdom of the Serbs, Croats, and Slovenes) and made it a monarchy. The negotiators did not recognize Bosnia as a separate geopolitical entity and that area was apportioned to the Croats and Serbs, who were thus able to increase their holdings and reinforce their claims to Bosnian lands. The issue of Muslim co-occupation was compounded for the Serbs because their portion of the new state of Yugoslavia contained many Muslims. Plans for a mass expulsion of Muslims from these areas were circumvented by the advent of World War II.

Throughout the 1920s and 1930s, tensions between ethnic and political groups continued to destabilize the Balkans. In 1934 a Macedonian under contract by the Ustasha Party, a radical Croatian group, assassinated the king of Yugoslavia. This event foreshadowed the dismemberment of Yugoslavia by the Nazis. In April 1941, Germany invaded and defeated the nation in twelve days, acting, on the demand of Hitler, "with unmerciful

harshness in order to destroy Yugoslavia militarily and as a national identity" (as quoted in Rummel 1994, 339). Yugoslavia was partitioned into
two zones. The Nazis controlled Serbia while Ante Pavelic, and his fascist,
nationalistic Ustasha party, ruled the new Independent State of Croatia. A
violent and chaotic civil war ensued as political and ideological conflicts
(between fascists, Communists, and nationalists) were aggravated by historical ethnic and religious animosities (between the Croats and Serbs).
The fascist Croatian regime used violence to implement an extremist form
of Catholic nationalism, sanctioned by the Church hierarchy, and characterized by the "ethnic cleansing" of Orthodox Serbs (in fact, the term
"cleansing" was actually used by the Ustashas). An estimated 600,000
people were murdered, 25 to 30 percent of all Serbs in Croatian lands.
Approximately two million Serbs were expelled from Croatia, and those
remaining faced forcible conversion or extermination. The Croatian fascists and German Nazis also exterminated thousands of Jews, Gypsies,
and Communists.

The Ustasha concentration camp at Jasenovac was notorious for its
brutality, and as word seeped out about the atrocities, references to Jasenovac consistently evoked rage from a guerilla group called the Chetniks,
"an official prewar force of volunteers and irregulars trained for warfare
behind enemy lines . . . largely Serbian, anti-Communist, nationalist, and
royalist" (Rummel 1994, 340). The Chetniks, who were mostly Serbs,
massacred both Croats (in retaliation) and Muslims (in accordance with
cleansing policies begun in the 1800s). The Chetnik leadership drafted an
ambitious policy calling for a "homogenous Serbia" that would encompass
not only pre-war Yugoslavia (including Croatia, of course), but also parts
of Bulgaria, Romania, and Hungary—despite the fact that the Serbs were
mostly minorities in these areas. The Muslims, particularly in Bosnia,
were subjected to mass killings and many joined the Ustashas in self-
defense. To compound the anarchy, Communist partisans, who had fought
with the Chetniks, broke away and fought against both the Ustashas and
the Chetniks, their former allies. Bosnia, which housed substantial numbers of all ethnic groups, became the "bloodiest killing ground of the
Yugoslav civil war" (Zimmerman 1999, 114).

By the end of World War II, the Communist partisans, led by Tito, had
taken over—a triumph not so much of ideology as of success in terrorizing
the population and extinguishing their nationalist rivals. According to the
statistician J. D. Rummel (1994), the Communists established control by
killing some 570,000 Ustashas, Croatian soldiers, Nazi POWs, ethnic Germans, Slovenian White Guards, anti-Communists, pro-Soviet Communists, collaborators, Chetniks, intellectuals, bourgeoisie, landlords, rich

peasants, rebels, critics, and innocents. In addition, hundreds of thousands of people were imprisoned between 1945 and 1952 by the post-war Communist apparatus and secret police, and many did not survive captivity. In all, Yugoslavia sustained a democide (death at the hands of government) of approximately one million people.

A new federated Yugoslavia emerged, a state traumatized by the bitter civil war between two factions of fanatical nationalism, and then by a bloody revolution in which another ideology, Communism, carried people to further extremes. Tito's Communist regime adamantly opposed nationalism and righteously rejected the wartime excesses of the Ustashas and Chetniks, conveniently ignoring the cost in human lives of implementing Communism. Socialist policies of "brotherhood and unity" were mercilessly imposed on a federation of six republics and two autonomous provinces. Communist doctrines and a centralized government dominated by Tito, a cult-like leader, held the units together. Perhaps in revulsion against years of ethnic strife, many Yugoslavians embraced Communism's promise of egalitarianism, internationalism, and multiculturalism. Nationalism became a dormant force, particularly in Bosnia, where one-fourth of the marriages crossed ethnic lines. Under Tito, it appeared as if the impulse behind old ethnic hostilities had been successfully transferred onto the outside world, to the west and east. The Yugoslavs built a powerful and professional army (the JNA) to protect their nation from these external enemies.

Nationalistic traces were retained only insofar as they were part of the folk heritage (folk dancing, the use of decorative motifs, local costumes), and religious identity remained intact (though discouraged). More overtly nationalistic tendencies were suppressed, as was a significant amount of historical memory. The crimes and grievances of World War II were not addressed; for example, the number of people (especially Serbs) killed at Jasenovac was never definitively established. In addition, Muslim claims to having lost 85,000 to 100,000 people during the war years in an attempted genocide by the Serbian Chetniks were ignored by the Communist government (Gutman 1993). A dangerous absence of established fact permitted moral accountability to fall by the wayside and subverted closure and reconciliation. Rather than an exercise in objectivity or the discovery of facts, historiography was a tool with which to build a socialist society. The Communists required certain versions of history to explain, bolster, and justify their roles. Thus, Tito had no compunction about presenting the Communist partisans' war as an honorable struggle against fascist nationalists, both domestic and foreign (Thompson 1994). Tito characterized all Croatian patriots as fascist Ustashas and Serbian patriots as racist Chetniks and ultimately encouraged the prototypical "remembrances" that would resurface in the 1990s.

In addition to their attitudes toward history, the Communists left behind ideological residue that was easily adapted to nationalist ends. Both dogmas are rigidly collectivist and militantly exclusivist (Zimmerman 1999). The individual counts for little, and violence is justified against all elements staking competing claims or standing in the way of sociopolitical mandates. Neither extreme nationalists nor Communists encourage divergent thinking or informed inquiry, and both groups exploit fear and call for constant vigilance. By suppressing the virulent nationalism of Serbia and Croatia, the postwar Communist regime did not expunge it, but instead preserved it in all of its virulence.

Yugoslav Communism began to crumble in 1974, when a new constitution weakened Yugoslavia's central government and, in addition to empowering the republics, fostered competition among them. Tito maintained control until his death in 1980, and then the centrifugal forces of decentralization, severe economic decline, and general malaise led to an explosion of nationalistic aspirations and an intense polarization of ethnocultural groups (Denitch 1994). The revolutionary utopianism of Communism was replaced in Slovenia by a reclusive nationalism, the Slovenians preferring to identify with Western Europe. Aggressive and expansionist nationalism was promoted in Croatia by President Franjo Tudjman, and in Serbia by Slobodan Milosevic. Denying a place for Muslims and for an independent multicultural Bosnia, both demagogues sought to expand their own group's territory by manipulating national myths, not caring that those myths could be overlapping, contradictory, or explosive (Zimmerman 1999). They ushered in an era of "history as terror, tormentor, and torch . . . and the discovery of the prison that bad or suppressed history can be" (Cohen 1998, xvi). Collision over mutually exclusive visions became inevitable.

NATIONALISM ON THE MOVE

After the post-World War II Communist takeover, Serbs were accorded privileged status in the bureaucracy, military, and economic infrastructure, and in the Communist Party throughout Yugoslavia. But, in the absence of a dominant heir upon Tito's death, the authoritarian centralization that recognized and mandated Serbian privileges unraveled. The other republics began to replace Serb officials with locals, a significant loss of power and prestige for the Serbs. By 1989, Yugoslavia had the highest inflation rate in the world—more than 3,000 percent on an annual basis (Zimmerman 1999). The floundering economy aggravated stress and confusion resulting from the official demise of Communism and the ensuing transformation of values. Because abandoning Communism required personal and political amnesia, a blotting out of that identity (Ugresic 1998), many sought meaning in reversion to ethnic identity and entitlements justified by their group's past victimizations. At this point Slobodan Milosevic, a lawyer and Communist-turned-nationalist politician, gained control of the Serbian government. He was a skillful speaker who appealed to fellow Serbs by calling upon idealized images of a glorious medieval past and playing on the Serbs' chronic sense of victimization (Balic 1993). A media campaign encouraged Serbs to see themselves as the scapegoats in an international conspiracy against the Serbian people and their homeland (Shawcross 1994).

Milosevic never reached the true cult status or totalitarian control of a Hitler, Mao, or Saddam. Neither was he a dedicated ideologue. He was, however, able to rally a critical mass of Serbs behind a political platform focused on Serbian identity and entitlements. Milosevic was masterful in using ideology—an exclusive, ethnocentric, religious nationalism that became racist—and the promise of a Greater Serbia to achieve his goals: personal power and power for Serbia. His defining moment, the point at which his ascent to power was assured, occurred in Kosovo in 1987. Videotapes by Western journalists show that minority Serbs orchestrated an incident by stationing a truck full of rocks near a meeting that Milosevic was attending on a mission to, ostensibly, dampen ethnic strife. The Serbs threw the rocks at the police, who then attempted to control the crowd. Milosevic strode to the microphone and assured the unruly mob of Serbs, who claimed to have been manhandled by the police, that they (and by proxy all Serbs) would never be beaten again. After this incident, some Serbs, raised as adoring followers within the cult of Tito, seemed to transfer emotional identification from Tito to Milosevic; indeed, some appeared to genuinely love him (Ramet 1996) and many paid "homage to Milosevic, whose stern but flap-eared visage and shaving-brush hair-style became the central artifacts in this new religion [of nationalism]" (Glenny 1992, 33). Other Serbs, however, including many writers and professionals who subsequently went into exile, viewed Milosevic as loving the power that he could attain with the people's backing: He was an "opportunist rather than an ideologue" and his espousal of Serbian destiny was utilitarian (Zimmerman 1999, 25). The BBC's Central Europe correspondent Misha Glenny (1992, 31) typified Milosevic as "a man without passion, without any real nationalist motivation (although on the surface, he appears to wallow in it), and . . . a man who has never shown any affection or regard for the masses upon whom he depends for support."

During the late 1980s, Milosevic cemented and extended his dominance by dismantling constitutional restraints on both *his* power as Serbia's president and *Serbia's* power within the federation. A key component in his plans was achieving control of the Yugoslav army. A powerful and respected force, the JNA had lost its focus when its mission, the protection of Yugoslavia's integrity and borders, became less compelling after the disintegration of Soviet communism. Of the 70,000 career officers, 70 percent were Serbs and Montenegrins. This percentage climbed in the 1980s as non-Serbs were forced out through use of covert and overt techniques, including intimidation and assassination. Identification with Serbia and its aspirations ensured job security in a downward spiraling economy; plus militarism had a central place in Serbian culture. By 1990, according to U.S. Ambassador to Yugoslavia Warren Zimmerman (1999, 87), the army, cut adrift from the rigidity of effective centralized Communist leadership, purged of non-Serbs, and left to indulge in anti-German, anti-Western fantasies, was becoming "doctrinaire, narcissistic, paranoid, flaccid, and unruly."

In addition, Milosevic seized control of the Serbian media, taking over radio and television stations and government presses and making it difficult for independent newspapers to operate. Because under the Communists, the media was ostensibly social property while actually coming under the control of the League of Communists, dismantling the official press posed no insurmountable problems. For many Serbian journalists and media figures, it was a small leap from one authoritarian dogma (socialism) to another (one-party nationalism) (Thompson 1994). For others, however, the choice posed the dilemma of choosing between career, emigration, or a dangerous path of dissent.

In the late 1980s, control of the content of television broadcasts, in particular, was key because Serbia was one-third illiterate. Coverage of news events involving ethnic conflict reinforced the rhetoric of vulnerability and images of real and staged Serbian victimization dominated the screen. Serbian television pushed the simple message that Milosevic was the defender of a Serbia threatened by Muslims and Ustashas, a message the viewers responded to enthusiastically (Maas 1996). Through radio, television, and print media, the Serbian people received a steady stream of propaganda in which Serbs were portrayed as having been misunderstood and abused throughout history and as currently facing a legion of enemies, some of whom (Muslims, for instance) were intent on exterminating them. "This dualistic self-view of superiority and accompanying vulnerability bordering on paranoia [—a common pattern for virulent nationalists—] can be a particularly explosive mix" (Cigar 1995, 78). The media employed the techniques of demagogy and headlong irrationality, using rhetorical questions and exclamations and citing the Serbs' destiny and mission: They were a "celestial people" confronting their fate. It was a definitive incitement to violence.

Control of the media, however, does not explain the enthusiastic affiliation of many Serbian intellectuals with extremist positions—particularly surprising since, according to scholar Bogdan Denitch (1994), Serbia was considered a center of liberal and democratic thinking in Titoist Yugoslavia. This reputation was "completely obliterated by an unprecedented level of conformist compliance with the nationalist celebration of primitive xenophobic fantasies" (Denitch 1994, 192–30). The Slovenian poet Ales Debeljak (1994, 31) wrote of this conformity, "Wherever collective memory based on the selective use of the past holds sway, everyone thinks alike. When everyone thinks alike, no one thinks at all. A society where no one thinks at all is little more than a frenetic and debauched, if picturesque, village bazaar." The heavily charged atmosphere is described in one observer's account of an official event:

> More than a million Serbs attend a frenzied rally on the battle site of Kosovo, where their forebears were humiliated *in 1389,* and hear former Communists rave in accents of wounded tribalism. Ancient insignias, totems, feudal coats of arms, talismans, oaths, rituals, icons, and regalia jostle to take the field. A society long sunk in political stagnation, but one nevertheless well across the threshold of modernity, is convulsed: puking up great rancid chunks of undigested barbarism. In this 1930s atmosphere of colored shirts, weird salutes, and licensed sadism, one is driven back to Auden, that period's clearest voice, who spoke of "The Enlightenment driven away" (Hitchens 1993, 5).

Those Serbian intellectuals who, disgusted and alarmed by the nationalist discourse, sought to voice divergent opinions and counterbalance the extremism, soon met the same fate as independent journalists. Choked out of the national discourse, many chose exile and left the country to complacent individuals, who, infected by nationalist fever, developed intensely anti-Islamic views. They used the machinery of academia to disseminate their pseudo-analysis of history and contemporary events, and they promoted their values by serving within the Serbian government. Novelist Dobrica Cosic, for instance, helped draft the Memorandum, the official blueprint for Serbian domination, and later became president of the post-secession Yugoslavia, composed of Serbia and Montenegro.

Members of the Serbian Academy of Arts and Sciences, the country's most prestigious intellectual forum, drafted the Memorandum in 1986. The document proclaimed that "the establishment of the Serbian people's complete national and cultural integrity, regardless of which republic or province they might be living in, is their historical and democratic right" (Cohen 1998, 185). Within the Memorandum was a denunciation of the "physical, political, legal and cultural genocide" of Serbs in Kosovo. The details of grievances incurred by the Serbs throughout history reinforced their position as victims and set the tone (at once self-pitying, morbid, and vengeful) of subsequent national discourse (Thompson 1994, 54). The Memorandum was part of a stream of propaganda, often disguised as scholarship, which justified a Greater Serbia and prepared the way for expansionism.

During the 1980s and 1990s intellectuals, as politically involved nationalists, did not provide critical and rational perspectives or fulfill the watchdog role often filled by the intelligentsia (Gutman 1993). They did, however, become key in the politics of rationalization and denial. A journalist recorded a telling anecdote about Nikola Koljevic, a Shakespeare scholar who became second-in-command under Karadzic (the Bosnian-Serbian leader, a psychiatrist who has been indicted for war crimes). Asked about Serbian atrocities, Koljevic claimed that they were all pseudo-events, created by the Muslims to garner media support. He made sure that he didn't see anything that would break through his myopia; hence, his comment about once seeing Serbs burning houses: "You don't really want to know, and so I stayed in Pale"(Cohen 1998, 480). In 1997, Koljevic committed suicide. It is possible that, in the end, Koljevic was unable to continue practicing the politics of ideas and maintain "the cool murderousness of the man of reflection, confident that the harm he does pays the necessary admission to the redeemed Future" (Pfaff 1993, 233).

Koljevic was not alone in his determined myopia. For example, academic Milorad Ekmecic defended Serbian policies and behavior as "carry[ing] within themselves *the invisible stamp of a struggle for biological survival. Fear governs us*" (as quoted in Hitchens 1993, 9). Quoted in a newspaper, poet and parliamentarian Brana Crncevic made a typical righteous and egregious statement: "The Serbs are not killing out of hatred, but out of despair. And to kill out of despair is the work of the killer and God, while to kill out of hatred is the work of the killer and the Devil. God is responsible for Serbian crimes, while the crimes of those others are the work of the Devil" (as quoted in Ugresic 1998, 43). In his book

Hearts Grown Brutal, Roger Cohen (1998, 130) wrote, "sometimes, listening to a diatribe in Belgrade, I wondered if the sheer accumulation of war in this country had not simply unhinged people."

By justifying rather than opposing nationalist madness, legitimizing paranoia and racism, and engaging in the language and discourse of war (Thompson 1994), intellectuals contributed to a homogenization of consciousness and the collapse of rational politics (Glenny 1992). There was no effective means of halting the pace of extremism because the hierarchy of the highly influential Serbian Orthodox Church also embraced nationalism and exhorted the population to stand against the Muslims. Religious enthusiasm was so intense in Serbia that several scholars have labeled the attack on Muslims in Bosnia a religious war. Far from being maverick, random behavior, the ethnocide, genocide, and libricide of the 1990s was sanctioned and legitimized by every level of Serbian society—governmental, religious, and civil.

LIBRICIDE IN CROATIA

When Communism was abandoned in the late 1980s, Milosevic used political means to weaken the multinational central government and to strengthen Serbian control. Although Montenegro and Macedonia, both with Serbian majorities, accepted the leadership of Belgrade, Serbian dominance posed a threat to the other republics of the federation, whose non-Serbian citizens also were experiencing a resurgence of nationalism. In June 1991, Slovenia and Croatia declared independence. After the international community recognized their sovereignty immediately, Milosevic, posing as the spokesman for Yugoslavia as a whole, mobilized the army to enforce the federation. For ten days the soldiers waged a confused "civil" war within Slovenia; forty-seven soldiers were killed. Because few Serbs lived in Slovenia and war could not be justified in ethnic terms, the Serb-dominated leadership lacked the will to continue fighting, and Slovenia was allowed to go its own way. The JNA retreated to Croatia, where it fought for six months against the newly independent state there. Here the will to fight centered on asserting dominance over Croatia as a lesser nation within Yugoslavia and securing contested lands for the exclusive use of Croatian Serbs. Serbs were pitted against Croats, who also were experiencing a surge of fervent nationalism.

Just as the Serbs had broken lose from the embrace of Communism to throw themselves into the arms of nationalism, so too had the Croats. Croatian nationalism, which had manifested itself in ethnocentric atrocities during World War II, had remained dormant under Tito. Just as Milosevic achieved power by appealing to Serbianism, Croatian president Franjo Tudjman rallied his people behind the promise of a great and independent Croatia. A general-turned-military historian-turned-university professor-turned-politician, he encouraged ethnic polarization by claiming that the "Croats, Serbs, and Slovenes are products of different civilizations, different cultures. Croats are Catholics and Europeans; Serbs are not" (Zimmerman 1999, 72). A Croatian writer, Dubravka Ugresic (1998, 81) wrote scathingly of the strategy of setting up frontiers and establishing differences: "We are different from them [the Serbs] because we are better, which is proved by our history; we always built, they always only destroyed; we are a European, Catholic, culture, they are only Orthodox, illiterate barbarians."

In the late 1980s, Tudjman began a process of "purifying" a Croatian civil society in which the Serbs, though only 11 percent of the population, held 40 percent of government positions, comprised 75 percent of the police, and almost completely dominated the press (Zimmerman 1999). Serbs were dismissed outright, or driven out by discrimination, intimidation, and required oaths; they were replaced with Croatian nationalists. Nationalist rhetoric dominated the public sphere. Writer Slobodan Novak explained the cultural cleansing that was deemed necessary: "Croatia is simply being restored to its original form and returning to its true self. If today it has to make painful incisions in its language, history, scholarship . . . that only shows the extent to which it was contaminated and how polluted were all facets of its life and all segments of its corpus" (as quoted in Ugresic 1998, 64). Patriotic librarians were quietly "putting books by Serbian writers into the cellars, cleansing the shelves of enemy Cyrillic, and also of Latin-script books imbued with the 'Yugoslav spirit'" (Ugresic 1998, 62). Volumes by Croatian writers, on the other hand, were featured and identified by a label with a folk motif in order to distinguish them from all non-Croatian books.

Tudjman's promotion of Croatian nationalism was tainted by the fact that Croatia, after eight hundred years of statelessness, had achieved independence for the first time during World War II under the violent Ustashas. Tudjman, like many Croats, had never really processed the Ustashas' legacy, and he glossed over war crimes in the interests of "national reconciliation." In published articles Tudjman drastically underestimated the number of Jasonevac Camp victims and represented the Croats' murderous campaign between 1941 and 1945 as "a form of Croatian patriotism, regrettable perhaps, but at heart a noble inspiration" (Cohen 1998, 308). Tudjman, who often appeared to be obsessed with symbols and protocol (Glenny 1992), alienated Serbs living within Croatia by reviving and blanketing the country with the Croatian flag and check-ered shield, which, while evocative of a more distant past, were never-theless symbols used by the Ustashas. For Croatian Serbs, these symbols called up memories of Viktor Gutic, the Ustasha prefect of western Bosnia, who had coined the term *"ciscenje"* (cleansing) to describe the process of ridding Croatia of Serbs through slaughter, eviction, and forced conver-sion (Cohen 1998).

Tudjman was hurriedly building the Croatian army when the Slovenes announced they would secede from a federated Yugoslavia. The Croats seized the opportunity to declare independence also, and Croatian troops fought the JNA, who posed their mission as quelling a civil war. But the JNA, while engaging the Croatian troops, irrevocably compromised its modern military traditions by participating in a systematic campaign to remove Croats and Muslims from Croatian lands claimed by Serbs. Its metamorphosis into an instrument for the expression of a Serbian nation-alism was complete. On orders from the Serbian capital, the JNA acted aggressively on behalf of the government, paramilitary forces, and local militias, participated in atrocities (several officers were indicted by the UN war-crimes tribunal for murder), and profited from looting and black-market activity.

Serbs living in Croatia joined forces with the JNA and seized the op-portunity to redress perceived ongoing discrimination and secure disputed lands; in turn, Croatians defended their property and also revived claims within Serb-controlled areas and pushed their "right" to live in ethnically homogeneous communities. Both factions followed a long tradition of ethnic cleansing, stampeding civilians and burning their homes behind them. For both groups, entitlement issues and rivalry were aggravated by bitterness over the ethnic violence that had occurred during World War II. Each group appeared to be avenging past atrocities: For the Serbs, con-temporary Croatian nationalists served as surrogates for the World War II Ustashas. The Croats typified JNA initiatives as irrational and unwarranted Chetnik aggression. Retaliation was mutual and provoked fresh hostilities on both sides. Both Croats and Serbs employed techniques aimed at ho-mogenization (village-burning, massacres, terror, forced emigration) and sought permanent resolution of historic disputes over territory. They pro-ceeded as if the physical removal of the "alien" population was not enough; all evidence of their ever having been present in any areas had to be permanently expunged. Cultural markers such as churches and li-braries were prime targets. It was a cold-blooded attempt to divorce iden-tity and place.

The Croats, for example, destroyed many seminaries and Orthodox churches. Most notably, the Croatian militia set up headquarters in the old

Bishop's Library in Pakrac (Slovonia—a Serbian area), throwing the books out of the library and burning them. This library was second only to the Library of the Matica (Novi Sad) in terms of the amount of ancient Serbian books, scripts, and poems it housed. It also held old texts taken from regional monasteries and parish churches and preserved in Zagreb during World War II. During the course of the conflict, however, the Croatian government, bruised by their own cultural and literary losses, began to display an awareness of the reprehensibility of such actions. The Croats seemed somewhat more aware of being out of sync with the rest of Europe, which had rejected excessive nationalism and was struggling to come to terms with multiculturalism. A departure from continental norms held much higher stakes than in the past: The highly publicized war between the Croats and Serbs was fought in full view of the international public. Global communications shaped public opinion, which condemned both the havoc wreaked on the people and the deliberate targeting, by both Serbs and Croats, of historical and cultural sites and artifacts. The Croatian Ministry of Culture and special groups such as library associations began to publicize Serbian assaults on cultural artifacts, thus scoring a public-relations victory in the eyes of the world as well as stiffening the national will to resist "the barbarians." One list chronicled the destruction of 210 Croatian libraries: ten research, nineteen memorial, one monastery, ten parish, thirteen special, thirty-three public, twenty-nine secondary school, and ninety-three primary school libraries (Miletic-Vejzovic 1994). Another listed 370 museums, libraries, and archives as damaged or destroyed (Tuttle 1992).

On the other hand, the Serbs, oblivious to backlash, intensified attacks on cultural sites. Intent on weakening the Croatian will to fight, the JNA attacked tourist and historical sites along the coast, far away from disputed areas. They displayed little concern, even of a superficial kind, for cultural values or public opinion even when their shelling of the ancient seaport of Dubrovnik resulted in international outrage. This attack damaged libraries dating back to the early sixteenth century and one (the Dominican Library) that dated back to the thirteenth century. Also damaged was the Dubrovnik public library network, five branches with approximately 70,000 books, many of which were donations by private collectors interested in supporting a city library. The buildings of the Inter University Center were burned and the literature looted (Peic 1995). Dubrovnik, though the most famous, was only one of several Croatian historic sites that were targeted. In the old coastal town of Split, the Serbs shelled the eleventh century St. Trinity Church, the cathedral converted in the seventh century from Diocletian's Mausoleum, and the newly excavated fourth century Palace of Diocletian (Tuttle 1992). However, it was the shelling of Dubrovnik, designated by the United Nations as a world cultural site, which was most incomprehensible to observers. One hypothesized that shelling the city may have been a gratifying way for the Serbs to retaliate against Croatia for breaking away from the federation—by depriving independent Croatia of its prestige and of tourist dollars (Detling 1993). The shelling indicated a profound ignorance of modern cultural sensibilities. After several months of shelling in which 40 percent of the inner city was damaged, a Serb allegedly made the statement: "We shall build Dubrovnik again, even lovelier, even older" (Ugresic 1998, 195).

Up the coast, the Zadar town library suffered a hit and the Zadar Research Library was shelled extensively: it had housed 600,000 volumes, 5,566 periodical titles, 926 newspapers, 33 incunabula, 1,080 manuscripts, 370 parchments, 1,350 rare books, 1,200 geographical maps, 2,500 photographs, 1,500 musical scores, and 60,000 advertisements (Aparac-Gazivoda and Katalenac 1993). According to a bitter Croatian resident, the guns were under the command of Serbian JNA officers who had been residents of Zadar for many years and appeared to be targeting "obvious witnesses of Zadar as a Croatian town . . . libraries, archives, churches. . . . In all those monuments, books, museums, they only saw something that did not belong to them and its existence nourished a gut hatred" (Stipcevik 1993, 7). When the JNA departed from the Zadar barracks, the Serbian commanders even ordered sixty computers to be demolished with axes and all the books of the military school library that were printed in Latin characters (the Serbs use Cyrillic characters) to be burned. Thousands of books were piled in the yard, doused with gasoline, and ignited in fires that burned for days (Stipcevic 1993).

In a highly publicized action, the Serb-controlled army also shelled the historic city of Vukovar and reduced it to rubble, taking pride in the fact that no building was left untouched. Human casualties included 261 non-Serb patients who were removed from Vukovar hospital and murdered. Cultural institutions that lost many books were the Town Museum Library, the Franciscan Monastery (which held 17,000 volumes from between the fifteenth and nineteenth centuries), and Vukovar's Public Library. Vukovar's old Eltz castle was blitzed, and its archives disappeared along with a valuable prehistoric collection (Tuttle 1992). Nearby, in Vinkovci, a large, varied, and unique collection of printed items, valuable manuscripts, and documents concerning writers from the area was lost (Aparac-Gazivoda and Katalenac 1993). The library had been shelled and set on fire; when extinguished, Serb troops shelled it again with inflammable bullets (Stipcevic 1993). Public libraries in both Vukovar and Vinkovci were burned to the ground. Churches, monuments, museums, archives, and libraries all came under attack. One Croat author who fled later heard that his personal library had been burned in a public spectacle. Armed Serbs forced his neighbors out of their apartments "to watch the burning of the 'Ustasha library of Ivan Lovrenovic,' a reference to the Nazi-era Croatian fascists" (Lovrenovic 1994, A19).

To some Croats, it seemed that the destruction of Croatian art and architecture was of a sinister nature. Indeed, the Serbian forces seemed bent on destroying everything that bore witness to Croatia's national identity—the more precious the site, the more vulnerable it was to attack (Tuttle 1992). Certainly, the destruction of their heritage had a tremendous psychological impact on the Croats. While the Serbs were settling scores from World War II and demonstrating dominance, they made a priority out of driving Croats from those areas of Croatia in which there were Serbian minorities. There, evidence of a concerted effort to eradicate ethnic memory began to accumulate. By destroying homes, razing churches, bulldozing graveyards, and burning documents, the Serbs were destroying the proof that non-Serbs had once resided, owned property, and had historical roots in this area—insurance against future claims by the dispossessed (Riedlmayer 1995). It was part of an overall strategy designed to secure territory in Croatia for the permanent use of Serbs by eliminating all reasons for Croats to return. By the end of six months, the Croats needed to regroup in order to continue their own cleansing of Serbs. The Serbs, on the other hand, were satisfied with their territorial gains and signed a peace agreement, confirming Serbia's occupation of one-quarter of Croatia's land. Serbia turned its attention to Bosnia, where a Serb minority coexisted with Croats and Muslims on lands that Serbia coveted.

LIBRICIDE IN BOSNIA

Of all the republics in the former Yugoslavia, Bosnia-Hercegovina had the most cultural diversity, with large concentrations of Serbs, Croats, and Muslims. It was touted as Yugoslavia in miniature—a multiethnic state in which three major ethnic groups lived together mostly in tolerance and civility, often inter-marrying (Zimmerman 1999). Of its 4.4 million people, 31 percent were Orthodox Christian Serbs (mostly farmers and shepherds) and 44 percent were Muslim Slavs, a group that included a secular, educated elite. Throughout the Ottoman and Austro-Hungarian periods, Bosnia had been a distinct political entity and had developed a national culture. Tito had reinforced its legitimacy by designating it a constituent republic, despite Serbian and Croatian claims to various sections. When

Slovenia and Croatia declared independence, Bosnia was left in an extremely difficult position. It could remain in a "Yugoslavia" dominated by Serbs, who each day manifested a more racist nationalism (as evidenced by their treatment of Muslims in Kosovo), or it could declare independence and face almost certain collapse at the hands of both Serbia and Croatia, who were likely to join forces with those locals who defined themselves ethnically as Serbian or Croatian rather than nationally as Bosnian. Multicultural Bosnian territories would then be divided into exclusive ethnic areas. In March 1991, 68 percent of Bosnians voted for independence in an internationally sponsored plebiscite. The Serbs, one-third of the population, abstained. Upon declaring independence, eastern Bosnia was invaded by the Serb-controlled JNA and Serbian paramilitary forces, which joined forces with Bosnian-Serb volunteers.

In many ways, the war in Bosnia was an escalation of what had occurred in Croatia, and yet it was also qualitatively different. By the end of the 1980s, anti-Muslim racism had reached a fever pitch in Serbia with the circulation of stories that Muslims were persecuting Serbs and preparing for a *Jihad,* a holy war. In 1994, British war correspondent Ed Vulliamy (1994) wrote that he had never heard a derogatory remark from a Serb about the Croats as people. They expressed hatred but never contempt. On the other hand, they referred to the Muslims as "gypsies," "filth," "bitches," and "animals." In his eyes, the Bosnian invasion "did not entail seeing the Muslims as an enemy—the threat of *Jihad* was all hot air—so much as subhuman" (Vulliamy 1994, 46–47). Hostility was fanned by propaganda from Serbian intellectuals and media that resonated with a racism rooted deep in Serbian culture. Serbian folk epics (required classroom reading) cited a history of grievances that called for the slaughter of Muslims and the destruction of Islamic culture. The combined efforts of the JNA, paramilitaries, and Bosnian Serbs were aimed at clearing the land of a people defined as subhuman. Perhaps as a result of this dehumanization, the campaign was extremely brutal, and 10 percent of the Muslim population was killed (Gutman 1993). Three-quarters of a million people were pushed from the 70 percent of Bosnian land seized by the Serbs.

The use of extreme terror was considered essential. Behind the ground-level chaos was a plan in which Muslim culture on many levels—biological, psychological, and symbolic—was to be eradicated. The line between ethnocide, the destruction of a group's culture, and genocide, the destruction of the group itself, blurred. When the Serbs took over Prijedor, Banja Luka, Zvornik, Bijeljina, Vlasenika, Foca, Trebinje, Brcko, Rogatica, and Sansksi Most, secular Muslim leaders and educated professionals were the first to be executed. The process consisted of rounding up the wealthiest people, the well-educated, and the political and religious leadership. For example, in Prijedor more than fifty people, including judges, businessmen, teachers, surgeons, and civil servants were taken to camps. Many "disappeared." At Kereterm, five or six of the intelligentsia were executed each night. The power structure in many towns was virtually eliminated. Religious leaders were humiliated and degraded: forced to make the sign of the cross, eat pork, and have public sexual intercourse. Many were executed. Lay Muslims were tortured, mutilated, transported in cattle cars, and confined in concentration camps (shades of the Nazis). In a new twist, the Serbs adopted rape, normally a corollary happening in war, as an official military practice. Rape became an authorized tool to incite terror and migration, to break the collective spirit, and to disrupt reproduction by dishonoring the women and causing a breakdown of Muslim families and culture (Allen 1996). Ten of thousands of women were victimized.

Serbian forces were also determined to remove all physical structures that symbolized Muslim culture. Ottoman quarters and mosques in Bosnian cities were prime targets, and literally all Islamic architecture east of Stolac was affected. By 1993, one thousand mosques had been damaged or destroyed and the rubble redistributed so as to preclude reconstruction (Balic 1993). The number of mosques lost was analogous to the hypothetical loss of one out of every two parish churches and cathedrals in Britain (Chapman 1994). Muslim cemeteries, burial monuments, and mausoleums were destroyed, bulldozed, and covered over by parks and parking lots.

Some sense of the scope of the destruction of books and libraries can be garnered from the losses in just one town, Stolac: rare manuscripts from as far back as the seventeenth century, historical documents, and illuminated calligraphic compositions were lost in the burning of the libraries of the Muslim Community Board, the Emperor's Mosque, and the Podgraska Mosque (Riedlmayer 2001). The libraries (many also containing unique manuscripts and documents), papers, and homes of the town's oldest families were lost also. In Janja, the culturally significant private library of the late Alija Sadikovic with its 100 manuscripts in Ottoman Turkish, Bosnian, Arabic, and Persian was burned along with the historic mansion it was housed in; the Sadikovic family graveyard was also destroyed (Riedlmayer 2001). As one commentator said: "It takes a few moments to understand what this means. They are murdering the dead as well as the living" (Fisk 1994, A-8). The willful destruction of books and libraries was also akin to murdering the dead. A journalist pointed out that *Kristallnacht* for the Bosnian Muslims came not in one or two nights, as it did for Germany's Jews in November 1938, but over many months (Gutman 1993, 81).

The Serbs were interested in destroying items that, simply by existing, confirmed the history of Muslim residency in Bosnia. Typifying Bosnia's Muslims as converted Serbs, and thus traitors against Serbdom, the Serbs were unwilling to admit that the majority of Bosnians—the Bosnjaks— had been Muslim by faith since the middle of the fifteenth century (Balic 1993). Their ancestors had lived in the independent Kingdom of Bosnia (1377–1463), which predated the Ottoman and Austro-Hungarian conquests. Within destroyed libraries, archives, museums, and mosques were handwritten accession registers and plat books from Ottoman times that demonstrated that Slavs professing Islam had lived in Bosnia for centuries. It was necessary to destroy documents demonstrating the validity of Muslim historical claims to Bosnia because they directly contradicted the Serbian expansionist claim that Bosnia had no legitimacy as a separate nation or civilization (Ali and Lifschultz 1993).

By shelling Sarajevo's Oriental Institute in 1992, the Serbs destroyed the largest collection of Islamic and Jewish manuscripts and Ottoman documents in Southeast Europe—primary sources documenting five centuries of Bosnia's history (Riedlmayer 1995). Losses included the Manuscripta Turcica, with more than 7,000 documents from the 1600–1800s, judicial documents, and deeds from nearly all districts of Bosnia in the 1800s (Zeco 1996). There were more than 5,000 oriental manuscripts, the eldest dating from the eleventh century. The institution was a major research center for Balkan studies. It had published its own magazine, catalogs, translations of the Koran, and an Arabic dictionary. By destroying this and other libraries, the Serbs were perpetrating the ultimate act of denigration of Turk or Ottoman civilization: eliminating all evidence of Muslim contributions to the development of culture (Balic 1993). The Serbs were chipping away at the very identity of Muslims from all angles: "An estimated 481,000 linear meters of record—the equivalent of a row of document storage boxes more than 300 miles long—were destroyed in attacks on historical archives and local registry offices during the 1992–95 war. Lost in the flames were hundreds of thousands of documents reording people's births, deaths, and marriages, their properties and businesses, their cultural and religious lives, civic and political activities and associations" (Riedlmayer 2001, 279). Personal documents were also seized, including passports, driver's licenses, letters, prescriptions, and diplomas. Muslims were forced to turn over property deeds in exchange for safe passage out of the region. In a curious perversion of bureaucracy, Muslims in Banja Luka had to obtain twelve different certificates to get out of the city, including one certifying that they had turned in all their library books. Then, for a fee of $200, they were transferred to the top of a mountain where they could walk to safety through an area controlled by Serbian paramilitaries and quasi-official bandits who robbed, raped, and sometimes executed them (Gutman 1993).

While Muslims were the main targets in Bosnia, Serbs also displaced Bosnian Croats and continued patterns of erasing evidence of Croatian presence. Catholic churches throughout Bosnia were destroyed as were any records showing that Croats had historical claims to lands coveted by the Serbs. For example, the monastery, church, and school of the Franciscan seminary in Nedzarici, a suburb of Sarajevo, had its scholarly collections and artistic artifacts destroyed or looted; many were sold in the local market (Lovrenovic 1994). Serbs shelled the Archives of Hercegovina in Mostar and 50,000 books were destroyed when the Roman Catholic archbishopric library was shelled. The communal records (boundary registers, documents, parish records) of 800 Muslim and Bosnian Croatian (Catholic) communities were torched (Riedlmayer 1995).

Out of concern over the heavy loss of life, the United Nations had placed an embargo on weapons purchases that locked in the Serb's 10-to-1 advantage. Serbian forces rapidly swept through the countryside where the Muslims were dispersed, but met with unanticipated resistance in the cities where the majority of Muslims lived. Bosnia did not have an army, a military tradition, or a significant arsenal of weapons, but it had two significant advantages. First, the Muslims knew their only chance for a viable homeland lay in Bosnia's survival as a pluralist, multinational, sovereign state (Ali and Lifschultz 1993). Secondly, there were a number of non-Muslims whose commitment to Bosnia as a multiethnic society made them willing to fight. Just as Serbia and Croatia had a tradition of exclusion and aggressive homogenization, Bosnia had a tradition of multiculturalism fostered by several decades of socialist commitment to "unity and brotherhood" backed by centuries of serving as a homeland for diverse populations. Many non-Muslim urban Bosnians (those rejecting identity as primarily Serbian or Croatian) thought of "Bosnia" as a geographical designation, rather than an ethnic one (Pfaff 1993). Thus, they joined forces with the Muslims under a wartime government committed to the ideal of a multicultural Bosnia.

The main pocket of resistance, and the headquarters of the Bosnian government, was the city of Sarajevo, which underwent a four-year-long siege from 1991 to 1995. Sarajevo stood in a narrow valley. By placing artillery units on the hills above, it was possible for Serbs to pinpoint targets. Snipers killed and maimed thousands of civilians as they crept through the streets trying to maintain life as usual. Universities, schools, research establishments, museums, and the finest Austro-Hungarian mansions were damaged; in contrast, the buildings around them, the Serb Orthodox church and cathedral, for example, survived unscathed, an indication that the targeting of Bosnian cultural sites was deliberate (d'Erm 1997). Andras Riedlmayer (2001) who has painstakingly collected information about losses, recounts this story: In September 1992, BBC reporter Kate Adie interviewed a battery commander and asked him why his men had shelled the Holiday Inn, where the foreign correspondents were housed. The officer apologized and said they were aiming at the roof of the National Museum across the street and had missed. Fortunately the museum's 200,000-volume library was evacuated despite shelling and sniper fire. Many other collections were not so lucky. For example, after shelling, 400,000 books and 500 periodical titles from the libraries of ten of the sixteen faculties of the University of Sarajevo were lost.

The multiculturalism of Bosnia as exemplified by Sarajevo was unacceptable to the Serbs, who considered Bosnia an illegitimate state (created from territory wrested from Serbia and Croatia). By shelling Sarajevo, the Serbs were continuing their attack on the Muslims as an alien race and religious group, but they were also attacking Bosnian national identity and legitimacy, which expressed the idea that Serbs, Croats, and Muslims could live together in peace. Serbia was uncompromisingly brutal in its attack on Sarajevo (the capital of newly independent Bosnia) precisely because it represented a unique phenomenon—a secular, prosperous, multi-ethnic society—in direct contrast to Serbian society. Some have proposed that the siege of Sarajevo (and indeed, the attack on Bosnia's Muslim population in general) was an attack on modern urban culture with its relative affluence and cosmopolitanism (Ali and Lifschultz 1993; Balic 1993). The Muslims and those Serbs and Croats defining themselves as Bosnian were mostly educated and secular. On the other hand, while their leaders were often highly educated, Bosnian Serbs and Serbian troops and paramilitaries tended to be poorly educated, from rural families, and devoutly religious. War in Sarajevo was "a struggle, above all, between the rural and the urban, the primitive and the cosmopolitan, and between chaos and reason" (Glenny 1992, 164). In this multi-layered clash of classes, cultures, and ideology, books and libraries can be counted as casualties.

Serbian nationalists were preparing a clean slate for the remaking of Bosnia according to their own design. "An entire way of life, a whole

civilization in the heart of Europe was being wiped out" (Ali and Lifschultz 1993, xvi). This society had been spotlighted by the 1984 Winter
Olympics, and, in a move designed to deny that distinction, on April 21,
1992, the Museum of the 14th Olympiad, housed in a beautiful historic
building and containing all the documentation of the Sarajevo games, was
shelled and destroyed (Bakarsic 1994). Of all the blows levied against
Bosnia's unique history and culture, the most symbolic was the August
1992 shelling and burning of the National Library of Bosnia and Hercegovina in Sarajevo. The Serbs cut off water to the surrounding district and
gunners shelled the National Library with incendiary rockets, using "constant, maniacal fire from machine guns and mortars" to keep citizens from
rescuing books from the flames and firemen at bay (Lovrenovic 1994,
A19). Devastated Sarajevans did what they could. Librarians and volunteers formed a human chain to pass out books despite the sniper fire. When
asked why he was risking his life, the soot-covered fire brigade chief
Kenan Slinic said: "Because I was born here [in Sarajevo] and they are
burning a part of me" (Riedlmayer 2001, 274).

Typically, national libraries testify to the intellectual and cultural vitality
and overall sophistication of a nation and link that nation to world culture
and history. National libraries tend to be housed in historic or aesthetically
distinguished buildings, and Bosnia's library was no exception. Founded
in 1945, the library had been placed in an Austro-Hungarian-era building
that was itself a symbol of the city. It was a former town hall, the site
where Archduke Ferdinand was assassinated. His death, of course, was
the trigger event for World War I. When images of the burning library
appeared on television screens worldwide, a global public experienced
grief over the loss, which they experienced more broadly as the destruction
of cultural heritage common to the world. The Serbs' shelling of Bosnia's
national library exemplified the generalized contempt for cultural sites as
universal patrimony that characterized their war.

Besides losing an important civic symbol, the nation (and the broader
community of scholarship) lost an institution that performed key roles in
preserving and disseminating learning and national and regional history.
Collections had included literary and scientific heritage in South Slavonic
languages, in Church Slavonic, in Latin, Hebrew, Spanish, Russian, German, Italian Turkish, Arabic, and Persian. The library housed an Austrian
Reading Room and the Study of the British Center, and provided literature
for seminars in Slavic Studies, Germanics, Augustics, and Romance language studies. Collections contained significant contributions from all
three ethnic groups: especially notable were texts from the Muslim cultural collection (the "Gajret") and Croatian and Serbian cultural societies

(Lorkovic 1992). The national library's rich and varied materials manifested in a "specific and original way the encounter and interweavement, the collision and exclusivism of cultures, civilization and religions which have existed for centuries . . . on the border between East and West" (Peic 1995, 12).

The library had served as the depository library for all Yugoslavian publications, maintained the national bibliography, and was in a unique position to serve as the central research and documentation center for university activities. It functioned as the central reference library for Bosnians and contained 1.5 million volumes, 155,000 rare books and manuscripts, 600,000 serials, Bosnia's national archives, and deposit copies of newspapers, periodicals, and books published in Bosnia. Its staff cataloged dissertations and scientific papers, maintained a microfilm laboratory, produced bibliographies, and provided technical training, courses, and seminars. The National Library was a depository for UNESCO documents and those of other international organizations, and provided access to international databases. Using up-to-date technology and international standards, the library had been automated and had cooperated with 250 libraries in the country and abroad. It had been a primary force in integrating Yugoslavian information systems into regional and international networks.

Very little of the collection, perhaps 10 percent, survived the three days of burning. The Serbs denied responsibility for shelling the library, just as they denied responsibility for most of their actions. The Bosnian Serb leader, Radovan Karadzik, a psychiatrist and poet turned nationalist, claimed that the Muslims had burned down their own library because "they don't like Christian civilization in their city. They never liked that library building. It is from the Austro-Hungarian times. It is a Christian building. They took out all of the Muslim books, left the Christian books inside and burned it down" (as quoted in Maas 1996, 160). Such an explanation seems impossibly simplistic and lurid, but it was typical Serbian rhetoric that the Muslims were actually responsible for atrocities that they blamed on the Serbs. If a shell exploded in the marketplace in Sarajevo, the Muslims were killing themselves to get sympathy; if Muslims were transported in freight cars, it was because they didn't ask for first-class passage. The Serbs continually made statements about the war that clouded its central issues, perhaps to sway public opinion, or perhaps as a means of "blurring the mind and so resisting the reproach of memory" (Cohen 1998, 251). A whole culture of lies was in force: Serbia's leading intellectual, Dobrica Cosic, characterized it thus: "Lying is an aspect of our patriotism and confirmation of our innate intelligence" (as quoted in

Ugresic 1998, 68). The diplomatic and humanitarian community appeared powerless before such obfuscation, and the destruction in Sarajevo and Bosnia was allowed to continue for four years.

Serbian forces were well rewarded for their efforts when formal hostilities were suspended in 1995 with the Dayton Agreements, crafted by American diplomat Richard Holbrook: the Bosnian Serbs were given 49 percent of the land in Bosnia for their Republic Srpska. The Bosnian federation was allotted the remaining 51 percent of the former state, and thus achieved a foundation on which to promote its vision of a unified, multicultural, and sovereign state. This tenuous peace in the Balkans would be disrupted once more in 1998 when the Serbs lashed out at Muslim Albanians in Kosovo and began another round of ethnic cleansing, massacre, and forced migration.

CONCLUSIONS

By pursuing the siren song of a powerful and homogeneous Greater Serbia, a possibility reintroduced by the demise of Communist unity in the 1980s, opportunistic Serbs shrugged off socialist unity and assumed offensive postures against their historic rivals (the Croats), their historic archenemies (the Muslims), and a modern force they underestimated: multiculturalism, which is defined by place, rather than ethnicity. For hundreds of years, Serbian nationalism and accompanying policies of exclusion and homogenization had involved Serbs in recurrent and bloody conflict, including the civil war in the 1940s. Upon the collapse of communism, nationalism reemerged as an ideology that rationalized the wars of expansion in the 1990s. The charismatic president of Serbia, Slobodan Milosevic, provided the machinery for mayhem. In a pattern reminiscent of German fascism in the 1930s and 1940s, the Serbs enacted their fantasies and fears in an ethnocidal, occasionally genocidal, frenzy that was nevertheless quite goal-oriented. To create an enlarged and "pure" homeland, terror was inflicted on expelled non-Serbs to dissuade them from ever returning. Extreme brutality, beyond the usual Balkans purging of ethnic groups, was similar to that demonstrated by the Ustashas in World War II and yet demonstrated a new pathological twist: cultural cleansing. Incomprehensible to much of the world where race often encompasses biological differences, the Serbs demonized groups that were genetically and linguistically identical. Conditioned to view sociocultural, religious, and political differences as the defining factor in identity, the Serbs' ethnocentrism escalated to virulent racism. Serbs tried to create a blank tablet on which to rewrite history, and thus legitimize their expansionism. Expunging all cultural links to the area—homes, churches, mosques, written records, and libraries—reinforced physical expulsion.

The Serb-dominated JNA attacked historical sites, a particular blow to Croatian pride. Croats were shocked by the pulverization of historic Vukovar, after which not one building was left standing, and by the shelling of the medieval city of Dubrovnik. The Croatian media responded with outrage, claiming that symbols of national culture such as books and libraries were being destroyed by uncultured vandals; homes and "hearths" were being destroyed and plundered; Croatia itself was being destroyed. The Croats launched a public relations campaign that distanced them from the "barbarism" of the Serbs and projected a profound difference in sensibility. While in the 1980s nationalism in Croatia and Serbia had developed in a similar fashion—with the revival of myths of a glorious past and subsequent victimization, centralized authoritarianism, control of the media, choking-off of dissent, militarization, and ideological co-option of the Church and intelligentsia—Croatian leaders somehow demonstrated an awareness of boundaries that the Serbs did not. Their patterns of cleansing differed qualitatively and quantitatively from those of the Serbs, especially in terms of rape and the use of concentration camps. It was as if the Croats took nationalism to the edge, wavered, and stepped back while the Serbs careened off it and went on to aggravated ethnocide (including libricide) and genocide. Serbs seemed indifferent to the consequences of their actions and blinded by their political and social agendas, self-interest, and early successes. But, in seeking to destroy a race, a nation, and its history, they would contaminate their present and jeopardize their future by eventually precipitating international condemnation and retribution.

While the Croats were also responsible for death, destruction, and cultural desecration, the scale, the consistency, and the brutality of the Serbian campaign against the Muslims (and, to a lesser degree, the Croats) are the grounds for this chapter's focus on Serbian culpability. In these three aspects, the Serbs' actions were without equal (Cohen 1998)—a judgment shared by the United Nations, human-rights organizations, and the global press. The fact that the Croatian government ultimately rejected the deliberate targeting of books and libraries in cleansing campaigns is of particular relevance to the subject of libricide. While gripped by a passionate nationalism, the Croats eventually expressed a more modern sensibility toward the importance of cultural monuments and records. The Serbs, on the other hand, were completely in thrall to an unbounded ideological commitment to racial and ethnic purity. The Serbs achieved many of their expansionist goals, but they miscalculated the revulsion that their campaigns would inspire in a world that believed modern Europe had outgrown such atrocities. Their behavior had an effect beyond violation of particular ethnic groups or individual victims; it was a direct affront to modernity and to a global culture that was struggling toward a new vision in the 1990s—an internationalism based on human rights, humanism, and multiculturalism.

REFERENCES

Ali, Rabia, and Lawrence Lifschultz. 1993. "In Plain View." In *Why Bosnia? Writings on the Balkan War*, eds. Rabia Ali and Lawrence Lifschultz. Stony Creek, Connecticut: Pamphleteer's Press, xi–lv.

Allen, Beverly. 1996. *Rape Warfare: The Hidden Genocide in Bosnia-Herzegovina and Croatia*. Minneapolis, Minnesota: University of Minnesota Press.

Aparac-Gazivoda, Tatjana, and Dragutin Katalenac, eds. 1993. *Wounded Libraries in Croatia*. Zagreb, Croatia: Croatian Library Association.

Bakarsic, Kemal. 1994. "The Libraries of Sarajevo and the Book That Saved Our Lives." *The New Combat* (July):13–15.

Balic, Smail. 1993. "Culture Under Fire." In *Why Bosnia? Writings on the Balkan War,* eds. Rabia Ali and Lawrence Lifschultz. Stony Creek, Connecticut: Pamphleteer's Press, 75–83.

Chapman, John, and Pavel Dolukhanov. 1993. "Cultural Transformations and Interactions in Eastern Europe: Theory and Terminology." In *Cultural Transformation and Interactions in Eastern Europe*, eds. John Chapman and Pavel Dolukhanov. Brookfield, Vermont: Avebury, 1–36.

Chapman, John. 1994. "Destruction of a Common Heritage: The Archaeology of War in Croatia, Bosnia and Hercegovina." *Antiquity* 68 (258):120–128.

Cigar, Norman. 1995. *Genocide in Bosnia: The Policy of "Ethnic Cleansing."* College Station, Texas: Texas A&M University Press.

Cohen, Roger. 1998. *Hearts Grown Brutal: Sagas of Sarajevo*. New York: Random House.

Debeljak, Ales. 1994. *Twilight of the Idols: Recollections of a Lost Yugoslavia*. Fredonia, New York: White Pine Press.

Denitch, Bogdan. 1994. *Ethnic Nationalism: The Tragic Death of Yugoslavia*. Minneapolis, Minnesota: University of Minnesota Press.

d'Erm, Pascale. 1997. "Sarajevo's Battered Soul." *UNESCO Courier* (July–Aug.):76–79.

Detling, Karen. 1993. "Eternal Silence: The Destruction of Cultural Property in Yugoslavia." *Maryland Journal of International Law and Trade* 17 (1):41–75.

Fisk, Robert. "The Cruelest War." *San Francisco Examiner* (July 3, 1994):A-8.

Glenny, Misha. 1992. *The Fall of Yugoslavia: The Third Balkan War.* London: Penguin Books.

Gutman, Roy. 1993. *A Witness to Genocide: The 1993 Pulitzer Prize-Winning Dispatches on the "Ethnic Cleansing" of Bosnia*. New York: Macmillan.

Hitchens, Christopher. 1993. "Appointment in Sarajevo: Why Bosnia Matters." In *Why Bosnia? Writings on the Balkan War*, eds. Rabia Ali and Lawrence Lifschultz. Stony Creek, Connecticut: Pamphleteer's Press, 4–11.

Judah, Tim. 1997. *The Serbs: History, Myth and the Destruction of Yugoslavia.* New Haven, Connecticut: Yale University Press.

Lorkovic, Tatjana. 1992. "National Library in Sarajevo Destroyed: Collection, Archives Go Up in Flames." *American Libraries* 23 (9):736, 816.

Lovrenovic, Ivan. 1994. "The Hatred of Memory." *The New York Times,* Saturday, 28 May, sec. 1A, p.19.

Maas, Peter. 1996. *Love Thy Neighbor: A Story of War.* New York: Alfred A. Knopf.

Miletic-Vejzovic, Laila. 1994. "The National and University Library in Zagreb: The Goal is Known—How Can It be Attained?" *Special Libraries* 85 (2):104–112.

Milosz, Czeslaw. 1990. *The Captive Mind,* trans. Jane Zielonko. New York: Vintage International.

Peic, Sava. 1995. "The Tragedy of Wanton Cultural Destruction." *The South Slav Journal* 18 (1/2):11–14.

Pfaff, William. 1993. *The Wrath of Nations: Civilization and the Furies of Nationalism.* New York: Simon and Schuster.

Ramet, Sabrina Petra. 1996. *Balkan Babel: The Disintegration of Yugoslavia from the Death of Tito to Ethnic War.* Boulder, Colorado: Westview Press.

Riedlmayer, Andras. 2001. "Convivencia Under Fire: Genocide and Book Burning in Bosnia." In *The Holocaust and the Book*, ed. Jonathan Rose. Amherst: University of Massachusetts Press.

Riedlmayer, Andras. 1995. "Erasing the Past: The Destruction of Libraries and Archives in Bosnia-Herzegovina." *Middle Eastern Studies Bulletin* (MESA) 29 (1):7–11.

Rummel, R.J. 1994. *Death by Government.* New Brunswick, New Jersey: Transaction Books.

Sells, Michael A. 1996. *The Bridge Betrayed: Religion and Genocide in Bosnia.* Berkeley, California: University of California Press.

Shawcross, William. 1994. Preface to *Forging War: The Media in Serbia, Croatia and Bosnia-Hercegovina,* by Mark Thompson. Avon, Great Britain: Bath Press, vii-xii.

Stipcevic, Aleksandar. 1993. "Instead of an Introduction." In *Wounded Libraries in Croatia*, eds. Tatjana Aparac-Gazivoda and Dragutin Katalenac. Zagreb, Croatia: Croatian Library Association, 5–8.

Thompson, Mark. 1994. *Forging War: The Media in Serbia, Croatia and Bosnia-Hercegovina.* Avon, Great Britain: Bath Press.

Tuttle, Alexandra. 1992. "Croatia's Art and Architecture Buried in Rubble." *The Wall Street Journal,* 16 January, sec. 1A, p. 11.

Ugresic, Dubravka. 1998. *The Culture of Lies: Antipolitical Essays,* trans. Celia Hawkesworth. University Park, Pennsylvania: Pennsylvania State University Press.

Vulliamy, Ed. 1994. *Seasons in Hell: Understanding Bosnia's War.* New York: St. Martin's Press.

Zeco, Munevera. 1996. "The National and University Library of Bosnia and Herzegovina During the Current War." *Library Quarterly* 66 (3):294–301.

Zimmerman, Warren. 1999. *Origins of a Catastrophe: Yugoslavia and Its Destroyers.* New York: Times Books.

Chapter 6

IRAQ, KUWAIT, AND THE POLITICS OF THUGGERY

"[I]t is neither the content, the leanings, nor the mixture of ideology that is the cause of disaster; it is the ideology carried to an extreme by those whose absolute power tolerates no alternative voices—animate or inanimate."

(Knuth, this chapter)

In 1989–90, Iraq invaded and annexed its tiny neighbor, Kuwait. Faced with acute economic and political problems, Iraq's president, Saddam Hussein, found the advantages of such aggression irresistible. To justify the invasion, Saddam turned simultaneously to Iraq's official ideology, the quasi-leftist Ba'thism; to regional Arabic mindsets; and to nationalism, the politics of the right. His facile jumble of rationalizations, many designed to appeal to fellow Arabs, generated great confusion and multiple responses, but the decisive one was a coalition that condemned Saddam personally (typifying him as a political thug—even a new Hitler) and opposed the Iraqi invasion as an aggressive and opportunistic act of nationalism and imperialism. Within the coalition, regional and international forces found enough common ground to launch a counterattack.

Eventually the Iraqis were expelled from Kuwait. But during the six-month reign of terror by 100,000 Iraqi troops, Kuwait's economic and cultural infrastructures were gutted, leaving the country a shell of its former self. The Kuwaitis were individually and collectively victimized as their personal possessions and cultural artifacts and institutions were devastated. Iraq removed thousands of Kuwaitis and resident expatriates as hostages, and 60 percent of the population (1.3 million) fled the country (Crystal 1995). Those who remained were subjected to the horrors of torture, rape, and summary execution. No aspect of Kuwaiti life was too small or too large to become a target of Iraq's campaign. Ninety-five percent of the animals in the Kuwait Zoo disappeared; troops machine-gunned many, and in the case of ten gazelles and a baby buffalo, ate them for food (Osborne 1996). The international time line between the two states was abolished. Residents were forbidden to grow facial hair, and some who did had their beards plucked out with pliers ("Horror in the 19th Province" 1990). Lampposts and traffic lights were knocked down, street names changed, and identity documents and license plates re-issued. Kuwait City was renamed *Kadhima,* an Arabic name (Tanter 1998). Virtually all of Kuwait's government buildings, utilities, homes, and businesses were vandalized. Many official documents were destroyed, including property deeds and college records. At Kuwait University, in the building that had housed the faculties of law and the arts, the Iraqis set up a detention and interrogation center (Joyce 1998)—an act of oblit-eration as symbolic as it was literal.

Cultural and educational institutions, including libraries and informa-tion centers, were particularly hard hit by the invasion. Schools were used as headquarters and ammunition dumps, and about 43 percent of the book stocks in school libraries were destroyed. According to one estimate, more than a million children's and educational books were lost. The dismantling and looting of public libraries, in which 133,199 volumes, or about 45 percent of their collections, were lost seemed prearranged and systematic (Salem 1992). Destruction was worse in academic libraries, where a num-ber of Iraqi academic administrators, faculty members, and librarians came to supervise and direct the removal of books (Al-Ansari and Con-away 1996). The Kuwait University Library collection, which contained 24,410 reference books and 540,955 volumes, reports, theses, audiovis-uals, microfiches, and periodicals, was decimated (McDonald 1993). In-deed, the university's entire physical infrastructure was shattered by troops who used classrooms as barracks and looted anything that could be trans-ported to Iraq—from computers to carpets and light fixtures. Library books and materials were shipped to Baghdad, burned in soldiers' cooking fires, or otherwise destroyed. Entire department offices and files disap-peared, and scholars lost irreplaceable research materials and private li-braries (Bollag 1994).

When a United Nations' coalition affirmed Kuwait's sovereignty, im-posed sanctions against Iraq, and increased pressure on Iraq to withdraw, the destruction of Kuwait's assets accelerated. Saddam's troops and officials continued to strike—at Kuwait's economy by setting fire to the oil fields, and at its cultural, intellectual, and national foundations as well. When Baghdad's Director of Museums arrived in Kuwait, he surveyed the collections of Kuwait's National Museum, shipped off artifacts of interest to Iraq, and then had the entire museum complex set ablaze. Losses included art books and manuscripts in a library prized by Islamic scholars. Troops burned the adjoining planetarium and laboratories. Many vestiges of ancient Arab culture were destroyed by this act (Drogin 1991). After the Iraqis were expelled, the museum's director Ibraheem Baghli likened his pain over the devastation to having "lost his father and his self." "It's not the money," Baghli said. "It's our civilization. It's our life" (as quoted in Drogin 1991, A11). Planetarium staff saw the destruction as part of Iraq's strategy of obliterating Kuwait's cultural heritage and uniqueness so that the country could be more readily absorbed into Iraq (Parker 1991).

Along with the physical damage to individual libraries, there was also systemic damage to national information systems that had taken years to develop. Shawky Salem (1991, 71) describes the loss of Kuwait's computer systems, libraries, and information as a "cultural catastrophe," pointing out that, during the last thirty years, experts and technicians had spent millions of hours developing these systems. Yaser Abdel-Motey and Nahia Al Hmood (1992) from the College of Basic Education echo this assessment and lament the loss of both human resources (including expatriate professionals) and work-hours spent in creating catalogues and providing technical services. The destruction short-circuited Kuwait's plans to switch the economy to more of an information base in preparation for the depletion of oil (Al-Ansari and Conaway 1996).

In fact, a concerted effort was made to dismember those "private and public institutions that used to make Kuwait a modern technological society" (Cassidy 1990, A15). The National Scientific and Cultural Center was looted, and then burned. Kuwait's Central Library, a depository for government and national publications that served functions relating to the preservation of national heritage, was also plundered. The Kuwait Institute of Scientific Research would be selectively dynamited by the retreating Iraqi army (McDonald 1993). Eighty-two offices that produced government publications and 25 private publishing houses were looted and destroyed. Kuwait lost an informatics sector that had supported 4,000 people; there had been 45 government computer centers, hundreds of smaller centers, and thousands of privately owned personal computers comprising an estimated prewar capital investment in computers of more than $115 million dollars (Salem 1991). The World Health Organization Center for the Gulf region was in Kuwait; its services, including bibliographical access to the medical databases MEDLINE/MEDLARS, were interrupted by the war. The war also disrupted UNESCO projects as facilities were destroyed and personnel scattered; this caused setbacks to plans for the establishment of ARISNET, an Arab information and library network. Kuwait City's newspapers were stripped of printing presses, computers, and news machines. The radio and television stations also were dismantled, so that no Kuwait media were left.

The intensity of the looting, while horrifying, at least has a rational component: Iraqis both resented and coveted Kuwait's expensive, modern infrastructure. What has been incomprehensible to onlookers is the wanton destruction of such things as public buildings, power and water installations, museums, and libraries. For example, antitank weapons blasted the clock tower at the seaside Sief Palace and then torched the wood-paneled library and elegant Moorish-style buildings (Drogin 1991). As a symbolic gesture of Iraq's spite and dominance, the devastation in Kuwait was reminiscent of the warfare of imperialism (similar to Nazi actions in Poland). Such gratuitous destruction severely compromised Iraq's protestations that the motivation for invasion lay in either restoring Kuwait's rightful place in the family of the Iraq nation or within the fold of Pan-Arabism. A more probable explanation is one author's speculation that Saddam was simply after the "the humiliation and spoliation of the domain of the Al Sabah [Kuwait's ruler]" (Tripp 1993, 29).

To date, literature about the invasion and Desert Storm (the response of a large international coalition after U.N. sanctions proved ineffective) has focused first on military and political events, and then on Kuwait's political destabilization and reorganization. Kuwait's recovery from material and ecological devastation also has been a topic of study. However, the sociocultural implications of the occupation, including the destruction of Kuwait's cultural environment, remain relatively unexplored. Damage to Kuwait's books and libraries is recounted in journals on library and information science (see cites in chapter reference section); these articles also provide descriptive information on preliminary reconstruction efforts and on the destruction's effect on information infrastructures, but little has been done to explain why the devastation occurred. One account, for instance, laments the loss of libraries and computer centers, which were either removed to Baghdad or destroyed and burned, but concludes the subject with the observation that "nobody understood the philosophy behind these decisions" (Salem 1991, 71).

What might bring us to a better understanding of causation and motivation in the occupation of Kuwait is careful consideration of social, psychological, and cultural (as well as political) factors. Further, analysis of these factors may provide insight or, at the least, thoughtful hypotheses as to why cultural materials became systematic targets in Saddam's campaign. The importance of this pursuit is that any individual case of libricide provides us with material for the comparison necessary for identifying common patterns of ethnocide, a process that aids in formulating strategies of prevention.

Thus, while keeping the degree of devastation in mind and also the daunting scale of reconstruction efforts, this chapter proceeds to inquire into the specific nature and cause of one Arab nation's attack against a neighboring nation of common language and culture. It explores the intersection of history, politics, and culture that sparked the devastation of Kuwait and its information infrastructure and material culture. The roots of the incident lie not in the victim country, but in the philosophical and ideological frameworks of the Iraqi state itself. This chapter posits that the root of violations perpetrated in Kuwait lies in the ideologically rationalized sociocultural violence perpetrated first within Iraq itself. The ideological extremism of Iraq's totalitarian system manifested itself first internally in the creation of its police state and in genocidal atrocities against the Kurd population, and then externally in a disastrous war with Iran. A profound militarism and impulse toward political violence finally resulted in aggression against Kuwait.

DISINTEGRATION AND THE RISE OF BA'THISM

The twentieth-century Arab world, slowly freeing itself from centuries of domination by foreigners, was unprepared for the severe social and economic dislocation that accompanied the process of adapting to a modern, secular world. Improved communication systems brought to the proud Arabs a stark view of their relative backwardness—a galling fact to a people who conceived of their identity as founded on a glorious past. This period, during which Muhammad passed on the revelations of God to the Arabs and united them within a rich and honorable high culture, had lasted from the 600s to the early 1500s (Brown 1993). Between this golden age and the contemporary Arab world came 400 years of humiliation under the Turkish-speaking Ottomans, who, though Muslim, were nevertheless outsiders. The Arab people then came under European domination, and only after World War II became independent. But even this independence was dictated by Western powers that divided the region into nation-states based on spheres of influence and economic and political interests. The resulting fragmentation of the Arab world has been an ongoing source of bitterness.

In the twentieth century, new mores and lifestyles resulting from industrialization and urbanization clashed with Muslim values and traditional Arab social patterns. As the Arab people struggled within the cognitive dissonance of incompatible paradigms, many fell back on a traditional conception of all Arab states as members of a unified Arabic world, a school of thought called "Pan-Arabism." Even as separate, bounded nations emerged as a result of the independence process, Arabs psychologically resisted Western patterns of nation-building based on geographic (and politically expedient) boundaries. Throughout the modern history of the Middle East, the notion of a common Arabic identity has prevailed, though it has taken different forms, and produced different outcomes, under each leader.

Pan-Arabism has been fueled by a powerful explanatory myth of the outsider as enemy. The myth was based on the premise that outsiders had caused cultural retrogression and division by conspiring to keep the Arab people weak (Zonis 1993), and it arose to make contemporary Arab history coherent—that is, to reconcile the glory of past civilizations with present entropy. Largely because of this myth, contemporary poverty, and indeed all social, economic, and political problems came to be seen as stemming from the machinations of outsiders; and the humiliation of contemporary military defeats, especially those by the Israelis, was assuaged. According to Paul Salem (1994), situating the source of failure or defeat outside oneself or one's immediate society has allowed the Arabs to maintain a reasonable self-image. In addition, the scapegoat mindset complements traditional Islamic worldviews that encourage an externalization of evil in a dichotomy of good (in *dar al-Islam*) and evil (in *dar al-harb*). Dichotomies are a common feature of ideologies; they simplify the disorder that occurs when traditional social and cultural systems collapse. Marxists, for example, pit exploiters against the exploited; nationalists frequently turn on a designated racial or ethnic group or on their neighbors. In the Middle East, targeting outsiders as scapegoats became a proven way to mobilize the masses, and authoritarian Arab leaders found it to their advantage to consciously promote this mindset because it deflected criticism of their own governments' failures.

Rejection of postcolonial regimes and outside influences led to political experiments and violent coups in the middle part of the twentieth century. Ultimately, a party espousing the revolutionary Pan-Arabic ideology called Ba'thism prevailed in Iraq. Since 1968, the Ba'thist Party fashioned a totalitarian state based on the notion that the true Arab nation transcends the boundaries of individual states. Like most totalitarian regimes, a cult leader, Saddam Hussein, dominated Iraq. But in a trend curiously incompatible with Ba'thist thought (perhaps reflecting the influence of patterns from the rest of the Middle East), Saddam's regime, though founded on principles of Pan-Arabism, also promoted a shadowy nationalism that sought to make Iraq unique (and even dominant) among Arab nations. By manipulating the historical record so as to claim direct links between contemporary Iraq and the ancient, illustrious Babylonia, Saddam crafted a unique and distinguished past for Iraq that substantiated belief in a glorious future. Saddam justified his policies and programs first on one ideological impulse (Ba'thism) and then the other (nationalism) as dictated by expediency; sometimes, he drew on both simultaneously, with little regard for consistency.

A mixture like this was bound to create great confusion for his allies, enemies, and ostensibly neutral observers. Thus, by the end of the 1980s, it was unclear whether Saddam was strategizing to achieve the Ba'thist unification of all Arab states into a truly revolutionary egalitarian meganation, or whether he sought such unification as a cover for a Greater Iraq empire. As Saddam positioned himself as the self-proclaimed leader of the Pan-Arab nation, the specter of Iraqi nationalism and imperialism reared its head. When neighboring Arab regimes responded conservatively to his post-Iran War efforts to mobilize the financial support he felt entitled to (for having defended all Arabs from fundamentalism), Saddam was bitterly disappointed. His anger, over the perceived recalcitrance of the other regimes in adjusting oil prices and providing him with funds, became focused on Kuwait. At this point, and even after the invasion, Saddam misread the political climate and seemed oblivious to the extent of major fractures in regional unity. However, even before the invasion of Kuwait, some of the leaders in neighboring Arab countries had witnessed Saddam's chronic shifting of alliances and Machiavellian conflating of ideologies and identities, and had come to mistrust his intentions. Saddam— insulated in a police state that had eliminated internal dissent and, thus, any elements of contradictory feedback—miscalculated the degree to which invocation of Pan-Arabism and the myth of outside domination could overcome rivalry and mobilize the support of other regimes. The growing divisiveness was concretely expressed when regimes chose sides during the Gulf War.

But let us go back to the founding of Ba'thism in Iraq, with its promise of Pan-Arab unification, and follow the processes by which it became the ideological center for a totalitarian state and was then partially displaced.

Throughout the Middle East, social and political collapse had begun with
the Ottoman empire, gained momentum during the fragmentation into
nation states supervised by foreign powers, and contributed to a climate
of victimization that reached devastating proportions in the middle of the
twentieth century when Palestine was lost to the Israelis and Arab forces
were defeated in the Six Day War of 1967. Some Arabs turned to revolutionary solutions, including Communism, but the homegrown socialist
doctrine of Ba'thism had greater appeal.

Ba'thism was established in Damascus in the early 1940s by a loosely
organized group of teachers and writers who had become estranged from
the Western-dominated establishment. Michel Aflaq, a Greek Orthodox
Christian schoolteacher, wove together an eclectic and appealing mixture
of Pan-Arabism, drawing on modern Western notions of nationalism,
mythical reconstructions of Arab history, and socialist ideas of egalitarianism and revolt against imperialist oppressors. Pan-Arabism offered the
vision of unity that twentieth-century Iraq (and, indeed, the entire Arab
world) needed: a social, economic, and cultural revolution that would
restore tranquility at home and strengthen the country and the region to
confront enemies (Brown 1993). "One Arab nation with an eternal mission" became the Ba'thists' motto. Unity, liberation, and socialism were
construed as the means to a spiritual rebirth of the Arab nation—a profound and revolutionary transformation that would extend beyond national
boundaries to encompass liberation of every Arab from former tribal, religious, and regional loyalties (Karsh and Rautsi 1991). It was a "seemingly uplifting message for downtrodden Arabs" (Al-khalil 1989, 245).
The group had its own daily newspaper by 1946, and in 1947 held its first
congress. The movement took the name *bi'ath,* or *ba'th,* which means
"renaissance" or "flowering," thus claiming to be the party of resurrection.

In 1958 Iraq's monarchy, established by the British in 1921, was de-
posed, and military coups followed in rapid succession. By 1968 the
Ba'thists had ultimately prevailed over all other factions because Ba'thism
provided a platform that resonated with traditional social patterns. Unlike
their rivals, the Communists, Ba'thists were able to make a shaky accommodation with Islamic religious identity. While Ba'thist doctrine was decidedly secular, the region so strongly defined itself culturally as
interchangeably Arab and Muslim that in Ba'thist Iraq, Islam was not
eliminated but became relegated to the realm of private worship and moral
training, similar to the place Christianity holds in the West (Salem 1994).
Socialism was to become an authentic Arab institution in its place. The
idea was to diffuse Islam as a political and social force while maintaining
its mantle of legitimacy. Religious doctrine was to be separate from the

affairs of state in the sense that clerics were not to be involved in politics (Baram 1991).

In general, however, Ba'thism requires a fervency of commitment to the Arab spirit that is similar to that aroused by religious belief. And like all ideologies, Ba'thism mandates standards of conduct for all aspects of life. But, from the start of his regime, the Ba'thist President Saddam Hussein's commitment to Ba'thism was elastic, and dogmatism was advocated only when expedient (for example, to justify creation of a police state). While demanding intense orthodoxy from all Iraqis, Saddam invoked Ba'thism (or not) in an opportunistic fashion; sometimes it was more expedient to identity himself with Islamic traditions. During the 1980s, for example, Saddam made a tremendous show of religious piety in order to strengthen his position against Iran, whose revolutionary clerics had launched a movement to restore fundamentalist Islamic principles throughout the region. Posing as the defender of the Arab world (Iranians are Persian not Arabic), Iraq waged a vicious eight-year war against Iran. However, since the Iranian fundamentalist revival had caused an upsurge of religious fervor throughout the region, an intensified religious identification was advantageous (regardless of whether he was the leader of a society governed by secular principles). Saddam went so far as to modify his family tree to demonstrate direct descent from Mohammed and take a highly publicized pilgrimage to Mecca. In 1990 Saddam reversed Ba'thist socialist policies on women's rights and restored traditional Islamic laws in which a male was permitted to murder a mother, daughter, sister, or maternal or paternal female cousin, for committing adultery (Karsh and Rautsi 1991). Both Ba'thism and Islam proved to be powerful and convenient tools for Saddam, and he used them with skill.

THE PATH TO TOTALITARIANISM

Early on in the Ba'thists' regime, Saddam occupied himself with suppressing dissent and institutionalizing the Party, exerting his influence from a powerful but secondary position. During this period he shaped doctrine and constructed a security apparatus of sufficient omnipotence as to achieve complete conformity to Ba'thist principles. When he had acquired enough political power, he stepped to the forefront, pushing aside his mentor, and promoted himself as a cult figure. Just as Ba'thism stimulated quasi-religious fervor, Saddam acquired a godlike status; eventually leader, ideology, and state became fused. As Ba'thism became a political religion, the Party's power progressed from authoritative to totalitarian, and by 1975—just seven years after the Ba'thists took power—Saddam had transformed Iraq from an autocracy ruled by successive, short-lived military regimes into a police state.

The transformation to a totalitarian state did not occur overnight, however. When the Ba'thists took over in the second of two political coups, there was no popular revolution and the Party's support base was narrow. Knowing this, the Party leadership embarked on an ambitious educational program that involved repeated and sustained campaigns to universalize education for the young and eradicate illiteracy at all levels. In enforcing compulsory education laws, the Ba'thists made illiteracy illegal, and literacy programs became a conduit for official propaganda. The goal of Iraqi education was to instill ideological adherence and loyalty to Ba'thism, bringing about the socialist transformation of society. Curriculum and intellectual agendas were, as a result, decidedly political. In the 1970s, a Ba'thist wrote "reactionary bourgeois and liberal ideas and trends in the syllabus and the educational institutions must be rooted out. The new generation must by immunized against ideologies and cultures conflicting with our Arab nation's basic aspirations and its aim for unity, liberty and socialism" (Al-khalil 1989, 85).

It will probably come as no surprise that in this sociocultural environment, historiography—methods and content of historical scholarship—was subjected to ideological imperatives. Prior to the Ba'thists' rise to power, there already was emerging drive in the region to retrieve Arab history from Western historians who chronicled an expatriate-driven Arab history in which "the inhabitants [Arabs] are spectators, and do not even get good seats at the show" (Rich 1991, xiii). The Ba'thists essentially hijacked this effort, wishing not only to assume ownership of Arab history but also to use it to their own ends. Husri, one of the original theorists, called boldly for mythmakers to construct "from the debris of the past a grand and glittering edifice to serve as a source of confidence and inspiration for the entire nation" (Salem 1994, 53). In the 1970s, emphasis was on the "nation" as being the Arab nation; by the 1980s, in Iraq, "nation" often meant the Iraqi nation. In Saddam's 1977 speech "On History" (subsequently published with great fanfare and supplemented by laudatory comments from sixteen Iraqi Ph.D.s), he stated that researchers and historians should not concern themselves with objectivity, nor should they leave their readers to draw their own conclusions about intellectual and social questions. Historical analysis and the writing and teaching of history must be rooted in the Ba'thist point of view:

> When we discuss the unity of Arabs, for example, we must not occupy the young student with details about fragmentation, thereby entering into a

discussion on whether or not we are one nation. It is sufficient to talk about Arabs as one nation, considering this an absolute truth, with a simplified summary on the role of [Western] imperialism in fragmenting the nation in order to weaken it and secure its control over it . . . without worrying the student at such a stage with complex theoretical, philosophical or political analyses (as quoted in Al-khalil 1989, 75).

Historians were to glorify the past of the Arab people, and history books that contradicted Ba'thist-oriented perspectives were to be burned. Dr. Al-Barak, who became head of the Party's intelligence network in 1982, wrote his doctoral dissertation as an exercise in Ba'thist analysis: The avowed purpose of his work was to "rewrite history in accordance with a new program" (Al-khalil, 1989, 181). His role, along with that of other scholars, was to provide "proofs" for use in ideologically based education. They promulgated a Ba'thist "truth" that was illusory, fictionalized, chameleonlike, and expedient (Al-khalil 1989).

As one might expect, academic excellence was an early casualty of the totalitarian state. Academic standards became a farce as Party members, including Saddam, awarded themselves advanced degrees. Non-Ba'thist students were denied vocational and higher education. The desired products of Iraqi education were either intellectuals who defended the regime out of Ba'thist beliefs, nationalism, or self-interest or "ambitious technocrats [who] readily took on the responsibilities of running a government, the horrors of which they either ignored or justified as necessary" (Henderson 1991, 78). Those who did not embrace orthodoxy were treated harshly. In 1979 the security services, given a free hand over cultural life, arrested 200 poets, storytellers, musicians, filmmakers, and painters; many died under torture or were poisoned by thallium, a lethal rat poison favored by the regime (Mohsen 1994). Soon after, 700 intellectuals fled the country. Those who stayed did so at their peril. Journalist and Saddam-specialist Simon Henderson (1991) writes of a recalcitrant university professor who was kept blindfolded for a week and then deliberately blinded by a powerful searchlight shone directly into his eyes. Following the argument that extremist ideology is inherently anti-intellectual, it is not surprising that those intellectuals who were unable or unwilling to relinquish the habit of thinking critically and divergently should be targeted.

The Iraqi government went to great lengths to impose Ba'thist conformity on all Iraqis. They controlled internal media and subsidized and exported great amounts of printed material. Three million copies of nineteen speeches by Saddam Hussein were distributed during 1978 alone (Al-khalil 1989). In 1980, Iraq claimed to have distributed through embassies, cultural centers, and the Party organizational structures almost ten million copies of the two national daily newspapers, more than four million periodicals, and eighteen thousand copies of every pamphlet or book published by the Ministry of Education. Internally, an annual output of ten million books was claimed, along with well over a hundred thousand magazines devoted exclusively to the welfare of Iraq's children (Al-khalil 1989).

At the same time, existing collections were purged of materials that reflected Western values and "imperialistic" accounts and interpretations, including encyclopedias. The West was considered dangerous not just because of its imperialistic tendencies, but also because of its philosophies and teachings. Post-Enlightenment values and perceptions, such as individualism and democracy, were a threat to collective and Ba'thist values (as interpreted by Saddam). New materials were generated that supported official claims and truths. As the regime's control over print matter became more and more ubiquitous, so did its control of intellectual life and social dialogue. The stories that normally circulate in the public domain as a way of spreading information and making sense of social, economic, and political events became too risky in Saddam's terror-ridden regime. Neighbors, colleagues, and family members were encouraged to inform on each other. All levels of discourse were effectively constrained as Iraqis fearfully conformed to Ba'thist ideology, the mores of the totalitarian state, and the demands of Saddam for public protestations of loyalty and adulation.

Of course, a key factor in transforming Iraq into a totalitarian state was the reorganization of political institutions. Saddam borrowed organizational structures and techniques from the Communists and the Nazis. Like them, he distrusted ground-roots revolutionary impulses and put together a cohesive political party to serve as a vanguard force responsible for perpetuating ideological doctrines. While the Ba'thist Party's legitimacy was ostensibly derived from the people and the revolution waged in their name, his party, which was entrusted with enforcing Ba'thist morals, was in fact bent on building a relatively amoral elite-driven autocracy. Thus, in Iraq, those who would "manipulate" the people by expressing dissent or deviating from the Party line were traitors and, for the welfare of the state, had to be swiftly stifled. In saving the people from themselves, the minority party asserted its own authority over the majority because only the Party knew what was best for the people (Salem 1994).

According to Efraim Karsh and Inari Rautsi's (1991) political biography of Saddam, his plan was that the Party would possess the organizational infrastructure and ideological basis for controlling people's actions and minds. While the Party controlled the masses and the state machinery, he would control the Party. Therefore, Saddam brought all state organizations—the army, the bureaucracy, trade unions, and mass organizations— under Party domination. These and other institutions formed the basis for a controlled media, and massive adult literacy, education, and propaganda programs aimed at inculcating absolute loyalty. Civil society was abolished and all individual rights, including rights to privacy, freedom of speech, and due process under law, were preempted in the interests of socialist unity. "We must ensure that the thirteen and a half million [Iraqis] take the same road," announced Saddam. "He who chooses the twisted path will meet the sword" (as quoted in Karsh and Rautsi 1991, 120). Politics came to an end, and institutionalized violence took its place (Al-khalil 1989).

Saddam's successful use of terror to bring about conformity became the distinguishing characteristic of contemporary Iraq (Henderson 1991). The omnipotence of security forces was a function of chronic surveillance made possible by the division of Baghdad into security zones. Each zone had a headquarters that was part of a security apparatus headed eventually by three agencies: the *Amn,* or State Internal Security (trained and supplied by the Russian KGB); the *Estikhbarat,* or Military Intelligence (operations against Iraqi or other nationals resident abroad, embassies); and the *Mukhabarat,* or Party Intelligence, the powerful and feared meta-intelligence agency that watched over other Iraqi networks and institutions like the army (Al-khalil 1989). The surveillance efforts of official security personnel were supplemented by information supplied by one's neighbors or colleagues. Even school children were encouraged to report the dissident comments of their parents. In the eyes of Saddam, no dissent was too trivial to warrant official reprisals (Karsh and Rautsi 1991), and an atmosphere of paranoia was deliberately cultivated.

Brutal suppression of anti-government plots was an excellent tool for both eliminating opposition and sending signals that dissent would be fatal. Security forces were encouraged to use torture and summary executions in suppressing anti-government activity. Reports by external human rights monitors are rife with accounts of beatings, starvation, sleep deprivation, electric shocks, maiming, killing, and frequent "suicides" of prisoners. The motive for torture was to discover information, but also to breed fear in the populace (Henderson 1991).

Racism, xenophobia, and a tendency to suspect conspiracies, all of which had a strong foothold in Iraqi culture, were in effect exploited by the government's high-profile denouncements of Zionist and imperialist conspiracies. The public witnessed hearings in which Saddam's political enemies were portrayed as pawns of outside forces, then tried, forced to confess, and sentenced to death. The few remaining Jews who had not emigrated to Israel were periodically accused of being Zionist pawns and victimized by bloody pogroms. Iraqis were subject to surprise raids; someone might simply disappear, and fear would prevent friends and family from inquiring into what had happened (Karsh and Rautsi 1991). Randomness, unpredictability, and secrecy increased the terror. The myth of eternal danger from outsiders was used to justify the maintenance of an omnipotent security apparatus, and Iraq became a "republic of fear" (Alkhalil 1989).

Among the political leadership, no one—even long-term friends and colleagues—was exempt from accusations of unfaithfulness to either Saddam or the state. Saddam would initiate purges whenever he felt threatened or thwarted, or just as preemptive measures. The purge of 1979 has been identified as the point at which Iraq crossed over from a politico-military dictatorship to a totalitarian state whose influence extended to every aspect of society (Karsh and Rautsi 1991). In this purge Saddam consolidated his power through the execution of nearly five hundred top-ranking Ba'thists who had been identified as disloyal, including one-third of the top-ranking Revolutionary Command Council (RCC) members. According to Karsch and Rautsi (1991) the RCC secretary, Muhyi Rashid, was the first to "confess" when his family was seized and held hostage; as a result, he and his whole family were shot. Surviving leaders were forced to join firing squads and execute their former colleagues. Members of the National Assembly, Iraq's parliament, were required to sign an oath of allegiance to Saddam in their own blood. Eventually no one would contradict the views of the man who simultaneously held the positions of President of the Republic, Prime Minister, Commander-in-Chief, Chairman of the Revolutionary Command Council, and Secretary-General of the Ba'th Party Regional Command.

Saddam promoted fear as an omnipresent fact of national existence. Part of his power lay in the fact that the people were programmed to simultaneously love and fear him. Soon after his ascension to power, Iraqis began to circulate stories about Saddam's personal involvement in the execution and torture of potential rivals. They exchanged tales of his prowess with guns and reported that "The Godfather" was his favorite movie and Stalin his personal hero. It is characteristic of Ba'thist Iraq that the truth content of a particular story may be less important than the fact that the people have come to believe it is true (Al-khalil 1989). Certainly, such stories were instrumental in fueling his mystique.

Totalitarian leaders tend to be larger than life. As progress is made from revolutionary fervor to institutionalized power, supreme cult figures emerge as centers of new "politico-social secularized religions" (Piekalkiewicz and Penn 1995, 20). Like other totalitarian leaders, such as Stalin or Mao, Saddam consciously developed a cult personality. His name appeared everywhere as a reminder of his authority: Saddam International Airport in Baghdad, Saddam Oil Field, and Saddam housing areas. Huge posters and murals of Saddam dominated every square and highway. A 140-foot pendulum in a new clock tower in central Baghdad was surrounded by statues depicting the seven stages of Saddam's life, from his birth to the cease-fire with Iran in 1988. His fists are reported to have been the model for the hands holding a pair of crossed swords in a huge *arc de triomphe* celebrating Iraq's "victory" in the war with Iran. Newspapers, pamphlets, and posters typified Saddam as the leader-president, the leader-struggler, the standard-bearer, the Arab leader, the knight of the Arab nation, the hero of national liberation, the father leader, and the daring and aggressive knight (Al-khalil 1989). Saddam was portrayed as the living embodiment of Ba'thist ideology and a modern day Nebuchadnezzar, the Babylonian king who fought the Persians (from whom fundamentalist Iran is descended) and conquered the Jews. Nebuchadnezzar represents everything that Saddam Hussein aspired to: glory, conquest, and regional hegemony; he was the embodiment of both Iraqi patriotism and wider Arab nationalism (Karsh and Rautsi 1991). To reinforce the identification, in the 1980s, Saddam ordered a reconstruction of the ancient ruler's Babylon made from thousands of bricks inscribed with Saddam's name. The monuments are clues to Saddam's delusions. He has been profiled as having a dangerous personality configuration called malignant narcissism, characterized by extreme self-absorption, a paranoid outlook, messianic ambitions, and the absence of a conscience and concern for the pain or suffering of others (Post 1993). It is a profile of the "destructive charismatic who unifies and rallies his downtrodden supporters by blaming outside enemies" (Post 1993, 54).

To outsiders, the posturing of totalitarian cult figures often seems surrealistic. In his book *Instant Empire,* Henderson (1991) comments on the startling proportions of Saddam's personality cult and the essential absurdity of the man whose image, decked in appropriate costumes, dominated the landscape. Samir Al-khalil (1989, 115) points to Saddam's revised family tree as signifying "total contempt for the populace, large numbers of whom he knew would accept this proof of ancestry." Others observe Saddam's need to be "at once the father of the nation and its glorious son, a fierce warrior and a thoughtful philosopher, a radical revolutionary and a practicing Muslim" (Karsh and Rautsi 1991, 151). True to totalitarianism, Saddam sought to dominate the public arena absolutely; he had to be everything and everyone to his people.

IDEOLOGICAL DRIFT AND NATIONALISM

The myth of Pan-Arab unity was appealing because it offered a common cultural identity like that once found in Islam. It promised a cultural renaissance, and it situated the enemy outside the Arab world. The myth was popular with political regimes because it allowed them to direct public attention away from pressing political and economic problems. However, it also distracted *governments* from addressing these problems and led to chronic undercurrents of instability. Pan-Arabism's claim that the only fully legitimate state is the one Arab nation caused disregard for outside nations, but also (potentially) for the boundaries and sovereignty of individual Arab states themselves (Salem 1994). Though, on one hand, individual Arab political entities were deemed "equal" by the doctrine of unity, size and political might could make it possible for leaders of large regimes to dismiss smaller entities and subsume them by arguing that they were arbitrarily created by Western Imperialism, and thus illegitimate anyway (Baram 1991). Thus, conditions were such that a single powerful state could annex others under the cover of the Arab nation—though of course this possibility was not publicly acknowledged. Small states were chronically vulnerable to coercion and threats while larger states jockeyed for power, and issues of security loomed as a major concern (Hassan 1999). The 1970s and 1980s were marked by continual crisis (actual and existential), and many Arab regimes began to drift quietly towards nationalism and the idea (though again, rarely spoken) of an Arab nation comprising loosely federated but autonomous states with common interests rather than one mega-state. Indeed, in the face of disillusioning events such as the 1967 Six Day War with Israel, Pan-Arabism seemed to have moved to the sidelines, a sort of bitter-sweet illusion that was difficult to renounce but that no longer served the rising political needs. But regimes realized that in the face of threats from fundamentalist Islamic factions, Pan-Arabism remained functional in posing an alternative utopian vision and assuaging the need for a sense of brotherhood and cultural belonging. Leaders were reluctant to abandon a tradition of demagoguery in which the regimes of neighboring nations were bypassed and Pan-Arabism, with its powerful appeal to the masses, was invoked to elicit grassroots support from Arabs as a whole.

In Iraq in the 1970s, tension was building over the ideological drift from Pan-Arabist nationalism (*cambia*) to Iraqi patriotism (*wataniyya*). While Ba'thism and its Pan-Arab philosophy still formed the doctrinal basis for Iraq's totalitarian regime, there were signs that the expression of Pan-Arabism was becoming a front for a nationalist movement and the extension of Saddam's power into the rest of the Arab world. In defense of a movement towards "Ba'thism in one country," Saddam argued that the completion of Iraq's transformation would entail the spread of the revolution, under Iraq's leadership, to the rest of the Arab world. A powerful Iraq was critical, he argued, because the glory of the Arabs stemmed from the glory of Iraq: throughout history, whenever Iraq had been mighty and flourished, so had the Arab nation as a whole. Saddam was positioning the Iraqis as a superior race. In 1974, Saddam was already proclaiming the Iraqi as "a new man who has evolved from ancient man in every respect. This is our achievement and this is the source of our confidence that the future belongs to us and not to any evil individual whether in Iraq or in the Arab homeland" (as quoted in Karsh and Rautsi 1991, 123–4). In 1985, a citizenship law was amended by the addition of an oath of allegiance for all citizens:

> I swear by Almighty God and by Iraq's pure soil, water and skies, that I shall guard Iraq against any foreigner that would engage in aggression against it, or plan to enslave it, or conquer it, or turn it into his vassal, and that I shall defend it by all means so that its banner remains high with no other banner higher, and its sovereignty elevated with no other sovereignty eclipsing it, and may God witness my words. (Baram 1991, 67)

This oath marked a new idea of Iraqi identity as eternal and distinct from other Arabs, and of Iraq as the destined leader of the Arab world by virtue of its illustrious history. It revealed "a clear-cut Iraqi centered Pan-Arab credo, that exposed occasional imperial tendencies" (Baram 1991, xiii), and the new image would serve Saddam well in the years to come. While building the infrastructure for nationalism and regional dominance, Saddam maintained appearances through the politically expedient mantle of Pan-Arabism, "Ba'thism in one country," and an egalitarian vision of a Pan-Arab alliance of independent and eternal states.

However, within Iraq, Saddam promoted national consciousness throughout the 1980s and gave Iraqi localism and identification with the ancient land between the Tigris and Euphrates rivers equal status with, and even priority over, Pan-Arabism (Baram 1991). Saddam promoted a new and specifically Iraqi identity—i.e. one tied to this geographic re-

gion—tracing Iraqi history back five thousand years to a glorious Mesopotamian period. A nationalist historiographical focus thus superseded a
Ba'thist one that identified with Pan-Arabism and the Golden Age of Arab
renaissance under Islam. Campaigns were launched to build cultural-
historical foundations for this new nationalistic impulse. Money was di-
verted to boost Iraqi folklore; modern versions of ancient Mesopotamian
spring rites were introduced; and artists who derived inspiration from this
period of antiquity were sponsored. Funding was plentiful for historians
engaged in writing corroborating texts and for archeological excavations
and reconstructions. Geographers revised maps and replaced contemporary place names with evocative ancient ones (Baram 1991). The docile
intellectual and educational apparatus accommodated both traditional
Pan-Arabic nationalism and a distinctive Iraqi national consciousness
and, certainly, few resident Iraqi citizens dared to point out doctrinal
inconsistencies.

THE IRAN-IRAQ WAR, 1980–1988

Since the arbitrary division of the Middle East in the early part of the
twentieth century, Iraq frequently engaged in border disputes, most often
over ownership of oil fields and access to ports. The country felt cheated
because it had only fifteen miles of ocean access and lacked a deepwater
port; it is surrounded by six other states, and its main port of Basra is only
accessible by 50 miles of contested waterway. Iraq has repeatedly sought
to gain control of the waterway from Iran. Also coveting Kuwait's oil
fields and seaport, Iraqi leaders intermittently encroached along poorly
defined stretches of the Kuwait-Iraq border. On two separate occasions a
disgruntled Iraq attempted to annex Kuwait—in 1961, after Kuwait declared independence from British supervision, and again in 1973, under
the Ba'thists. Both attempts on Kuwait were rebuffed with the support of
the British and other Arab nations, but tension defined the relationship
between the two states.

By 1980, Saddam had consolidated his political control over Iraq, and
the nation was riding the crest of a wave of development. Al-khalil (1989)
describes Saddam at this point as self-confident, armed to the teeth, motivated by an impulse to violence, and primed for war. Any war. Saddam's
habit of violence and the country's emerging nationalism (with attendant
notions of persecution, past greatness, and a glorious destiny mandated
by historical and biological determinism), provided the perfect breeding
ground for an amplification of existing tendencies toward militarism and
imperialistic aspirations. Like Imperialist Japan and Nazi Germany before,

Iraq had come to glorify violence, feed off of a sense of thwarted destiny, and seek direction from a powerful, godlike leader who could provide a direct path from intention to action.

At this point in Iraq's history, Iran seemed a relatively easy target and, in 1980, Saddam invaded the country and soon was immersed in a long-term war. Saddam posed Iraq's aggression as a response to threats from Islamic fundamentalist leaders who hoped to spread the revolution in Iran to the Arab nations. And these threats were real; they were both personal and ideological. Iran's Ayatollah loathed Saddam, and secular Ba'thism was ostensibly an anathema to the fundamentalists. But Saddam's opportunism was also evident in the invasion. He wanted to gain control of the contested waterways and possibly enable Iraq to annex the oil-rich province of Khuzestan and return its three million Arabs from the Persians to their rightful family. Were history to Saddam a lesson rather than a blank tablet, he might have known that attacking a civil society in the throes of revolution would most likely unify it and elicit a fierce response, internal enemies suddenly appearing far less threatening than those without (Karsh and Rautsi 1991). Iran struck back ferociously, and the two countries became locked in a vicious eight-year war reminiscent of the trench warfare of World War I.

The war caused an immediate escalation of militarism within Iraq. In two years the Popular Arm, a paramilitary force, grew from 100,000 troops to 450,000. Millions of citizens were trained through its programs and through induction into the army; according to Saddam, "the use of weapons should be an essential component of the new man and the new society" (Al-khalil 1989, 32). Iraq would eventually field one million soldiers. Within Iraq, the regime advanced militarism through the manipulation of culture. The state-run printing houses in the 1980s pumped out "military victory literature" or "battles literature" that romanticized war. More than forty festivals were held to revive popular poetry, including Bedouin *rajiz* poems that celebrated tribal values, revived the old violent language, and prepared the rural masses for war. According to poet Abd al-Wahid, a fighting language that was wounded was being replaced: "An arrogant, colourful, victorious language is present now. Blood, bullets, the names of weapons, cannons, armoured vehicles. With such words we live daily. I remember that one of the military commanders told me: 'You made us love our weapons because you made them into people, you made them living humans.' This means that language is so elastic that it can humanize iron and fire" (as quoted in Mohsen 1994, 15).

Saddam mobilized support within Iraq and from other Arab states by emphasizing that Iraq was not the only Arab nation terrified by the po-

tential of a fundamentalist revolution. In addition, he characterized the
war as a racial war dating back to pre-Islamic times, a second *Qadisiyya*
or continuation of ethnic Arab-Persian conflicts (Baram 1991). Adopting
the stance of a lone Arab knight facing Persian (Iranian) expansion, he
transposed personal interest in his own political survival and imperialistic
interest in acquiring natural resources into a war to "protect the eastern
gateway to the Arab nation" (Algosaibi 1993, 8). Any wavering of Arab
support was tantamount to a betrayal of Pan-Arabism. As a result of the
war, Saddam was able to unify his country, build a massive war machine,
and gain leverage from posing as the defender of the Arab world. Many
Arab governments gave him diplomatic, logistical, and financial support.
Western nations such as the United States, which had its own issues with
Iran after the 1979 hostage situation, became allies and turned a blind eye
on Saddam's experiments with ever more lethal weapons and tactics. Because of political self-interest, the world's democratic nations stood by
while he used chemical weapons on the rebellious Kurds, his own people,
and significantly expanded Iraq's biological, chemical, and nuclear warfare capabilities. Saddam's use of chemical weapons finally prompted Iran
to agree to a cease-fire in 1988. Saddam immediately declared a glorious
victory.

Iraq had paid a high price for this victory. Iran's stubborn resistance
and use of human wave attacks had debilitated Iraq's war machine. Iraq
lost more than 100,000 troops, and possibly twice as many were wounded.
The country was left with massive debts and a leader so primed by the
war that disaster was inevitable. Saddam's pretensions and fantasies concerning Iraq's superiority in the Arab world had only increased as the war
continued, as did his sense of military prowess. Perhaps Saddam had come
to believe that his arsenal of chemical and biological weapons had given
him the "destructive powers akin to that of a superpower" (Haselkorn
1999, 33) and would deter foreign intervention in any future military
action. Saddam's pretensions, his psychological state, and a context of
unstable financial and social conditions served to bring on another war
that would bring Iraq face-to-face with a global coalition of nations whose
political and economic interests were in direct opposition.

FACTORS IN THE INVASION OF KUWAIT

With the long war behind him, Saddam now faced a desperate economic
situation. Oil production had fallen, oil prices were going down, and Iraq
could not begin to repay debts worth billions of dollars, much less get
new loans for reconstruction or for pursuing his political aspirations. Sixty

thousand POWs were still in Iran, and on the home front troops were demanding demobilization and peacetime jobs. A population that had tripled in thirty years had high expectations concerning the promised fruits of victory. Clannish conspiracy in the armed forces and simmering family feuds were symptoms of cracks in Saddam's autocracy and an indication that Saddam's inner circle was weakening (Tripp 1993).

Saddam's personality was one of the most powerful forces behind the direction these conditions took. Experts such as Karsh and Rautsi (1991) have posited that beneath the outward bravado, Saddam is very insecure because of an extremely cynical view of politics as a ceaseless struggle for survival against plots and enemies—the "destructive charismatic" syndrome mentioned earlier (Post 1993). When domestic crisis escalated in Iraq, Saddam attributed it to the country's sacrifices for the Arab cause in the war with Iran, hoping to be bailed out by the Arab neighbors he had "defended." When debt subsidies and reductions were not forthcoming, heroics and pleas for help gave way to anger, resentment, scapegoating, and obsession. He began to focus his anger on rich Kuwait, which he had always resented for its unsocialist retention of great wealth in the face of the needs of poorer Arabs (a Pan-Arabic position) and Kuwait's possession of natural resources that were rightfully Iraq's (a nationalistic stance that expanded the scope of contested boundaries—an issue throughout the century). When his escalating demands for money, debt forgiveness, and modification of oil policies remained unsuccessful, Saddam became furious at what he perceived as disrespect and indifference and obsessed with Kuwait's wealth and geostrategic advantages.

Further exacerbating his frustration, countries that had been sympathetic during Saddam's war with Iran were turning away. The U.S. and Great Britain, alarmed at Saddam's quest for military supremacy, began to confiscate weapons shipments and interfere with his efforts to create a supergun. In 1981, for similar reasons, the Israelis had bombed an Iraqi nuclear facility. These actions only fueled Saddam's resentment of non-Arab nations and strengthened his belief that they were attempting to sabotage Iraq, this time by cutting off its livelihood. "For the Arab nation," he stated, "the need for scientific advancement is tantamount to the need to live" (as quoted in Karsh and Rautsi 1991, 126). Postwar armchair analysis is always problematic, but nevertheless, this assumption is probably warranted: In the end, Saddam ordered the invasion because he needed natural and financial resources to ward off domestic crisis, but he cloaked his imperialism by claiming that Kuwait's rejection of his demands constituted an act of war and that Kuwait was plotting with his enemies. After the invasion, Saddam would assert to a British interviewer,

"We took our action because the ruling family in Kuwait is good at black-mail, exploitation, and destruction of their opponents. They had perpetu-ated a grave U.S. conspiracy against us . . . stabbing Iraq in the back with a poisoned dagger" (as quoted in Karsh and Rautsi 1991, 1). In Saddam's "Victory Day" address of August 8, 1990, his paranoia and demagoguery are powerfully evident:

> This is the only way to deal with these despicable Croesuses who relished possession [oil wealth] to destroy devotion [to Islam, to Pan-Arabism] . . . who were guided by the foreigner instead of being guided by virtuous standards, principles of Pan-Arabism, and the creed of humanitarianism. . . . Two of August has come as a very violent response to the harm that the foreigner wanted to perpetrate against Iraq and the nation. The Croesus of Kuwait and his aides became the obedient humiliated and treacherous dependents of that foreigner. . . . Iraq will be the pride of the Arabs, their protector. (quoted in Post 1993, 53)

Despite this later rhetoric, the invasion was first publicized as an attempt to support an indigenous Kuwaiti uprising against the monarchy, a fabri-cation designed to support Saddam's plan to set up a puppet regime in Kuwait and claim that Kuwait was undergoing a Pan-Arab revolution. However, he could not find any prominent Kuwaiti willing to man such a regime. Global public opinion also rejected this rationalization and iden-tified the invasion as an illegal action against a sovereign nation. During the ensuing uproar, Saddam took refuge in yet another myth of his own creation (a nationalist one), claiming that the Kuwaiti civil government had appealed to their kinfolk in Iraq, "the valiant men of Qadisiya, the honorable, generous, chivalrous guards of the eastern gateway of the Arab homeland, led by the knight of the Arabs and the leader of their march, the hero leader President Field Marshal Saddam Hussein—to approve the return of the sons to their family, the return of Kuwait to great Iraq, the motherland" (Karsh and Rautsi 1991, 222). Thus, the myth of the "pro-visional revolutionary government" became "the return of the branch to the root" (Algosaibi 1993, 69), and on August 28, 1990, Kuwait was officially declared the nineteenth province of Iraq.

Invocation of myths and conspiracies, the use of Islamic slogans, the linking of his cause with anti-Zionism and anti-Imperialism, and promises that he would redistribute oil wealth to the Arab poor failed to elicit a critical mass of support. Even before the Kuwait invasion, Iraq had be-come, to many Arab regimes, a rogue state and Saddam a rogue leader—dangerous and uncontrollable. For thoughtful Arabs, his credibility as an

Arab and as a socialist or revolutionary ideologue first had been compromised by his genocidal treatment of the Kurds. The post-invasion rape and pillage of his fellow Arabs, the Kuwaitis, merely solidified the perception. The Arab world reeled under "the shattering effect of one Arab state invading and in effect attempting to obliterate another . . . [some Arabs felt] a sadness and anger that is equal to and in some respects worse than we felt in 1967 and 1982" (Said 1991, 97). The prominent scholar Edward Said (1991, 101) traces this mood to Saddam's failure to build on what the Arabs had achieved: "Kuwait after all was a thriving society, its people a vital part of the Arab nation, its institutions prosperous and liberal. What good has it done to attack all this? How can violence against Kuwait have ever been justified? The failure of creativity, morality and principle are so profound as to trouble us all. . . . There is loss to be mourned and regretted. All Arabs share in the general diminishment." Arab intellectual Fouad Ajami (1998, 146) later would decry the tendency by some Arabs to choose to have politics remain an instrument for "fighting the other rather than a means of self-criticism and self-discovery." Ajami (1998, 166) emphasizes the distinctiveness of certain regional mindsets by quoting a poem, "Who Killed Kuwait?" by Souad al-Sabah; the last line queries "Didn't we all take part in the chorus of the Regime?"

AFTERMATH OF INVASION

Saddam's grandest professions to be serving the goal of cultural renaissance could not cloak the spite and brutality revealed in the occupation of Kuwait nor the national degradation it caused. The Iraqis' disgust, rooted in Ba'thist philosophy, for Arab reactionary forces and the wealthy oil sheiks fed unbridled greed. Over the years, Saddam had expended massive resources on portraying Kuwait's royal family as the avaricious puppets of the imperialists. Millions of dollars were spent to put hundreds of Arab journalists on Baghdad's payroll in order to fan resentment over the lifestyle of the well-to-do Kuwaitis who had been relatively unaffected by a recession in the 1980s, which had been disastrous for poor and middle-class Arabs (Rezun 1992). According to Ajami (1998, xiii), "that drive to the gold *souk* [trading area] of Kuwait that Saddam Hussein's soldiers took in August of 1990 was a brigand's gift, an offering to all those who had been taunted and denied by an era of astounding fury." Wealthy Kuwaitis suffered particularly extreme cruelties at the hands of Saddam's troops. One Kuwaiti banker had his eyes gouged out and was quartered by a chain saw in full view of his family; his limbs and torso were mounted on a stake and his head thrown into a nearby gutter (Rezun 1992).

Just as Ba'thism rationalized social violence in Iraq, the destruction in Kuwait had byproducts that served ends of ideological extremism. First, the looting could in some perverse way be posed not just as a Robin Hood response, but as a way of turning Kuwait away from its independent, materialist identity that was antithetical to revolutionary Pan-Arabism. By destroying its Western-oriented technological and cultural base, it could be more easily transformed into an essentially Arab (Ba'thist) entity. In addition, the destruction of Kuwait served nationalistic and imperialistic ends that were furthered by obliterating the separate Kuwait nation as such. The Kuwaitis, posed as inferior to the Iraqi "new man," were occupying land "rightfully" belonging to Iraq (their claims to dominance harkening back to ancient Mesopotamia) and profiting from natural resources that Iraq desperately needed in order to achieve its predestined supremacy. By annexing Kuwait, Iraq gained oilfields and a harbor, and made giant steps toward achieving a Greater Iraq. By destroying everything that supported a separate political, economic, or cultural identity, the Iraqis were transforming Kuwait into a pacified, relatively primitive nineteenth province.

CONCLUSIONS

The extreme social and cultural violence wreaked on Kuwait was the extension of the decades-long subjugation and terrorization within Iraq itself. Western influences, expressed in humanistic values that supported, at least to some degree, critical thinking and free access to information, long extinguished in Iraq, had to be rooted out in Kuwait. The quickest path to asserting control of information, history, the media, and intellectual life in Kuwait was to strip the nation to ground zero and then reconstruct (or not) according to Iraqi specifications. As identity markers and sociocultural stimuli, libraries presented logical targets. Before the 1990 invasion, Kuwait had 23 public libraries, 572 school libraries, 29 academic libraries, and 69 special libraries and information centers. All of these were deliberately devastated—victims of policy, not of battle.

After the fact, it is obvious that the looting and destruction of Kuwait's information systems was essential to the dual processes of elevating Iraq and negating Kuwait as a sovereign nation and as a regional leader. What is sobering is the ripple effect of Iraq's actions. Let us examine, for example, Kuwait's role as a leader in information technology and informatics development in the Middle East. The invasion and destruction of its information infrastructure was a severe setback not only to Kuwait but also to Middle Eastern librarianship and information and knowledge systems in general, because the coordination of information systems is as dependent on civilized international relationships as are political and economic policies. Great harm was done to the growth of regional library services and to promising plans for Middle Eastern networks, because August 1990 marked "the time when real [information] development and cooperation within the region as a whole and in the Gulf in particular was arrested" (Sliney 1990, 912). Previous to that date, Kuwait was performing various services to the region's libraries; for example, its librarians were collecting Bahrain's publications because Bahrain had no national library (Young and Ali 1992) and planning for a regional inter-library loan service involving Bahrain, Kuwait, and Saudi Arabia (Sliney 1990). Ironically, these networks would have facilitated the unity and advancement of Arab countries, a goal of a benign form of Pan-Arabism.

The Gulf War, like all wars, had a retarding effect on information dissemination by the aggressor, victim, and surrounding nations. Thus, while the publishing industry in Kuwait suffered as a direct result of loss of infrastructure, it also was stifled in Iraq, where resources were redirected towards the war, and throughout the Middle East, where funds for education and social services were reallocated to security. Research activities were "halted, delayed, abandoned," and total publication of Arab monographs dropped by 50 percent (Young and Ali 1992, 459). Intellectual development within the entire Arab world suffered. But, of course, empowerment of other Arab countries, and their technological advancement, assumption of Western patterns, and unfettered intellectual growth did not serve Iraq's interests.

Paradoxically, while destructive in the short term, the war may have had a positive influence in convincing governments of the need for mastering all forms of technology and building structures for the dissemination of knowledge. Development could be justified as a strategic underpinning for the technological growth essential for national defense and, indeed, librarians seized the opportunity to promote the role of libraries in eradicating computer illiteracy. In addition, the Gulf War was advanced as an argument for the value of information as a tool for assessing risks and costs, forging strategy, and swaying decision-makers and the public (Aman 1992). These rationales for library and information development implicitly acknowledge that relations between Arab states are often conflict-oriented and that information systems can be desirable as tools for defense (or offense). Modernist library leaders, such as Mohammad Aman (1992), stressed also humanistic and social goals, decried the confidentiality and secrecy of the Arab world, and optimistically speculated that the Gulf War might cause regimes to promote freer circulation of information. But the dilemma for authoritarian leaders, before and after the war, remains whether the benefits of an informed citizenry is offset by a decrease in malleability and whether a regime can develop library and information technology systems without opening the door to challenges to their control of society and its social discourse. Saddam, of course, had some success in harnessing the potential of information technology without succumbing to its Trojan horse effect because of his judicious use of terror; the intense violence of the Iraqi invasion signaled the intent of exporting that terror to Kuwait. In a way, expressing the perverse logic of extremism, the intense censorship within Saddam's own nation and the massive devastation wreaked on information systems in Kuwait stands as a tribute to the power of written materials.

While Saddam's personal proclivities and thuggery certainly influenced the invasion of Kuwait, the destruction in Kuwait followed the universal political logic and processes that occur within libricide. In summary, faced with social trauma associated with the onset of modernity, Iraq's frustrated population had turned to an ideology that promised solutions to existing problems and a vision of renaissance. This ideology was compatible with existing cultural mindsets and predispositions, among these the desire for a common Arabic identity, xenophobia, and a tendency to see conspiracies. An authoritarian leadership used the ideology to cement its power and justified the creation of a totalitarian nation as necessary to counteract enemy conspiracies. Intellectual and cultural life was forced to acquiesce to ideology as all alternative visions, dissent, and information contradicting official doctrine were eradicated. Because they served as repositories of memory and supported critical thinking, books and libraries also had to be brought into line, if necessarily, ruthlessly and violently. This process of control was achieved incrementally by purging collections and, then, controlling authorship and publishing. As the mindset became increasingly nationalistic and imperialistic, it became imperative that mechanisms for the control of information and ideas be extended beyond Iraq's borders. Libricide was used as a tool of subjugation, and part of a concerted effort to destroy identity because identity, of course, serves as a rallying point for resistance.

The destruction of information is, in effect, the removal of access to ideas. And ideological extremism is the kidnapping of these avenues by those whose desire for power is so great that they admit of no other fixed principle. In his classic book *Ideas are Weapons,* Max Lerner (1939) discussed this very phenomenon: In the interests of *Realpolitik,* he explains, ideas are used and discarded as if they were tools suited only to specific jobs. While Lerner was writing in the context of the rise of Fascism and

Nazism, his observations also hold true for Saddam Hussein's ideological brew. Pan-Arabism, nationalism, imperialism, and totalitarianism alternately overlapped, competed for dominance, and clashed outright, drowning and reinforcing each other in a process that would leave a "bitter legacy" for the region (Salem 1994, vii). Like Hitler, Stalin, and Mao, Saddam proved himself lacking in humanity—but also in ideological commitment. His only commitment was to retain power at all costs; indeed, by his own admission, he was ready to start World War III rather than voluntarily relinquish any of his power. Such extreme narcissism, when buttressed by absolute power, has disastrous consequences on the human community. Iraq's destruction of Kuwait's libraries is a reminder that it is neither the content, the leanings, nor the mixture of ideology that is the cause of disaster; it is the ideology carried to an extreme by those whose absolute power tolerates no alternative voices—animate or inanimate.

REFERENCES

Abdel-Motey, Yaser Y., and Nahia Al Hmood. 1992. "An Overview of the Impact of Iraqi Aggression on Libraries, Information and Education for Librarianship in Kuwait." *Journal of Information Science* 18 (6):441–446.

Ajami, Fouad. 1998. *The Dream Palace of the Arabs: A Generation's Odyssey.* (First Vintage Books Edition, July 1999). New York: Vintage Books.

Al-Ansari, Husain A., and Charles William Conaway. 1996. "Projections of Library and Information Workers in Kuwait in Its Post-War Development." *Technical Services Quarterly* 13 (2):25–39.

Algosaibi, Ghazi A. 1993. *The Gulf Crisis: An Attempt to Understand.* London: Kegan Paul International.

Al-khalil, Samir. 1989. *Republic of Fear: The Politics of Modern Iraq.* Berkeley, California: University of California Press.

Aman, Mohammed M. 1992. "Libraries and Information Systems in the Arab Gulf States: After the War." *Journal of Information Science* 18 (6):447–451.

Baram, Amatzia. 1991. *Culture, History and Ideology in the Formation of Ba'thist Iraq, 1968–89.* New York: St. Martin's Press.

Bollag, Burton. 1994. "Rebirth From the Ashes." *The Chronicle of Higher Education* 40 (23):A47–A48.

Brown, L. Carl. 1993. "Patterns Forged in Time: Middle Eastern Mind-Sets and the Gulf War." In *The Political Psychology of the Gulf War: Leaders, Publics, and the Process of Conflict,* ed. Stanley A. Renshon. Pittsburgh, Pennsylvania: University of Pittsburgh Press, 3–21.

Cassidy, John. 1990. "Back to Year Zero: Saddam Eradicates Kuwait but Bush Must Hold Fire." *The Sunday Times,* 7 October, sec. 1A, p. A15.

Crystal, Jill. 1990. *Oil and Politics in the Gulf: Rulers and Merchants in Kuwait and Qatar.* (Cambridge Middle East Library: 24, Reprinted 1995). Cambridge, England: Cambridge University Press.

Drogin, Bob. 1991. "In Seven Months, Iraqis Stole 'The Very Soul' of Kuwait." *Los Angeles Times,* 11 March, sec. 1A, p. 11A.

Haselkorn, Avigdor. 1999. *The Continuing Storm: Iraq, Poisonous Weapons, and Deterrence.* New Haven, Connecticut: Yale University Press.

Hassan, Hamdi A. 1999. *The Iraqi Invasion of Kuwait: Religion, Identity and Otherness in the Analysis of War and Conflict.* London: Pluto Press.

Henderson, Simon. 1991. *Instant Empire: Saddam Hussein's Ambition For Iraq.* San Francisco: Mercury House.

"Horror in the 19th Province." 1990. *The Economist* 317 (7686):48.

Joyce, Miriam. 1998. *Kuwait 1945–1996: An Anglo-American Perspective.* London: Frank Cass.

Karsh, Efraim, and Inari Rautsi. 1991. *Saddam Hussein: A Political Biography.* New York: The Free Press.

Lerner, Max. 1939. *Ideas are Weapons: The History and Uses of Ideas.* New York: Viking Press.

McDonald, Andrew. 1993. "Post-disaster: Rebuilding the Information System in Kuwait." *Serials* 6 (2):73–79.

Mohsen, Fatima. 1994. "Cultural Totalitarianism." In *Iraq Since the Gulf War: Prospects for Democracy,* ed. Fran Hazelton. London: Zed Books, 7–19.

Osborne, Christine. 1996. "Send the Bactrian Camel to Baghdad." *The Middle East* 259:38–39.

Parker, Sharon. 1991. "The Casualties of War: The Kuwait National Museum." *The Planetarian* 20 (4):8–11.

Piekalkiewicz, Jaroslaw, and Alfred Wayne Penn. 1995. *Politics of Ideocracy.* Albany, New York: State University of New York Press.

Post, Jerrold M. 1993. "The Defining Moment of Saddam's Life: A Political Psychology Perspective on the Leadership and Decision Making of Saddam Hussein During the Gulf Crisis." In *The Political Psychology of the Gulf War: Leaders, Publics, and the Process of Conflict,* ed. Stanley A. Renshon. Pittsburgh, Pennsylvania: University of Pittsburgh Press, 49–66.

Rezun, Miron. 1992. *Saddam Hussein's Gulf War: Ambivalent Stakes in the Middle East.* Westport, Connecticut: Praeger.

Rich, Paul. 1991. Introduction to *Iraq and Imperialism: Thomas Lyell's The Ins and Outs of Mesopotamia,* by Thomas Lyell. Cambridge, England: Allborough Press Ltd., vii-xxx.

Said, Edward. 1991. "Shattering Effects of Saddam's Invasion." In *The March to War,* ed. James Ridgeway. New York: Four Walls Eight Windows, 97–101.

Salem, Paul. 1994. *Bitter Legacy: Ideology and Politics in the Arab World.* Syracuse, New York: Syracuse University Press.

Salem, Shawky. 1991. "Inside the Gulf Crisis: Destruction and Looting in Kuwait." *Information Development* 7 (2):70–71.

Salem, Shawky, ed. 1992. "Tables and Photos on the Iraqi Aggression to the Library and Information Infrastructure in Kuwait." *Journal of Information Science* 18 (6):425–440.

Sliney, Marjory. 1990. "Arabia Deserta: The Development of Libraries in the Middle East." *Library Association Record* 92 (12):912–914.

Tanter, Raymond. 1998. *Rogue Regimes: Terrorism and Proliferation.* New York: St. Martin's Press.

Tripp, Charles. 1993. "Iraq and the War for Kuwait." In *Iraq, the Gulf Conflict and the World Community*, ed. James Gow. London: Brassey's, 16–23.

Young, Harold C., and S. Nazim Ali. 1992. "The Gulf War and Its Effect on Information and Library Services in the Arabian Gulf with Particular Reference to the State of Bahrain." *Journal of Information Science* 18 (6):453–462.

Zonis, Marvin. 1993. "Leaders and Publics in the Middle East: Shattering the Organizing Myths of Arab Society." In *The Political Psychology of the Gulf War: Leaders, Publics, and the Process of Conflict,* ed. Stanley A. Renshon. Pittsburgh, Pennsylvania: University of Pittsburgh Press, 269–292.

Chapter 7

CHINA'S CULTURAL REVOLUTION

". . . [I]s it true that a nation cannot cross a desert of organized forgetting?"

(Kundera 1981, 159)

Ironically, twentieth-century China experienced libricide by extremists of both the right and the left. Japanese imperialists destroyed books and libraries during attempts to subjugate China in the late 1930s and early 1940s. They expressed their nationalism, racism, imperialism, and militarism in vicious vandalism, looting, burning, and bombing that resulted in the loss of perhaps ten million books. After the Japanese were expelled in 1945 and the Communists took over in 1949, libricide became internal and ongoing, sanctioned by leaders who demanded that China's books, intellectuals, and cultural traditions conform to Party orthodoxy. While we will never know exactly how many books, manuscripts, and documents were destroyed, the indicators are that the Communists' destruction subsequently eclipsed the damage done by Japan. In both cases, the link between extremism, mass murder, and libricide was explicit: Both regimes sought to make their political ideas dominant and used extreme violence, physical and cultural, as the means to that end.

Sociopolitical conditions often determine the extent to which libricidal impulses are acted upon. War provides a chaotic and highly charged forum for violent destruction, and the Japanese took full advantage of its cover. However, the libricide committed by the Communists occurred under cover of political campaigns that provided a heightened emotional climate in which any act was justifiable if it furthered the process of revolution. An escalation of these campaigns signaled the temporary ascendancy of Party radicals. Typically, a totalitarian state is constructed around one ideology, but subject to ongoing factional power struggles over the proper policies to implement that ideology (Taylor 1985). In China, socialist transformation was alternately governed by the policies of first radical and then more moderate factions of the Party. The subsequent ebb and flow of repression affected print culture because the factions had vastly different approaches to accessing written materials and to their preservation or censorship (the ultimate censorship being, of course, annihilation of entire libraries). These approaches were linked with notions of the desirable pace and nature of revolutionary change. Moderates sought incremental reforms primarily directed toward economic growth, and they allowed intellectuals and learning institutions to fulfill some traditional roles. On the other hand, the radicals, led by Mao Tse-tung, used power to advance profound transformation and when they held sway, the use of libraries by intellectuals, including scientists and educators, was curtailed, and libraries were directed to serve the masses and to operate as political rather than intellectual or economic instruments. Struggles over the pace and orientation of socialist programs ultimately fractured Party unity and set the stage for a show-down, the Cultural Revolution (1966 through 1976), that polarized the nation and threatened the very existence of the nation's libraries.

For Mao the Cultural Revolution was the final battle. He urged that all moderation be cast aside. He convinced the educated youth of China that true revolution could only be achieved by rejection of anything "old." A sort of ideological hysteria, akin to religious fanaticism, took hold. Extremism is the natural enemy of books, and when the Maoists spun out of control, the consequences were tragic. This chapter tells the story of the loss of books and libraries within China proper during this infamous decade. It is the story of the collision of left-wing extremism with traditional culture, of how an ancient society with a profound reverence for learning could, in a relatively short period of time, be induced to abandon its tradition of arts and letters and destroy its own books and libraries. It is a cautionary tale about the threat to cultural heritage posed, and even mandated, by revolutionary fanaticism.

CHINA BEFORE 1966

China has a long tradition of literacy. Its oldest written records date from the Shang dynasty (about 1766 B.C. to about 1122 B.C.), and the first major history of China was written in about 100 B.C. Since ancient times, the Chinese kept detailed records of major events and dynasties and produced important works of literature under the auspices of the state. Most of the important writers prior to 1900 were in government service, an occupation conferring the greatest prestige. Indeed, government exams tested the applicants' skills in composing both prose and poetry. Most pre-Communist works of Chinese literature, including those on Confucianism, taught a moral lesson or expressed a political philosophy (Knechtges 1996), so politics and literature were traditionally linked.

During the nearly 4,000 years of rule by centralized, autocratic dynasties (1766 B.C. to A.D. 1912), relative stability would give way to violent transitional periods as one dynasty replaced another. Administrative and philosophical reforms accompanied these transitions, and cultural vitality waxed and waned. Libraries were routinely assembled by each new dynasty, and just as routinely dispersed or destroyed by the next. Nevertheless, the basic structure of autocracy remained the same. Beginning in the 1800s, China's isolation and autonomy were jeopardized by foreign merchants and their colonialist governments, including the British, the French, and the American. The Manchus, who had established their dynasty in 1644, were forced to sign treaties that accorded special privileges to the much-resented foreigners; great shame was felt at the foreign domination. Tension mounted, and an upsurge in nationalism led to a series of rebellions, the most serious being the Boxer Rebellion of 1900. The Boxers, members of a secret society, went on a xenophobic rampage and were subsequently crushed by Western forces. The Manchus lost a significant amount of prestige and had to pay stupendous fines. Realizing that regaining autonomy required accommodation of Western political ideas, systems, and technologies, they initiated a series of reforms (Pfaff 1993). However, the pace of these reforms was too slow and revolutionary discontent intensified. After a revolt by the army, the last emperor, 6-year-old Pu Yi, gave up the throne in February 1912, and ceded control to a new Republican government.

This regime lacked consensus and was too weak to suppress the escalating conflicts that would keep China in turmoil. Struggles for control of the vast nation consumed the first half of the century. Statistics in China, of course, have always been hard to come by because of secrecy, the vastness of the country, inadequate collection procedures, and the tendency of local figures to falsify numbers, but all indicators speak to China as having been drenched in blood throughout this period. By 1922, rivalry between warlords had brought anarchy and civil war, and the Republican regime, plagued by internal struggles, lost control. Two political groups came to the forefront: the Nationalist Party and the Communist Party. The two parties engaged in almost constant civil war, vying for the support of the people and recognition by world powers. Meanwhile, in 1931, the Japanese, sensing the preoccupation of the Chinese with internal conflicts, occupied Manchuria and set up a new, "independent" state, Manchukuo, which, of course, functioned under their mandate. In 1937, in a further attempt to extend their military influence, the Japanese launched the Sino-Japanese War. This precipitated an alliance between the Nationalists and Communists, which resulted in the defeat of the Japanese in 1945. Despite the success of their combined efforts, a ferocious civil war immediately erupted and lasted until 1949.

During this civil war, traditional Chinese ways of life, under severe stress during previous conflicts, eroded further with forced conscription, lost crops, high inflation, and widespread famine. Under Chiang Kai-shek, the corrupt Nationalist Party managed to alienate a substantial portion of the population because their tactic of choice was brute force. Mao Tse-tung and the Communist Party, on the other hand, had come to the conclusion that brute force alone would not be effective—they needed a "cultural front" to appeal to all segments of society (Boorman 1966). As a result, they tended to treat the peasants well and to court the intellectuals. They offered revolutionary zeal and ideological (and personal) rectitude as an antidote to corruption, and they capitalized on the loss of popular faith in the Nationalists.

Mao was already firmly established in the Party as a fighter, revolutionary, and strategist. Born in 1893 to a land-owning peasant, Mao received a rudimentary education before rejecting rural life and heading to the city to train as a teacher. In 1918 he moved to Peking to work as an assistant in the library at Peking University. His work was mundane, his status low, and he spoke in a thick, barely intelligible rural accent. There he brushed shoulders with and, he would later claim, was shunned by China's intellectual geniuses (Thurston 1987). There he learned more about an exciting political movement, Marxism, and pursued this interest by connecting with a radical librarian, Li Ta-chao, who conducted Marxist study groups in his office, the "Red Chamber" (Nelson and Nelson 1979). In 1921, in Shanghai, Mao and eleven others organized the Chinese Communist Party and eventually put together an army. Mao's position as leader of the movement was cemented by his tenacity and endurance during the 1934 Long March, a 6,000-mile epic yearlong trek to escape encirclement by the Nationalists. In remote Shaanxi, he rallied the surviving 20,000 Communists (out of the 100,000 who set out). From this camp, Mao shaped and articulated the tenets of a uniquely Chinese Communism. He restructured Marxist-Leninism (originally conceived as an urban working-class movement) into a peasant-based revolutionary doctrine.

The Communists emerged victorious and, in 1949, the Nationalists retreated to Taiwan. The Chinese people, exhausted by chronic social and political turmoil, violence, and war, looked to the Communists for stability and reform. Mao, the chairman of the Communist Party, became a highly acclaimed national hero, the first Chairman of the People's Republic of China. In the process of creating a totalitarian state in the early 1950s, radical changes were made daily. In an effort to continue this pace and even escalate the speed of reform, Mao began to chafe at restraints imposed by moderates, but his power at this time was not absolute. Seeking to build his power base, he capitalized on the tendency within totalitarian societies for ideologies to evolve into secular quasi-religions revolving around an omnipotent cult figure. Under Mao's guidance, the Chinese were urged to reject traditional religion—including the ethics of Confucianism—for Maoism, a messianic form of Communism. Maoism fulfilled many of the traditional functions of religion (Zuo 1991) and Mao served as a living deity. While physically reclusive, he projected an image far less remote than an abstract deity, and provided the people with the illusion of intimacy and divine partnership (Buchheim 1968). The relationship between Mao and the people was likened to that of the sun and sunflowers, and Mao was hailed as the "Great Helmsman," "the Great Teacher," "the Red Sun," and "the Messiah of the Working people." By the onset of the Cultural Revolution in 1966, any public appearance would elicit ecstatic outpourings of adulation from the crowds. His writings, Mao's *Little Red Book,* became a sacred text that the entire population studied and carried as an amulet. Morning and night, families performed ritual activities before Mao's picture, asking for his instructions and confessing their sins; they wore badges imprinted with his image and performed sacred songs and dances to honor him. By the decade of the Cultural Revolution, the Chinese-American wife of the U.S. ambassador observed with horror the people "singing the praises of the Chairman with a hypnotic fervor so primitive, so extreme, that it seemed . . . as if China had reverted to a time when the nation was not yet civilized" (Lord 1990, 171).

Although Mao's political regime was ostensibly centered on them, and his charisma was enhanced by identification with them, he exhibited contradictory attitudes toward the peasant classes. At one point, he described China's 600 million people as having two remarkable peculiarities: "They are, first of all, poor, and secondly blank. That may seem like a bad thing, but it is really a good thing. Poor people want change, want to do things, want revolution. A clean sheet of paper has no blotches, and so the newest and most beautiful words can be written on it . . ." (as quoted in Short 1999, 488). On the one hand, he appeared proud of his peasant background and comfortable in projecting an earthy image. But while he lauded the peasants in public speeches, his policies demonstrated a general contempt for them. When it suited his plans, Mao allowed millions to perish in famines that he refused to acknowledge.

In relation to Mao's views on the use of violence, however, he showed no discrepancy between his philosophy and his policies. In 1927, he was already gesturing toward the ruin he would later bring about: "To put it bluntly, it is necessary to create terror for a while. . . . Proper limits have to be exceeded in order to right a wrong . . ." (as quoted in Thurston 1987, 118). By the 1940s he had refined the justification: "The anti-Revolutionary does not disappear from history on its own. It is like sweeping the floor: if there is no broom, the dust will not disappear" (as quoted in Luo 1990, 286). Since the revolution was ongoing, violence became a permanent feature of Chinese Communism. Mao fostered a paranoid environment, using the threat of the 5 percent of the people (at any one time) who were enemies of the state to justify brutal social policies. He and his followers intensified repressive measures whenever they could muster enough power. They usually targeted intellectuals, political rivals, and, indeed, any dissenters, whose supposed or actual recalcitrance could be blamed for the always-insufficient progress to a transformed society. In the name of love for Mao, no cruelty or oppression was spared in the struggle to inculcate absolute loyalty and orthodoxy (Jiaqi and Gao 1996). "No single person was able to escape it: one was either condemning [others for a lack of devotion] or condemned" (Zuo 1991, 105). In general, campaigns functioned as opportunities for extending the Party's totalitarian grip on the people. And the power of the Communist government ultimately required that the entire population be terrified of becoming among the 5 percent that Mao believed were the enemies (Thurston 1987).

The Communist Party began its rule in 1949 by initiating a "dictatorship of the proletariat," in which the Party supervised all mechanisms of security—the police, courts, prisons, and army. Harnessing the population was essential to the next step: tearing down existing bureaucratic and social arrangements and rebuilding them according to socialist models. To the Communists, the same people inspiring the revolution were materials to be used, like mortar and bricks or lumber and nails, to create the new social structure (Rummel 1994). And some of those materials were not suited to the new structure. The Party became fanatically devoted to identifying class enemies. Cadres, officials that were usually Party members, engineered "class struggle sessions," public meetings where the peasants and workers were encouraged to confront the old upper classes verbally and physically. The meetings followed a pattern of accusation and forced confession, and frequently culminated in summary executions. In the first several years of Communism, between two and five million people, loosely categorized as "landlords," were shot, hanged, beheaded, battered to death, nailed to walls of buildings, buried alive, or covered with water and left outside to freeze in the winter (Becker 1996). "Seeing conspiracy, having an enemy, defining the clean people and the unsalvageably dirty ones, 'dividing one into two,' all became state policy. . . . It meant labeling people with good and bad names, monitoring them so that the good ones might be nurtured and the bad restricted, and running campaigns to inspire some and scare others" (White 1989, 315).

From 1950 to 1956, the government concentrated on categorizing citizens as being of either the "proletarian class" or the "class enemies." The proletarian class was composed of five Red categories: workers, poor and lower middle-class peasants, revolutionary soldiers, revolutionary cadres, and revolutionary martyrs. The class enemies fell into seven "Black" categories: landlords, rich peasants, reactionaries, bad elements, rightists, traitors, and spies. Later an eighth category, "capitalist roaders in authoritative positions," and a ninth category, intellectuals (scientists, teachers, artists, and writers), were added (Lin 1991, 3).

Once a person was classified, the whole family was given the same label and each person's political and economic activities were recorded in dossiers maintained by the Party. People in the Black categories (nonproletarian) were considered to be socially degenerate and, therefore, irretrievable outlaws. Newspapers, radio broadcasts, and the speeches of local officials spread the word that these class enemies were to be treated brutally and, if necessary, wiped out. Mandatory study groups, which could last two to three hours per day, supported campaigns that institutionalized this categorization and discrimination. The people were expected to internalize socialist doctrines and then demonstrate their commitment by participating in confrontations orchestrated by the cadres—even at the expense of relations with neighbors, co-workers, and family members. A climate of fear and suspicion replaced normal intercourse. The format of the struggle sessions was intensified in prison settings, re-education sites that often took the form of huge labor camps similar to the Soviet gulags.

Few Chinese, swept up in their own fates, were aware of the power struggles that racked the Communist Party. Power over policy shifted back and forth between hard-line leftists, the radicals—those, including Mao Tse-tung, who wanted rapid and radical changes—and those more moderate and cautious leaders who believed that changes should be implemented slowly and incrementally. Ostensibly both factions had the same end goals, but the radicals sought the immediate imposition, whatever the costs, of a classless society, while the moderates stressed the importance of maintaining food stocks and developing the economy so that the nation could survive during the transformation period. While preserving outward appearances of Party unity, radicals and moderates became more and more polarized: The radicals secretly condemned the moderates as counter-revolutionaries, while the moderates could barely restrain their disgust at the consequences of the radicals' impulsive and impractical programs. The ebb-and-flow of these alternate visions, reflected in Party policy, affected every level of society. When the radicals set policy, the emphasis was on ideological goals—in education, for example, the creation of Reds, the political education of peasants. When the moderates held sway, the emphasis shifted toward technical education, academic standards, and content, on "creating experts." In the economic arena, policies instituted by radicals for ideological reasons, such as the precipitous creation of communes, often had devastating effects on growth and development. This was the case in a movement called the Great Leap Forward (1958 to 1961), when a national famine resulted from sudden and dramatic reforms.

The path that Chinese radicals took during the Great Leap Forward (GLF) mirrored that of the Soviets twenty years earlier. Stalin's collectivization campaign, beginning in 1929 and focusing on the Ukraine, was designed to revolutionize Russian agriculture and create grain surpluses that would advance industrialization. Based on Marxist-Leninist ideas, it assaulted all aspects of private ownership and rural life. When the *kulak*s, land-holding peasants, resisted the Communists' plans, the central government seized their grain. Such seizures and the ineffectiveness of the new communes set in motion a famine that killed eleven million people. The famine, which was allowed to run its course, was instrumental in crushing the *kulaks,* Ukrainian nationalism, and, in fact, all peasant resistance. The extent of the famine became a state secret, and totalitarian controls were instrumental in suppressing all evidence of the regime's cruelty and mismanagement and the dire results of implementing its ideological theories.

The secretive handling of the famine set a pattern for the suppression of information that became typical of Communist regimes. It was unthinkable to disseminate information that reflected badly on either basic tenets of Communism or Party management. Admissions of error or failure could jeopardize the credibility of the socialist theory on which the whole structure of the state rested. Therefore, as novelist Boris Pasternak wrote in *Dr.*

Zhivago, to conceal the failure of collectivization, "people had to be cured, by every means of terrorism, of the habit of thinking and judging for themselves, and forced to see what didn't exist, to assert the very opposite of what their eyes told them" (as quoted in Conquest 1986, 331). Even Party members had to learn to shut their eyes. In 1937, three years after the famine, one million Party members were purged in what came to be known as Russia's Great Terror, an effort to ensure that all adhered to this code (Rummel 1994).

Some twenty years after the Russian famine, Mao's collectivization campaign benefited from the silence that surrounded the Ukrainian famine. Mao must have known the Russian experiment had been a disaster, but he seemed to attribute this failure to errors in implementation rather than flaws in socialist theory. By setting in motion the GLF, Mao wanted to demonstrate that the Chinese, by sheer force of will and total commitment, could achieve Communism more successfully than the Soviets. Like Stalin, Mao seemed to view the masses as malleable to the point of self-duplicity, and he used the mechanisms of absolute power to enforce reforms. Unlike the Soviet leader, however, Mao exercised charismatic leadership to inspire the poverty-stricken Chinese with the hope of prosperity and a utopian future. Wildly enthusiastic urban workers devoted numerous hours of overtime labor to boost production, while other urbanites, including students and academics, went down to the countryside to perform grueling manual labor on farms and dam-building projects. In the interests of self-sufficiency, everyone was urged to build backyard furnaces and produce their own steel. The lifestyle of rural peasants, who were not quite as enraptured, was revolutionized as private property was abolished and traditional social patterns disrupted. Families were forced to eat in common kitchens, and children were cared for collectively; religious practices and folk culture were banned. Indeed, identification with any of the traditional foundations of society (such as family, gods, local agricultural practices) was suppressed, as was any expression of individuality. Loyalty to the collective and efforts toward creating a socialist society were paramount.

Collective efforts did bring initial, apparent increases in grain and steel production, but these artificial levels could not be maintained. They were based on unsustainable worker sacrifices; shortsighted planning that eventually exhausted natural resources; and delusional approaches that ignored traditional or empirical knowledge. Mao's disdain for reliance on "bookish learning," first expressed in his book *Oppose Book Worship,* was expressed in GLF policies. The Party radicals advised the masses to forget theory and book learning in favor of adding imagination to science, acting "recklessly," and employing "peasant enthusiasm" (Becker 1996, 62). After the first year, agricultural production began decreasing; the much-touted backyard furnaces consumed metal utensils and iron but produced useless grades of steel, and peasant-designed dams collapsed. However, early successes had been praised and publicized to such a degree that it became impossible to acknowledge the emerging reality. Falsified production figures and exaggerated reports of bumper crops masked the truth.

Mao and radical Party members rejected reports of starvation as the fabrication of counterrevolutionaries and rightists. A "climate of megalomania, make-believe, lies and brutality" prevailed as persistently inflated information on yields led to larger and larger tax levies on grain (Becker 1996, 87). When peasants were unable to meet the levies, Mao accused them of hoarding and of resisting the revolution. Grain was ruthlessly seized in payment, even while the peasants were starving. Soon, however, people began dying in the streets and resorting to cannibalism (Yi 1996)—difficult circumstances to deny. Still, information on the famine was suppressed in an uncanny replay of the Party's response to the Ukrainian famine. Perhaps Mao agreed with Lenin, who had opposed aid to famine victims, arguing that hunger would radicalize the masses. Lenin had said earlier, "Psychologically, this talk of feeding the starving is nothing but an expression of the saccharine-sweet sentimentality so characteristic of our intelligentsia" (as quoted in Conquest 1986, 234). Perhaps Mao saw the famine, as had Stalin, as just punishment for an uncooperative peasantry (Jonassohn and Bjornson 1998). Certainly for Maoists, the necessity for a "great leap forward" in production and social transformation outweighed costs to human life.

Then the sweep of the Party's pendulum reversed. The moderates, appalled by the famine and falling grain yields, reversed many of the collectivization initiatives, permitted some degree of private ownership and individual initiative, and managed to stabilize the economy. When these leaders pulled back on Mao's policies, Mao withdrew somewhat from the national scene and used the next few years to rebuild and extend his power base. To Mao, the moderates were revisionists who were betraying the revolution and its promise of socialist transformation. When they retreated from his visions, he saw them as both personally and ideologically disloyal. According to his doctor, Li Zhisui (1994, 125), "Mao was the center around which everyone else revolved. His will reigned supreme. Loyalty, rather than principle, was the paramount virtue." Those who crossed Mao over the Great Leap Forward would later pay dearly.

The famine generated by the GLF movement may have been the greatest trauma suffered by the Chinese under Communism (Becker 1996).

Peasants talk about the famine as if it had been an apocalypse—as indeed it was: between 27 and 30 million died. To this day, however, the Party attributes problems during the "bitter years" of the late 1950s and early 1960s to natural disasters and discourages circulation of information about the period. In the early 1960s, few Chinese had any idea of the scope of the famine and few blamed it on Mao's policies. As a result, he was able to continue to direct their enthusiasm for his leadership into his personality cult. However, the GLF aggravated existing splits between moderates and radicals at every level of the bureaucracy, and these differences culminated in a civil war—the Cultural Revolution (1966 to 1976)—which has been described by some as nothing more than a delayed purge of those who had been responsible for ending the famine, and a device to restore Mao's authority (Becker 1996). It was a last desperate attempt to force radical Communist restructuring of society and to seize and maintain power by the extreme left.

BOOKS, LIBRARIES, AND THE FATE OF INTELLECTUALS

Throughout most of imperial China's history, royal libraries existed as cornerstones for systems of control over information and knowledge. Collections were built and purged according to the prevailing mindset of the regime. While the royal libraries became targets of violence in times of rebellion or dynastic change, imperial libraries and information systems were always reconstructed and persisted nevertheless, along with private libraries, in providing cultural continuity. And while individual emperors varied in the degree of intellectual control they exercised, traditional learning, scholars, and texts were generally held in high esteem.

After the overthrow of the last dynasty in 1912, attempts were made to introduce to Chinese culture modern institutions like public and academic libraries. In spite of the violence and civil war that racked the nation before 1936, libraries experienced an eightfold increase during this period. The progress was undone, however, during the war against Japan (1937–1945). Invading Japanese troops, who killed somewhere between two to six million Chinese during their occupation, destroyed or dispersed between 2,000 and 2,500 libraries (Lin 1998). College and university libraries were prime targets; for example, a quarter of a million valuable books and manuscripts (some irreplaceable) were lost in the Japanese bombing of the Nankai University in Tianjin in 1937. Throughout China, many books were looted and sold to Japanese collectors (Fung 1984); some were simply casualties of the devastation caused by troops.

By the time the Japanese had been driven out and the nation was "liberated" by Communism, the library situation in China was dire. Altogether, the thousands of libraries had been reduced to less than 400. As part of their social engineering project, the Communists quickly began to rebuild libraries in accordance with Chinese-Marxist objectives, which necessitated the involvement of libraries in the revolutionary process (Barclay 1995). Libraries were decentralized and directed to focus on the dissemination of political materials. They were purged of "reactionary, obscene and 'absurd' publications"—those whose contents contradicted Communist interpretations of historical events or supported Western claims to China and its territories, for example (Ting 1983, 139). Some books were pulped or otherwise destroyed; others were placed under restricted access. While classic texts were to be preserved, the political value of the content was to be placed above the "bibliophilic love of literary treasures" (Barclay 1995, 30). Libraries were expected to foster political literacy by disseminating Marxist-Leninist principles and pushing socialism as the desirable substitute for religion and other traditional influences on everyday behavior (Buchheim 1968).

Public libraries in particular, typified by the Party as "cultural enterprise organs," were to be instrumental in the Communist reconstruction of China by providing access to "culture"—in this context referring to materials that met the needs of the masses as defined by Communist ideology. The Communists knew that print was an excellent medium for disseminating their messages. As part of the propaganda apparatus, libraries provided symposia, lectures, exhibitions, study groups, texts, and reading lists. Mobile libraries called "culture carriers" supplied print materials to field and factory. In 1950, thousands of rural libraries were founded to support reading-campaign efforts designed to bring literacy to the 70 percent of men and 99 percent of women in the countryside who couldn't read (Thurston 1987). By 1956, more than 180,000 rural libraries had been established, and during the Great Leap Forward (1958–1961), while millions starved to death, the number rose to more than 300,000. Many were quite primitive and short-lived.

Just as economic and social policies were at the mercy of power shifts between Party factions, the mission of China's libraries had to adapt repeatedly to the prevailing mindset. In the first few years of Communist rule, when Marxist-Leninist models were being established, librarians were urged to practice radical librarianship and focus on supporting mass political literacy. Directing services to intellectuals was considered erroneous (Ting 1983, 139). During the first Five Year Plan (1953–57), which reflected the moderates' influence, the priority placed on technological and scientific development allowed libraries to extend services to intellectuals and the scientific community. However, in 1957, when the radicals launched the Great Leap Forward movement, they targeted intellectuals as rightists (scapegoats for the slow progress of the Five Year Plan), and the emphasis on mass political education was restored. Those who had worked under the previous mandates were censured or purged. Then, in the brief moderate-dominated period between the failure of the Great Leap Forward and the launch of the Cultural Revolution in 1966, library services swung back. For nearly two decades, political correctness one day was sabotage the next, and China's librarians paid a heavy price with each tide.

Educators and intellectuals were also affected by these shifts in political agenda. Educators were caught between the moderates' pressure for academic and scientific excellence and the radicals' demands for practical, ideologically correct, and peasant-based education (in other words, between educating experts or educating Reds). Librarians, intellectuals, and educators were constantly scrutinized for ideological correctness, but the criteria for adequacy in this area was subject to the relative influence of the two Party factions, and their fate hung in the balance. When policies shifted to the left, members of all three groups were inevitably defamed or purged; when the moderates assumed control, these professionals were often "rehabilitated"—considered to have adapted to new, correct ways of thinking—and encouraged to resume some traditional practices. Communism is essentially anti-intellectual in the liberal humanist sense; the moderates and the radicals basically agreed on that. They disagreed on how much of a threat the traditions of literate culture posed and on the use that could be made of intellectuals.

Literary policy was so important to Mao that he had begun reforms many years before the takeover in 1949. He knew that throughout Chinese history, authoritarian rulers had dictated that political, ideological, and cultural worlds coincide. He simply continued this totalitarianism in a new guise. Classic Chinese texts, because of their identification with pre-Communist dominant classes, were suspect. In fact, Mao believed that those who advocated the reading of Confucian classics aligned themselves with the old imperialist culture and should be eliminated (Zhang and Schwartz 1997). Books designated as serving the bourgeois class were denounced and censored, while those that overtly served the proletariat were promoted and circulated (Leys 1979). Writers (typically of bourgeois background) were required to concentrate on socialist realities. They required strict monitoring because, like all intellectuals, they tended toward independent thought. The Communists were aware of a strong literary

tradition behind the conception of a writer as permanently alienated from
political authority—the writer as the thorn in the flesh of the establishment. According to the venerated writer Lu Hsun, "The statesman hates
the writer because the writer sows seeds of dissent; what the statesman
dreams of is to be able to prevent people from thinking, and thus he always
accuses the artists and writers of upsetting his orderly state" (as quoted in
Leys 1979, 44).

Under the Communists, Chinese writers began to display a quality that
one observer characterized as "mental furtiveness" (Moraes 1953, 33).
Creativity was dangerous and, in any event, nearly impossible because
the entire sociopolitical fabric of life was so tightly woven as to leave no
room for this pursuit, either in terms of material leisure and privacy or in
terms of psychological or spiritual autonomy (Leys 1979). Mao addressed
this issue:

> But will not Marxism destroy any creative impulses? It will; it will certainly
> destroy the creative impulses that arise from feudal, bourgeois and petty-
> bourgeois ideology, from liberalism, individualism and nihilism, from art-
> for-art's sake, from the aristocratic, decadent and pessimistic outlook—
> indeed any creative impulse that is not rooted in the people and the
> proletariat. So far as proletarian artists and writers are concerned, should
> not these impulses be utterly destroyed? I think they should; indeed they
> must be utterly destroyed and while they are being destroyed, new things
> can be built up. (Mao 1967, 103–4)

By the 1970s, guidelines, formulas, and prohibitions for writers had become extremely rigid and doctrinaire. The leading figures of Chinese literature became silent in tacit acknowledgement that in totalitarian
regimes, "the humblest truth is revolutionary, mere reality is subversive"
(Leys 1979, 46). Jean-Francois Revel (1977, 52) has written of such regimes: "Totalitarianism does not condemn a work of art because it con-
ceals a political motive. It is because the regime is totalitarian that in its
eyes a work of art always has a political dimension—more accurately,
only a political dimension: for or against the regime." Any novel, however
seemingly apolitical, makes a statement by merely portraying a world in
which the extremist state's values and concerns are absent, because it
presents an alternative (Stieg 1992).

The work of historians was another focus of the Communists' cultural
policies. After their takeover in 1949, history was rewritten to reflect
Marxist perspectives, and historians were ordered to participate in the
revolution by minimizing the use of classic sources and concentrating

instead on the modern revolutionary period (Dutt and Dutt 1970). However, an official directive in the 1960s explicitly forbade them from writing a history of the Chinese Communist Party—a practical prohibition in light of ongoing purges and regular accusations of revisionism. Many historians, unable to keep up with the rapidly shifting official line, took a "lengthy intermission" from writing on modern China (Leys 1979). Others found refuge in relatively nonpolitical areas such as archeology. In fact, archeological discoveries made during the Cultural Revolution were admirable and, ironically, highly publicized to the world as proof of the regime's interest in culture. Those historians who couldn't or wouldn't observe political correctness underwent lengthy re-education programs involving grueling manual labor. In any event, the notion of objective history was denounced as a bourgeois prejudice and respect for original or primary sources was viewed as a puerile superstition (Leys 1977).

The Party was deeply concerned about all intellectuals, the approximately 5 percent of the Chinese population with a middle school or university education. Moderate officials recognized that it needed intellectuals to bring about industrialization; but at the same time, the Party as a whole considered intellectuals highly dangerous because of their bourgeois tendencies (many came from upper-class families), their connections to Western culture (many had been educated abroad or had foreign friends), and their propensity for articulating and expressing dissent. In Germany, Hitler had described the dilemma of intellectuals thus: "When I look at the intellectual classes here in Germany. . . . [W]e need them. Otherwise, I don't know, we could wipe them out or something. But unfortunately we need them" (as quoted in Schoenbaum 1966, 288). The Chinese Communist leadership was far less pragmatic.

After the Communist takeover, some scholars with strong Nationalist ties were killed or imprisoned immediately. By late 1951, most intellectuals were swept into a yearlong Thought Reform Campaign. Thought-reform processes (what we would call brainwashing in the West) involved public "struggle" sessions (Lifton 1961). Those who made sufficient progress in becoming Red were allowed to resume their careers. Actually, many teachers and professors had welcomed Communism as an alternative to fascism under the Nationalists. Some actively participated in the abrupt reorganization of campuses as Party members supervised and reoriented education from Western to Russian patterns. In this process, private universities were closed or absorbed into state institutions. Liberal-arts education by and large disappeared, as did the liberal arts universities. The social sciences—including world history, Western philosophy, and logic—were abolished. Political studies (i.e. of Communist doctrine) became a mandatory component of all remaining programming. Admission was opened to worker and peasant children, rather than determined exclusively by competitive examinations, the traditional method that favored children of the elite classes. The announced goal was the proletarianization of scholarship and science.

Those who could not adapt to these changes were killed or imprisoned indefinitely. The number of intellectuals in the Chinese *gulags* (labor camps) swelled periodically by the campaigns, organized by radicals, which regularly identified them as rightists, reactionaries, and counterrevolutionaries. Throughout Chinese history, traditional folklore glorified learned martyrs who had stood up to autocrats (Thurston 1987). It was precisely this recognition of the intellectual as potentially a subversive element that made scholars a prime target of the Communists, regardless of whether or not they demonstrated disloyalty. In the camps, intellectuals and political prisoners were treated more harshly than real criminals, who were considered easier to reform and indoctrinate (Becker 1996).

One of the most virulent campaigns against intellectuals occurred after Party leader Zhou Enlai circulated data among Party members that 10 percent of the academic community was still "backward" and opposed socialism, and another 10 percent were downright counterrevolutionary (Thurston 1987). These recalcitrant intellectuals were blamed for impeding educational reform and derailing the proletarianization of higher education (Nee 1969). A trap was set. In mid-1956, in what appeared to be a stunning reversal of previous totalitarian controls on speech, Mao and the Party began urging intellectuals to speak out and criticize the government under the slogan "Let a hundred flowers bloom, let a hundred schools of thought contend." Promises of freedom abounded—freedom of thought, of debate, and of creative work; freedom to criticize and express opinions (Nee 1969). But it functioned merely as a trap to expose counterrevolutionary trends—in Mao's words, to lure "freaks and monsters" into stepping forward so that the people could struggle against them (Cheng-Chung 1979, 122). When, after initial hesitation, floods of criticism poured out, the government responded by labeling those who had spoken out as "rightists." Educational institutions from the primary level up were assigned quotas of between 5 to 10 percent of their faculty to be so identified. An estimated half-million intellectuals were brutally assigned their fates: ostracism, demotion, exile, or execution. The Party followed up by putting cadres, some of whom were barely literate, in control of all institutions of higher learning. Political reform had priority over learning.

For some, history seemed to be repeating itself. Most modern Chinese were familiar with the phrase "He burned the books and he burned the scholars," a reference to Ch'in Shih-huang, the first Emperor of China and the individual responsible for the construction of the Great Wall. In 213 B.C., alleging that certain texts were being used to criticize his government, the emperor ordered his officials to collect and burn all books. By reducing their access to information, he hoped to unify and control his people. But then the paranoid emperor accused his scholars of studying the past in order to criticize the present. For this crime he executed 460 scholars by *keng,* burying them alive from the neck down (Guisso and Pagani 1989). As leftist repression of intellectuals waxed, Mao brazenly acknowledged kinship with the first Emperor. In a closed meeting of Party cadres in 1958, he boasted:

> Well, and what was so remarkable about Ch'in Shih-huang? He executed four hundred and sixty scholars. We, we executed forty-six thousand of them! This is what I answered to some democrats: you think you insult us by saying that we are like Ch'in Shih-huang, but you make a mistake, we have passed him a hundred times! You call us Ch'in Shih-huangs, you call us tyrants—we grant readily that we have those qualities; we only deplore that you remain so much below the truth that we have to fill out your accusations! (as quoted in Leys 1977, 145)

For a brief period in the early 1960s, after the Great Leap Forward, when the Party's moderate faction was in control, many of the intellectuals that were persecuted in 1957 were declared "rehabilitated." The moderate-directed efforts to reinstate an academic orientation in Chinese higher education were, however, broadsided by the Maoists' launch of the Cultural Revolution in 1966. This virulently anti-intellectual movement struck forcefully at books and libraries, persistent witnesses to the past and alternate realities.

With the exception of Pol Pot's Cambodia, no contemporary society has so deliberately, thoroughly, and rapidly rejected its history and traditions as China did during the Cultural Revolution. But in spite of their efforts to abolish all things old, the Communist Party could not negate the power and persistence of history, either in their own practice or in the minds of the people. Political leaders themselves used historical analogies and allusions to China's most famous tyrant as precedent. Among themselves they whispered that Mao was less a revolutionary than another autocrat. Some astute non-Party dissenters realized that the Party was but another privileged dynasty, because, ironically, after dismantling the old bureaucracy in the interests of egalitarianism, they succeeded merely in creating a whole new one. The Party had thirty hierarchical classes, each with special privileges and prerogatives (Leys 1977). Designated bosses, often cadres, had extensive patronage networks that fostered dependence.

Like many dynasties before them, the Communist Party's path to achieving absolute control required institutionalization of the politics of violence. Their brutalization of society prepared the way for the Cultural Revolution, which was, at least in part, "an expression of rebellion and wrath" in response to the politics of the past seventeen years (Yi 1996, 130). The people were repressed, frustrated, angry—and ripe for manipulation. Flashpoint occurred when Mao, his designated successor (Lin Biao), and the Gang of Four (a demagogic group that included Mao's wife) once more tried to "put politics in command" and implemented drastic policies to speed realization of a Communist state (like those implemented in the Great Leap Forward). This pitted them against Liu Shaoqi, Deng Xiaoping, and others who favored a more moderate socialization and gradual reform. Mao expertly directed the people's frustration by acknowledging it and claiming as its cause those reactionary forces, including Party moderates, who continually thwarted the promised revolution. This polarized conflict became the Cultural Revolution.

THE CULTURAL REVOLUTION

The Great Proletarian Cultural Revolution (GPCR) was many things. It was a revolution of the masses, an orchestrated attack against traditional culture, a class struggle, a chaotic civil war, and a convulsive effort on the part of the existing leadership to maintain power. Set in motion by a flawed, all-too-human god, it was ultimately an act of violence by and against millions of people (White 1989, 7). The GPCR was formally launched in May 1966 with a sixteen-point directive issued by the Chinese Communist Party. Its author, Mao, sought to transform education, literature, art, and all other parts of the cultural superstructure. He targeted the Party's old, moderate leaders who were getting in the way of his economic and political policies, and in his opinion, abusing their privileges and status and thus becoming bourgeois. His other target was the educational and cultural specialists whom he viewed as valuing academic standards and professional competence above ideological commitment and thus retarding reform. Non-Communist ideas and learning in all forms came under attack in the Cultural Revolution. The GPCR was the enforcement of orthodoxy to Mao's ideas of a permanent revolution (Jonassohn and Bjornson 1998)—total, irreversible.

In early June 1966, the leading national newspaper, the *People's Daily*, called for mass participation in purges of anyone opposing Mao's policies and thoughts. Initial fire was directed at the university and middle school faculty under whom, after the Great Leap Forward, academic standards and advanced training in science and technology had been reinstated. Some colleges, like Wuhan University, had even returned to a broad curriculum, including philosophy, world history, psychology, and logic. To Maoists, these courses contained "ancient and foreign things, things feudal, capitalistic, and revisionist" (Nee 1969, 35). They were taught by the "stinking ninth element" (the term of opprobrium for intellectuals) and by "ox ghosts and snake spirits"—the name for reactionaries.

By late 1966, four million copies of textbooks in Chinese language, history, philosophy, economics, pedagogy, political education, and foreign languages—all "branded as poisonous weeds"—had been pulled from the shelves (White 1989, 296). Universities and middle schools, first in Peking and then throughout China, closed down as student revolts, incited by Mao, spread and led to the suspension of classes. The students suddenly had a great deal of free time. At the time, there were 534,000 students enrolled in 434 universities and 6.4 million students in 56,000 middle (secondary) schools (Lin 1991). Millions of these students, whose ages ranged from 14 to 23 years old, joined the Red Guards. Literally, "Red Guard" meant a student from a Red category who was regarded as a guard of Chairman Mao and his great socialist cause (Lin 1991).

It is crucial to note that many of the students involved in this movement were born after 1949 and had been raised in a society scored by the Communists' violent class discrimination. They grew up in an environment where beatings, torture, executions, and imprisonment were commonplace, and every action was measured against correct ideology. In fact, the process of socialist transformation justified *anything*. "It is a small matter," wrote one member, "to beat someone to death, but it is very important to conduct revolution, to uproot revisionism, to preserve redness. These cow ghosts and snake demons [the instructors] are all anti-Party, anti-socialist, and Anti-Mao Tse-tung thought. The more of them that die, the less peril there will be" (as quoted in Bennett and Montaperto 1971, 28). Raised to believe that a glorious utopia was just around the corner, the students needed someone to blame for the broken promises of socialism and were just as frustrated by impediments to the revolution as elder Party members, and perhaps even more so, with the effects of general social repression compounded by competing political and academic demands on their time.

The various campaigns that the Communist Party had launched since 1949 had a far deeper effect on China's youth than on older generations. The absoluteness of the students' allegiance to Mao was a product of their having been raised in a culture—albeit a fabricated one—that openly denigrated identification with family and with religious and ethical traditions. With such basic nurturing structures denied them, they grew up with a profound psychological need for approval and direction; and with right and wrong always distinguished by violence, destructive fantasies no doubt consumed their imaginations. Planting the idea that campus authority figures and other reactionary forces were to blame for the slow pace of the revolution was easy for Mao. And it was just as easy to mobilize the students behind his agenda simply by validating them as true and autonomous revolutionaries. At an enormous rally in August 1966, and in seven subsequent gatherings, Mao endorsed the Red Guard movement. His appearances thrilled millions of students, who held up their *Little Red Book*s and chanted "Long Life Chairman Mao" until they were hoarse. He spoke of them as "the morning sun" and the hope upon which the future of China and the fate of humanity depended (Yang 1997, 121), and he urged them to further the revolution using any means available. They felt emancipated, human, and free (Yi 1996, 124). They were being given a chance to prove themselves *and* to save the revolution.

In one memoir, former Red Guard Rae Yang (1997, 115) wrote: "[T]hose seven months were the most terrible in my life. Yet they were also the most wonderful! I had never felt so good about myself before, nor have I ever since." Ken Ling (1972, 44), another former Red Guard, described this period as the one time in their lives when the students could "enjoy anything, whatever people had and more. If we could not enjoy something, then we would destroy it so that everyone would be equal." A talented surgeon described an encounter with fanatical Red Guards thus: ". . . the ringleader announced that he was going to teach me a lesson, to put a stop to my crimes of conceit, to humble me once and for all. With the same supreme indifference a righteous elder exhibits when snapping the bit of chalk filched by a naughty boy to doodle on walls, he broke my thumb [thus assuring I would never operate again]" (as quoted in Lord 1990, 172).

"To rebel is justified" became the slogan of the Red Guards. All those who had wielded authority over them were pushed aside, using the kind of violence Mao had long advocated. In public struggle sessions the students accused teachers and administrators of being freaks, monsters, exploiters, intellectual aristocrats, and tyrants, (Cheng-Chung 1979). They paraded these authority figures through the streets in dunce caps and beat and tortured them. Common was "the spectacle of well-known and universally respected people being fitted up with placards and grotesque, ignominious headgear and forced on all fours to lap food from a bowl on the ground" (Leys 1979, 118). Some teachers were beaten to death during these sessions— Peng Kang, the president of Jiaotang University in Xian, died in one such beating. Some were murdered outright, including the entire senior faculty of the history department at Zhongshan University. Others committed suicide. Precipitated in part by an estimated 20,000 "sightseers" that came to the campus daily to abuse staff and administrators, 200 suicides occurred at Peking University between August and October 1966 (Foreign Expert 1966). At the Hunan Medical College, a third of the senior faculty of the Department of Psychiatry committed suicide. Intellectuals were arrested, imprisoned, and exiled to labor camps. For some, the imprisonment would last a decade.

At the same time as they were attacking teachers and academics, the students were turning on the material expression of the past, burning and shredding "bad books and bad pictures"—the primary competition to Maoist ideals (Jiaqi and Gao 1996, 66). Part of their education having been to distrust and attack China's traditions, they quickly learned to extend their intolerance to any reverence for books or learning. In the eyes of the revolutionaries, classical works promoted feudalism, Western materials advanced capitalism, and Soviet works encouraged revisionism. In post-revolution accounts, participants in the Cultural Revolution repeated the same refrain in explaining their actions: I attacked the enemy. What could be wrong with that (Terrill 1996, xv)? The link between abusing their professors and destroying books was often quite explicit. Former Red Guard Yan described one book burning:

> Finally the books—by now a small mountain—were set on fire by the Red Guards. . . . Excited and passionate slogans accompanied the thick smoke rising up into the sky. Perhaps the Red Guards felt that the act of merely burning books was not "revolutionary" enough. In any case, using their belts, they prodded the "Black Gang" [instructors] to the edge of the fire and made them stand there with their heads lowered, bodies bent forward, to be "tried in the raging flames of the Great Cultural Revolution." . . . What I had witnessed was the Beijing No. 11 Middle School Red Guard book fire. (Yan 1996, 328)

First, the students sacked the academic and school libraries. Then they removed thousands of books from public libraries. Accounts of former Red Guards describe the excitement they felt at having access to closed shelves and coveted books. Many secretly carried away books for their own nighttime reading while spending their days pulling similar books off the shelves, labeling them as "counterrevolutionary," and consigning them to huge bonfires (Ling 1972). One non-Red Guard student described a scene at Nan Yang Model Middle School in Shanghai: "Now this center of education had become the new frontier of the war that had been declared on civilization. On the playground, the road, the roof of the library, even under the grapevines in the school's vineyards, people were burning books. The sky turned red" (Luo 1990, 25). It was their teachers, members of an earlier generation, who grieved when books were burned. The distinguished professor You Xiaoli, who was physically tortured and then assigned to clean campus latrines for years, said later that the burning of books was worse than the physical and emotional abuse (Thurston 1987, 206). Also grieving were the Black-category families, often educated people who valued books and education. They were stripped of their collections and forced to publicly denounce learning. Their children, while often pressured by peers to participate in anti-intellectual activities, were nevertheless excluded from full participation as Red Guards. But Black-category students often had retained close ties to their parents and had less need for Mao as a father figure. They were more emotionally capable of rejecting violence. Their post-Cultural Revolution memoirs stress how they and their families survived persecution and clung to their beliefs and allegiances while the more narcissistic memoirs of the Red Guards focus on the thrill of participation in a revolution, the bonding with other Guards and Mao, and, finally, the crushing disillusionment felt when legitimacy was lost.

While some books during this period were lost because of personal looting and chaotic civil war, most were lost to government-condoned Red Guard actions. For libraries, it was a time of unrelentingly high-risk conditions. The most dangerous time for collections was 1966–1968, when the Red Guard was waging its campaign against the "Four Olds"— old ideas, old culture, old customs, and old habits of the "exploiting classes." Sometimes the presence of Marxist-Leninist books and books by Mao prevented the Red Guards from burning entire buildings to the ground; but many other times there was no such obstacle. At Zhongshan University in Canton, the Red Guards first burned all the books from the collection of Western classics; then they burned all texts not obviously Communist or Maoist; and then they burned the library building itself (Thurston 1987). The Red Guards destroyed vast numbers of archival collections and entire research libraries. For example, at the Soochow Middle School of Kiansu Province, a school with a 900-year history and a 100,000-volume collection, 80,000 books were lost in one night (Barclay 1979, 108). Academic libraries actually sustained more damage than public libraries; however, collections in public libraries at the county level and above were probably reduced by one-third (Lin 1998).

Librarians and staff occasionally succeeded in protecting their collections by taking personal risks—either openly confronting Red Guards or hiding books. For example, after having observed the burning of books from a nearby Catholic Church, the staff of Shanghai's Xujiahui Library was waiting when the students began an attack on their library. They guarded the doors and talked the students into sparing their historic collections. The library was then closed down until 1977 and the contents were preserved, although staff members suffered persecution, imprisonment, and physical harm simply because, as librarians and educated individuals, they were presumed to be reactionaries (King 1997).

All libraries were closed for various lengths of time (UNESCO 1996), and some remained closed for the entire decade. Closures pleased the radicals by ensuring that the libraries not serve as "the paradise of the capitalist class" (Ting 1983:148), But closures also allowed moderate officials to protect some of the major libraries, including the provincial public libraries. The collections in Beijing Library, for example, survived relatively unscathed. And despite the political and cultural goals of Mao, some of the great literature of the past was preserved, including the Shanghai Library's collection of some 130,000 volumes of Chinese classics on fragrant camphor wood (Castagna 1978).

For many libraries, deliverance came when books could be safely stored in rooms sealed with *fengtiao*—two long narrow paper strips in an X bearing information and an official seal of closing by the government. A fascinating story about one sealed collection is told in *Turbulent Decade: A History of the Cultural Revolution* (1996), written by Yan Jiaqi and Gao Gao (scholars with political connections): Mao's wife, Jiang Qing, an immensely powerful member of the Gang of Four, attempted to wipe clean her early career as a film actress in Shanghai in the 1930s, a time when she may not have been sufficiently Red. She destroyed letters and pictures and arranged for the death and persecution of people who had known her in those days. All books, newspapers, magazines and documents of the 1930s in the Xu Jia Hui collection of the Shanghai Library were officially sealed and ten staff members with ties to this collection, including a janitor, were interrogated and underwent various degrees of mental and physical torture. However, the collections were preserved and when the Gang of Four was put on trial, the Shanghai Library staff was able to use this collection and other texts to provide documentation for 300 of the Gang's "crimes" dating back thirty years and more (Castagna 1978, 791).

The story illustrates the threat that collections, as guardians of public memory, can pose and, sadly, also demonstrates how dangerous association with certain collections can be for the custodians of such records.

Another story illustrates the power of collections as witness and the impulse of librarians towards preserving knowledge. Librarians at the Beijing Library protected its more traditional collections from the Red Guards by convincing them of the importance of the library as a center for the preservation of revolutionary GPCR materials. They put a nationwide call out for three copies of pamphlets, circulars, petitions, and materials related to the Cultural Revolution—thus assuring materials for future scholars (Jiaqi and Gao 1996, 76).

The Red Guards soon carried their rebellion out of the schools and into the larger community, and Mao endorsed them by commanding the police to refrain from intervention. Although those in Black categories and out-of-favor moderates were the preferred targets, no one was exempt from persecution. Individuals were attacked both in their homes and on the streets. Throughout a reign of terror lasting from 1966 to 1968, the Red Guards, assisted by officials who knew that they could be the next targets if they thwarted Mao's "children," formed an extra-Party quasi-dictatorship of the proletariat that forced the cowed populace to comply with all demands. All allegiances, interests, and individuality were to be abandoned. According to one memoir, "'Relaxation' had become an obsolete concept: books, paintings, musical instruments, sports, cards, chess, teahouses, bars—all had disappeared" (Chang 1991, 332). All were labeled "bourgeois" and along with family life and socializing were displaced by revolutionary activity. Workers were required to attend hour after hour of exhausting, sometimes violent, study and struggle sessions in which they repeatedly reaffirmed their total allegiance to Mao. If, during these sessions, parents were condemned as rightists or counterrevolutionaries, their children shared that condemnation.

All things reactionary, bourgeois, and Western were considered evidence of resistance to the revolution. Both modern and traditional clothing and hairstyles were unacceptable, and the entire population donned Mao outfits and cut their hair. Compliance was enforced rigorously and indiscriminately. The Red Guards accosted women on the streets, many of them elderly, and subjected them to rough haircuts; young girls had their pigtails cut off. As an added humiliation, one side of the head might be completely shaved. Everything in the environment had to promote Maoism, and loudspeakers blared revolutionary messages night and day. Shrubs and flowering plants were uprooted and killed. Pets were beaten to death. On an experimental dairy farm, cows imported from Holland (also bourgeois!) were killed (Thurston 1987). Red Guards raided homes, usually at night to maximize the terror, and confiscated valuables such as jewelry, watches, cameras, and radios. They smashed china, glassware, lamps, mirrors, and musical instruments. Many Black-category families were stripped of most of their belongings and evicted from their homes or squeezed into one room.

By waging war on personal possessions and traditional cultural objects, the students felt they were articulating their contempt for the old system's corruption and making room for Maoism (Zhang and Schwartz 1997). Pieces of art and literature, no matter how old or intricate, were confiscated or destroyed (Luo 1990). Their victims were devastated:

> They searched our home and took father's entire art collection and his reference books. They smashed his faithful green reading lamp. There were eleven "death searches" that year. They would come after midnight, beat us, shatter anything made of glass, and shred any book or paper in sight with the exception of Mao's works. (Luo 1990, 100)

> On the state farm where I lived there was very nice man who played accordion very well. He came from a landlord's family . . . the Red Guards charged into his house, finding several books with musical notes, which they did not understand. They claimed the books were "account books using secret code to register their past property and revenge on the proletariat once they have a chance to overthrow the [P]arty and socialism." He was immediately taken to a hilltop and shot. (Lin 1991, 24)

> All my books and my manuscript were burned . . . But the book [that I had been working on] had become my life. How could I let it go? Though they had burned my library and my papers, they had not burned my memory, and I began to write in secret, recalling the words I had chosen before, and hiding the pages in my quilt. (Lord 1990, 56)

> I looked out the window and saw bright, leaping flames in the garden. A bonfire had been lit in the middle of the garden and the Red Guards were standing around the fire carelessly tossing my books onto the flames. "My heart tightened with pain." (Cheng 1986, 79)

In anticipation of Red Guard incursions, many families preemptively destroyed anything written or printed that would reflect the "Four Olds." As a protective measure, one family sold several hundred copies of their

English and French books by the pound to a waste recovery station. Books, letters, and journals were stealthily burned and the ashes flushed down the toilet (Yang 1997). Destroying one's own books sometimes exacted a terrible price. A daughter describes her father's agony:

> He had lit a fire in the big cement sink, and was hurling his books into the flames. This was the first time in my life I had seen him weeping. It was agonized, broken, and wild, the weeping of a man not used to shedding tears. Every now and then, in fits of violent sobs, he stamped his feet on the floor and banged his head against the wall. . . . I did not know what to say. He did not utter a word either. My father had spent every penny on his books. They were his life. After the bonfire, I could tell that something had happened to his mind. (Chang, 1991:330)

Political correctness (and in some cases, survival) mandated the prominent display of Mao's image and works. The attack on anything old was an attack on anything that demonstrated or stimulated divided loyalties and competition to Mao and Maoism. On a house-by-house level, Red Guards defaced family photographs, claiming that looking at photos of loved ones or ancestors was a feudal act. In a repudiation of religion, Red Guards destroyed every reminder of Confucianism, including images and sacred texts. Public places were cleansed of the poison of the past as temples, churches, graveyards, statues and monuments were desecrated and smashed. Museums were looted and their artifacts turned into a "gigantic burnt offering"—a tribute to the iconoclastic frenzy of the Red Guards (Leys 1979, 91). The only museums to survive intact were the selective few, such as the Imperial Palace in Peking, which were closed down and protected by government troops.

By far the worst of the violence and destruction occurred in the first three years of the Cultural Revolution, during which time the conflict metamorphosed rapidly into civil war. As the revolution progressed, "it began somersaulting, flipping this way and flopping that, like a fish out of water, as the revolutionaries of one stage of the movement became the counterrevolutionaries of the next, the persecutors during one phase the persecuted of the next" (Thurston 1987, 108). Finally, the Party leadership used the army to quell the turmoil, and the most extreme violence was over by April 1969. The oppression, however, did not ease until Mao's death in 1976—the event that marked the end of the Cultural Revolution.

For libraries and librarianship, the devastation, after the initial few years, is best described as utter retrogression. Professional activities, including participation in associations and conferences, were terminated. All but two library schools were closed, and these were radicalized. Library school-academics were persecuted. Progress toward modern librarianship was reversed as emphasis shifted from mastering professional knowledge and information management skills to adapting socialist theory to library organization and management. Future librarians were not to become "watchdogs of imperialism" as had past librarians; indeed, library students were not allowed to learn about libraries in any other period or country (Ting 1983). Library systems that had begun to move toward networking, cooperation, and automation were dismantled, and libraries surviving Red Guard destruction and purges had severely curtailed functions.

Cut off from national and local networks and from international information systems, collections in Chinese libraries rapidly stagnated. Foreign exchange schemes and purchases of non-Chinese materials were banned. Libraries ceased collecting serials; indeed, Chinese scholarly and professional journals largely suspended publication. The national bibliography ceased publication from 1966 to 1970. The politicized Chinese Library Classification System was developed to replace the "semi-feudal, semi-colonial" decimal system (Barclay 1995, 101). Knowledge was divided into five principal groups, according to Marxist-Leninist-Maoist doctrine. Gang-of-Four thought was reflected in the fields of philosophy and social sciences, where unique subclasses and divisions were invented to suit the radicals' views (Ting 1983).

Many basic reference and reader services ceased because intellectual activities were discouraged. As late as 1975, academic librarians were forced to abolish faculty reading rooms and forbidden to assist instructors in research work (Ting 1983). Libraries were no longer needed to support research because research results were to rise from the masses, not trickle down from "rarified" research institutes or individual scholarship (Broadbent 1980, 30). Attribution of authorship was "unnecessary." The role of libraries in supporting education (in serving as sterile "archives of theory") was denigrated because education was not about mastering a body of knowledge as much as it was about developing into a good socialist. Intellectual activity for its own sake was highly suspect. Since reading was a political act, the circulation records of university students were scrutinized and students were discouraged from reading at all—"no-use was in large part politically instigated and founded on fear" (Barclay 1995, 99). Libraries were expected to serve as ideological instruments or not at all. They, like other institutions, conformed to a decade in which China became a "blank nation intellectually" (Lin 1998, 16).

IN THE AFTERMATH OF THE CULTURAL REVOLUTION

In its wake, the Cultural Revolution left a devastated society. Between 20 and 25 million urban youth (many of them former Red Guards) had been sent to labor in remote areas—partly to temper their revolutionary zeal, but also to alleviate pressure on a stagnant job market. Many were never allowed to return to the cities. For most, their education was permanently interrupted, and they became known as the "lost generation." The Party's credibility was severely damaged by the revolution; in terms of basic decency, Communism had proved to be an utter failure. Further, in terms of replacing Confucianism, the family, and traditional values with a viable alternative, Communism had been ineffectual. The Party admits that over the course of the decade, some 100 million human beings suffered some kind of harassment or persecution. Up to 10 million may have died; over a half million died in battles alone (Rummel 1991).

With the trial of the Gang of Four in 1980, the Party managed to salvage some of its image. By characterizing the Cultural Revolution as "a severe and disastrous event wrongly launched by leaders and manipulated by a counterrevolutionary group" (Becker 1996, 284) and by calling upon the people "to criticize the Gang of Four for its anti-history fallacy of breaking completely with all the cultural heritage. . ." (Zhang and Schwartz 1997, 203), the Party deflected criticism of both socialism *per se* and its regime's implementation of socialist policies. By typifying the GPCR as a sudden deviation from normality engineered by a minority faction, the government attempted to evade admission of the real roots of the upheaval: China's historical predisposition to authoritarian rule, the policies of the Communists' totalitarian regime that institutionalized discrimination and violence, the corruption of Mao's personal quest for untrammeled power, and the frustration of a people exhausted by revolutionary demands and disappointed by broken promises (Terrill 1996, xvi). In 1978, the Communist Party abandoned Mao's 'class struggle' and organizations across China burned the personal files that had institutionalized categorization and discrimination: "bonfires were lit to consume these flimsy pieces of paper that had ruined countless lives" (Chang 1991, 506).

Twenty years later, the Party is still leery of releasing too many details about the Cultural Revolution. Librarians were reminded of the Party's sensitivity about the era by the arrest of Yongyi Song in August 1999. Song, a librarian at Dickinson College and a soon-to-be naturalized citizen of the United States, had returned to Beijing to gather first-hand materials on the GPCR, mainly newspapers ("China Releases . . . " 1999). He was released after six months in response to widespread protests from the West. Uncensored, substantive accounts of events and critical analyses of Cultural Revolution policies are only available *outside* of China, as are the often-poignant survival stories of victims and memoirs of former Red Guards. The Party does not want the people of China to be informed about events that reflect so badly on their regime. They do not wish the people to think autonomously, process their personal experiences during this time, or be exposed to the "scar" literature, because "It is through the small scenes, the individual evidence, the private testimony, that human tragedy on this scale can be reduced to manageable, meaningful proportions" (Thurston 1987, 33).

Within China, the Party maintains a firm control on modern history. While willing to acknowledge that the Cultural Revolution was a political mistake engineered by a renegade faction, the Party is still deeply reluctant to confront the appalling loss of life, 20 to 30 million people, that occurred in the Great Leap Forward, 1958–1961. Official denial of the loss of almost 5 percent of the population has given the famine "a ghostly existence in the collective consciousness of the Chinese" (Becker 1996, 286). For nearly two decades, there was a blackout of all Chinese population statistics gathered during that time and "problems" with food supplies during the GLF era were downplayed and attributed by the Party to natural disasters. Indeed, officials had taken advantage of the Cultural Revolution to burn large quantities of materials from the State Statistical Bureau and other evidence of the famine.

The magnitude, and often the reality of the famine itself, is still not acknowledged, and therefore neither is its role in precipitating the Cultural Revolution. Both the Great Leap Forward and the Cultural Revolution are too closely tied to Communist China's greatest hero, Mao Tse-tung, to permit uncensored analysis. Any realistic accounting of either event would expose Mao to charges of culpable stupidity at best, or, at the very worst, crimes against humanity—the equivalent of indicting the Party and Chinese Communism in a country where many remnants of Maoism remain. For this very reason, in 1981 the Party's Central Committee attempted to foreclose discussion of Mao by issuing a summation of his life. Mao was officially classified as a great revolutionary whose contributions empirically outweighed the costs of his mistakes: He was 70 percent good and 30 percent bad.

For survivors of the Cultural Revolution, the Party's assessment of the great leader brought little closure. Many still struggle with "a profound sense of loss—loss of culture and of spiritual values, loss of status and honor, loss of career, loss of dignity, of hope and ideals, of time, integrity, truth, and of life; in short, of nearly everything that gives meaning to life" (Thurston 1987, 208). It has been particularly difficult for former Maoists to move from worship of Mao, to doubt, and finally, in recent years, to assimilating tales of his hypocrisy and corruption. Published in the West, a memoir by Mao's personal doctor, Li Zhisui, revealed his betrayal of the peasants and Red Guards and traced Mao's descent into "a shadow world" of seclusion and paranoia, where his great visions for humanity became father to great crimes against the same (Li Zhisui 1994, xiv). Many of those who had worshipped him, and perhaps still did, were devastated when Li Zhisui's anecdotes about Mao's predilection for indolence, dancing parties, promiscuous bedding of young country girls, and utter ruthlessness made their way back to China. They found it difficult to reconcile Mao's personal life with the public image of self-sacrifice and austerity that he modeled and promoted.

While China's Communist infrastructure remained in place after 1976, the radical element's struggle for the hearts and minds of the people of China was lost. The exhausted and disillusioned Chinese Communist Party, including many radicals, appeared ready to accept the pragmatic revisions that seem an inevitable development in revolutions. Libraries were reopened; scholars were released from labor camps and rehabilitated once again; intellectual development, specializations in technology and science, and some modern values were restored in education. Unlike Cambodia, where Pol Pot's Communist regime reduced the nation to ground zero culturally, China stopped at the brink of complete disaster. And so, while China's new society hardly expresses the full range of its rich cultural heritage, neither is it a blank slate; its surviving cultural patrimony and bibliographic legacy seem secure. However, by not coming to terms with the past, remnants of Party radicalism have the potential to resurface, as the 1989 massacre of student protestors in Tiananmen Square illustrated. The Party still maintains control through its "Technique of Forgetting History"—a device of rule in which the whole society forgets history, especially the history of the Communist Party (Fang 1990, 268). For example, new generations have no specific knowledge of the radicals' Anti-Right movements and purges in 1942, 1957, 1970, 1979, and 1989, because details of these events have been suppressed in the interest of the Party's "one correct belief." Even recent history is barred from influencing political and social actions.

The fate of libraries in China has always been tied to government policies. When the pendulum swung back to a new pragmatism, liberalism, and openness to the West after 1978, a revived acceptance of the importance of some cultural continuity and rejection of isolationism resulted in an injection of funds for the expansion of China's libraries and publishing industry. In the next twenty years, the number of registered publications jumped from 150 to 4,000. Libraries were given an important role in helping to make the past, although a sanitized past, serve the present and "things foreign serve China" (Barclay 1995, 123). The government called upon libraries to support the "Four Modernizations"—of science and technology, defense, agriculture, and industry. Chinese librarians were reinstated, and many were exonerated of the crimes that they had been accused of during the Cultural Revolution. They were urged to put the Cultural Revolution behind them and modernize and computerize operations, apply management principles, and engage in networking. Librarians and libraries were no longer the enemy.

Now an embarrassing shadow in the background of contemporary China, the Cultural Revolution was nevertheless a watershed event in modern cultural history. It stands as a frightening example of left-wing extremism, as the Holocaust stands for right-wing extremism. In Germany, totalitarian-based utopianism led to the ultimate abuse of social engineering, the genocide of the Jews and their culture and the Poles and Polish culture. In China, totalitarianism led the Chinese people first into political indoctrination, then into social brutalization, and, finally, into alienation from their cultural heritage and auto-ethnocide. While the Nazis purged some of their own books, they primarily destroyed other people's books and libraries because the German vision of utopia required the preservation (albeit censored) of a glorious past; for the Nazis a sanitized history and literary heritage was a pillar of the longed-for triumph of the Third Reich. The Chinese Communists, on the other hand, went far beyond purging, because to them the past served as a reactionary force, tethering the revolution and the new world it promised. To Party radicals in the first two decades of Communist China, as to other socialist regimes in predominantly rural nations, the written record was at best, of little importance, at worst, an enemy of the people.

Perhaps the Cultural Revolution's ultimate significance lies in its warning about the predilection of violent regimes to align behind an extremist ideology that justifies annihilation of anything standing in the way of its visions. Ultimately that regime savages its own people and culture and/or other peoples and cultures. This savagery endangers not only the specific individuals and cultures under attack but, ultimately, all the peoples of the world, because just as the decimation or extinction of one species diminishes a region's ecological integrity, destruction of any group's books, the keepers of memory, diminishes the common cultural heritage of the world.

REFERENCES

Barclay, John. 1979. "The Four Modernisations Embrace Libraries in the Peoples [sic] Republic of China." *The Australian Library Journal* 28 (7):102–110.

Barclay, John. 1995. *The Seventy-Year Ebb and Flow of Chinese Library and Information Services: May 4, 1919 to the Late 1980s.* Metuchen, New Jersey: Scarecrow Press.

Becker, Jasper. 1996. *Hungry Ghosts: Mao's Secret Famine.* New York: Henry Holt.

Bennett, Gordon A., and Ronald N. Montaperto. 1971. *Red Guard: The Political Biography of Dai Hsiao-ai.* Garden City, New York: Doubleday.

Boorman, Howard L. 1966. "The Literary World of Mao Tse-tung." In *China Under Mao: Politics Take Command: A Selection of Articles from The China Quarterly*, ed. Roderick MacFarquhar. Cambridge, Massachusetts: MIT Press, 368–391.

Broadbent, K.P. 1980. *Dissemination of Scientific Information in the People's Republic of China.* Ottawa: International Development Research Centre.

Buchheim, Hans. 1968. *Totalitarian Rule: Its Nature and Characteristics,* trans. Ruth Hein. Middletown, Connecticut: Wesleyan University Press.

Castagna, Edwin. 1978. "A Visit to Two Chinese Libraries." *Wilson Library Journal* 52 (10):789–792.

Chang, Jung. 1991. *Wild Swans: Three Daughters of China.* New York: Doubleday.

Cheng, Nien. 1986. *Life and Death in Shanghai.* New York: Penguin Books.

Cheng-Chung, Li. 1979. *The Question of Human Rights on China Mainland.* Republic of China: World Anti-Communist League, China Chapter, Asian Peoples' Anti-Communist League.

"China Releases Wife, Detains Dickinson College Librarian." 1999. *Library Hotline* 28 (49):6.

Conquest, Robert. 1986. *The Harvest of Sorrow: Soviet Collectivization and the Terror-Famine.* New York: Oxford University Press.

Dutt, V.P., and Gargi Dutt. 1970. *China's Cultural Revolution.* Delhi: National Printing Works.

Fang, Lizhi. 1990. *Bringing Down the Great Wall: Writings on Science, Culture, and Democracy in China.* New York: W.W. Norton.

Foreign Expert. 1966. "Eyewitness of the Cultural Revolution." *China Quarterly* 28:1–7.

Fung, Margaret C. 1984. "Safekeeping of the National Peiping Library's Rare Chinese Books at the Library of Congress 1941–1965." *The Journal of Library History, Philosophy and Comparative Librarianship* 19 (3):359–371.

Guisso, R.W.L., and Catherine Pagani (with David Miller). 1989. *The First Emperor of China.* New York: Birch Lane Press.

Jiaqi, Yan, and Gao Gao. 1996. *Turbulent Decade: A History of the Cultural Revolution,* trans. and ed. D.W.Y. Kwok. Honolulu, Hawaii: University of Hawaii Press.

Jonassohn, Kurt, and Karin Solveig Bjornson. 1998. *Genocide and Gross Human Rights Violations in Comparative Perspective.* New Brunswick, New Jersey: Transaction Publishers.

King, Gail. 1997. "The Xujiahui (Zikawei) Library of Shanghai." *Libraries and Culture* 32 (4):456–469.

Knechtges, David R. 1996. "Chinese Literature." In *World Book Encyclopedia,* Vol. 3. 511–512.

Kundera, Milan. 1981. *The Book of Laughter and Forgetting,* trans. Michael Henry Heim. New York: Alfred A. Knopf

Leys, Simon. 1979. *Broken Images: Essays on Chinese Culture and Politics,* trans. Steve Cox. New York: St. Martin's Press.

Leys, Simon. 1977. *Chinese Shadows.* New York: Viking Press.

Li, Zhisui. 1994. *The Private Life of Chairman Mao: The Memoirs of Mao's Personal Physician,* trans. Tai Hung-chao with the editorial assistance of Anne Thurston. New York: Random House.

Lifton, Robert Jay. 1961. *Thought Reform and the Psychology of Totalism: A Study of "Brainwashing" in China.* New York: W.W. Norton.

Lin, Jing. 1991. *The Red Guards' Path to Violence: Political, Educational and Psychological Factors.* New York: Praeger.

Lin, Sharon Chien. 1998. *Libraries and Librarianship in China.* Westport, Connecticut: Greenwood Press.

Ling, Ken. 1972. *Red Guard: From Schoolboy to "Little General" in Mao's China,* trans. Miriam London and Ta-ling Lee. London: MacDonald.

Lord, Bette Bao. 1990. *Legacies: A Chinese Mosaic.* New York: Knopf.

Luo, Zi-Ping. 1990. *A Generation Lost: China Under the Cultural Revolution.* New York: Henry Holt.

Mao Tse-Tung. 1967. *Mao Tse-Tung on Art and Literature.* Calcutta: National Book.

Moraes, Frank. 1953. *Report on Mao's China.* New York: MacMillan.

Nee, Victor (with Don Layman). 1969. *The Cultural Revolution at Peking University.* New York: Monthly Review Press.

Nelson, Diane M., and Robert B. Nelson. 1979. "'The Red Chamber': Li Ta-chao and Sources of Radicalism in Modern Chinese Librarianship." *Journal of Library History* 14 (2):121–128.

Pfaff, William. 1993. *The Wrath of Nations: Civilization and the Furies of Nationalism.* New York: Simon and Schuster.

Revel, Jean-Francois. 1977. *The Totalitarian Temptation,* trans. David Hapgood. Garden City, New York: Doubleday.

Rummel, R.J. 1991. *China's Bloody Century: Genocide and Mass Murder Since 1900.* New Brunswick, New Jersey: Transaction Publishers.

Rummel, R.J. 1994. *Death by Government.* New Brunswick, New Jersey: Transaction Publishers.

Schoenbaum, David. 1966. *Hitler's Social Revolution: Class and Status in Nazi Germany, 1933–1939.* New York: Doubleday.

Short, Philip. 1999. *Mao: A Life.* New York: Henry Holt.

Stieg, Margaret F. 1992. *Public Libraries in Nazi Germany.* Tuscaloosa, Alabama: The University of Alabama Press.

Taylor, Simon. 1985. *Prelude to Genocide: Nazi Ideology and the Struggle for Power.* London: Duckworth.

Terrill, Ross. 1996. Foreword in *Scarlet Memorial: Tales of Cannibalism in Modern China*, by Zheng Yi and translated by T.P. Zim. Boulder, Colorado: Westview Press, xi–xvii.

Thurston, Anne F. 1987. *Enemies of the People.* New York: Knopf.

Ting, Lee-hsia Hsu. 1983. "Library Services in the People's Republic of China: A Historical Overview." *Library Quarterly* 54 (2):134–160.

UNESCO Memory of the World Program. 1996. *Lost Memory: Libraries and Archives Destroyed in the Twentieth Century.* Paris: UNESCO.

White III, Lynn T. 1989. *Policies of Chaos: The Organizational Causes of Violence in China's Cultural Revolution.* Princeton, New Jersey: Princeton University Press.

Yan, Liu. 1996. "Burning Books." In *China's Cultural Revolution, 1966–1969: Not a Dinner Party,* ed. Michael Schoenhals. London: M.E. Sharpe, 327–329.

Yang, Rae. 1997. *Spider Eaters: A Memoir.* Berkeley, California: University of California Press.

Yi, Zheng. 1996. *Scarlet Memorial: Tales of Cannibalism in Modern China*, trans. T.P. Zim. Boulder, Colorado: Westview Press.

Zhang, Tong, and Barry Schwartz. 1997. "Confucius and the Cultural Revolution: A Study in Collective Memory." *International Journal of Politics, Culture and Society* 11 (2):189–212.

Zuo, Jiping. 1991. "Political Religion: The Case of the Cultural Revolution in China." *Sociological Analysis* 52 (1):99–110.

Chapter 8

TIBET:
A Culture in Jeopardy

"[T]he incremental demise of this distinct group of people depletes the world's reservoir of enduring wisdom"
(Apte and Edwards 1998, 131).

Immediately after taking control in China, the Communist Party sought to secure vital border areas. Chinese troops invaded Tibet in 1949, claiming the isolated state as an inherent part of the Chinese motherland. But, distinct by virtue of linguistics, race, culture, geography, history, and religion, Tibet resisted China and set in motion an epic battle over irreconcilable world views: Buddhism versus Communism, with the latter heavily overlaid with nationalism and colonialism. Through a government in exile in India and resistance by locals, Tibet has maintained its right to political self-determination (i.e., independent nationhood and cultural sovereignty), and the two civilizations have been locked in unrelenting conflict. Chapter 7 covered the development of Communism as an ideology, the processes by which China became a totalitarian state, and the background and promulgation of internal libricide in China. This chapter discusses Tibet's culture and written materials and China's ideological responses to that culture. It explores the respective worldviews that made conflict inevitable and resulted in ethnocide and libricide, the deliberate and ongoing destruction of Tibetan culture and texts.

TIBETAN WORLDVIEW AND CULTURE

Isolated by mountain ranges and uninhabitable wilderness, Tibet evolved over several thousands years into a unique, highly focused civilization based on an adaptation of Indian Buddhism. Beginning in the 600s, the kings of Tibet were concerned with introducing to their country the whole of active Indian Buddhist beliefs and culture, including forms of literature, monastic organization, medicine, painting, and architecture. Scholars and craftsmen then turned the borrowed culture in a specifically Tibetan direction by mixing it with indigenous influences (Snellgrove and Richardson 1986). Buddhism came to inform the Tibetans' views on the origin and nature of the world, the role of the individual in society, the relation between mind and matter, the principles of ethics, the arts, medical science, religion—the whole of life (Batchelor 1987). By very deliberate efforts, Buddhism came to form the basis for Tibetan culture, the "intricate living web of customs, beliefs, rituals, tools, history, and necessity" (Hicks 1988, 91)—and Tibetan identity. Of all the bonds that defined Tibetans as a people and nation, religion was undoubtedly the strongest (Government of Tibet in Exile 1999).

The centrality of religion was most evident in the figure of the Dalai Lama, an incarnated monk. By the 1600s, religious and political powers were fused in his person. The Dalai Lama, other monks, the aristocracy, and government officials were connected in a tightly woven web that made no clear distinction between worldly and spiritual pursuits (Gyaltag 1991). Thus, in pre-1959 Lhasa (Tibet's capital city), the bottom floor of the Central Cathedral housed 50 chapels filled with religious artifacts and scriptures, while above were the offices of the Mayor, the Regent, the Cabinet, the Foreign Bureau, and the Departments of Finance, Customs, and Agriculture and hundreds of documents—centuries-old treaties and tax records filed in bunches tied to red-lacquered pillars (Avedon 1997). The cellars of the Dalai Lama's home, the Potala, were reserved for storing government records and held thousands of religious and historical texts that testified to the life and development of Tibetan culture—parchments, palm bark books, and volumes of sacred texts written in a special ink made from blends of gold, silver, iron, or copper powder (Pema 1997). The Potala with its 1,000 chambers was "less a home than a living museum" (Avedon 1997, 21), containing the tombs of nine previous Dalai Lamas and archives of Tibetan culture.

Throughout Tibet, signs of Buddhism were pervasive. There were more than 6,000 monasteries, multitudes of shrines, *chortens* (the spire-topped reliquaries of Buddhist saints), *stupas* (domed platforms containing religious objects), and piles of *mani* stones (stones carved with invocations). Statues, frescoes, and *thankas* (Tibetan icons painted on rolls of silk or fabric) decorated the temples; outside, prayer flags waved in the breeze and passing Tibetans regularly set prayer wheels in motion. Religious observances and festivals punctuated each year, and a constant flow of pilgrims connected religious sites and Tibetan society. Daily life was infused with spirituality (Norbu 1987). For many Tibetans, religion was an expression of "universal responsibility and the good heart"(Hicks 1988, 10). Based on logic and understanding rather than on blind faith, Buddhism was integral in their worldview. Older Tibetans remember pre-Communist Tibet as a place with deep social unity and spontaneous friendliness to all and sundry, grounded on the simple notion that "we are all but men" (Snellgrove and Richardson 1986, 258). Tolerance was the rule, but retribution was swift when one offended society or tradition.

Mid-twentieth century Tibet has been described as "redolent of the Middle Ages" (Craig 1999, 167) and similar to Western Europe up until the point at which that region experienced the Renaissance and an ensuing freedom of style that led to modernity (Snellgrove and Richardson 1986). Unlike Renaissance-period Europeans, Tibetans had remained steadfastly resistant to change. Tibetan feudalism (different from Western feudalism in that it was not military-based) functioned as a "safety net" of security protecting the lower classes from starvation and complete destitution (Hicks 1988, 31). Foreigners' pre-1949 color films and photographs of official occasions in Tibet portray a "world like that of the late mediaeval miniature brought back to life with its display and luxury at the apex of a society, sophisticated and ordered but with a limited technology and no doubt a poverty cheerfully borne and perhaps also not as extreme as elsewhere" (Zwalf 1981, 126).

While underdeveloped economically and technologically, Tibet had advanced psychological and spiritual mechanisms of support. Behind the unpretentious lifestyle of the Tibetans was an elaborate network of laws, codes, and ethics based on concepts of non-violence, compassion, the cyclic nature of all living things, and the interdependence of the earth's living and non-living elements—what many now call "an environmental ethic" (Apte and Edwards 1998). For Tibetans ecological principles were integrated into their daily lives. For example, a respect for all forms of living beings and a belief in reincarnation led to the prohibition of fishing and hunting and thus to an abundance of life forms, including more than 500 species of birds. After hundreds of years of living like this, it was difficult for Tibetans to differentiate between the practice of religion and concern for the environment (Atisha 1991). Careful stewardship and skill in adapting to the environment enabled generation after generation to sustain both human life and Tibet's fragile ecosystems, and real famine was unknown.

In general, spiritual matters dominated material concerns in Tibetan society. Fully one-fourth of the male population was monks or lamas (spiritual teachers) who devoted their lives to pursuit of enlightenment and compassion as personified by Buddha. They practiced the Dharma, the path revealed by Buddha in which wisdom is supported by generosity, ethics, tolerance, energy, and meditation. The monasteries held the "rare-precious-three"—the three most highly valued objects connected with religious beliefs: the teacher (the Buddha), his teachings, and a community of lay and monastic followers (Aldridge 1999a). For the layperson, "[t]o be able to support institutions and individuals who were actively pursuing enlightenment as a full-time job was the most virtuous possible use of one's life" (Patt 1992, 26). The monasteries owned 40 percent of the land and were supported by taxes and contributions from tenant farmers. Most of the disposable wealth of the country was invested in statues and art objects to grace the temples and shrines. Tibetans constantly gave offerings of butter to burn in the lamps that lit holy places; they went on pilgrimages; they made perambulations around religious sites, their continuous prostrations on hands and knees expressing commitment and piety. Almost all Tibetans had a personal connection with a monastic community through a close relative or son.

The monasteries served important religious, cultural, and educational functions; most importantly, they supplied and cultivated the basic doctrine on which the political and social order of Tibet rested (Gyaltag 1991). A Tibetan script was developed in the 700s so that Buddhist scriptures could be translated from Sanskrit, a task that took scholars 600 years. The resulting translations of the scriptures of the Buddha and 750 Indian pundits, assembled in more than approximately 4,500 individual works, were so accurate that modern scholars have been able to produce adequate reconstructions of lost Indian Sanskrit works from the Tibetan versions (Alterman, Alterman, and Gewissler 1987). By the thirteenth century, when Buddhism was disappearing from India and dwindling in Nepal, Tibetans felt uniquely privileged to be the guardians of the entire corpus of their religion, probably the richest collection of religious literature in the world (Pema 1997). Maintenance of these texts thereafter became a priority.

The Tibetans had assembled a canon with an extraordinary range of teachings. They had the full scope of *sutras, tantras,* their accompanying liturgy, and, most critically, the guru-disciple lineages founded on oral transmission, which served as an unbroken link to the origin of the oldest of the three world faiths (Avedon 1997). They possessed 108 volumes of discourses called the *Kangyur* or "translation of the word," and a further 227 volumes of Indian commentaries on those discourses, called the *"Tengyur."* Four to five thousand pages long, these scriptures were printed on tough, fibrous paper, placed between wooden covers, and wrapped in cloth. Chapels routinely contained shelves of texts that were worshipped as reverently as other holy objects. It was a very poor Tibetan temple indeed that did not possess an 18-volume set of the "Perfection of Wisdom" texts (Batchelor 1987). *Stupas* might contain scriptures as well as religious relics; the white *stupas* at Drepung Monastery contained 100,000 verses (Batchelor 1987). While few villagers could read them, sacred texts were often carried in a yearly procession around the village in order to ensure a good harvest (Snellgrove and Richardson 1986). Tibetans cherished their books and considered it a sin to place anything upon a book or even step over one and books were reverently stored in high places within any Tibetan abode (Alterman, Alterman, and Gewissler 1987). Many homes had a few religious books, kept respectfully by the shrine and sometimes read to their owners by mendicant monks (Snellgrove and Richardson 1986). For the wealthy, having a private library of sacred Buddhist books was considered an act of merit; for those who were well educated, it was also an indispensable aid to spiritual practice (Aldridge 1999b).

The Tibetan literati absorbed the construction and styles of Indian works and also developed their own linguistic materials to produce a highly complex religious and philosophical vocabulary (Snellgrove and Richardson 1986). After the initial translations were complete, Tibetan lamas began to compose commentaries and dissertations, and every important lama authored his own *"Sungbu"* (collected works), often ten to twenty volumes, exploring the meaning of Buddhist doctrine, philosophy, and logic as well as secular subjects (Batchelor 1987). Second only to the Dalai Lama in power was the Panchen Lama, or "precious scholar," most of whom were prolific writers (Snellgrove and Richardson 1986). Monasteries were known for their associations with famous scholars. For example, Samding Monastery was associated with the eminent poet and scholar Lama Bodong Chokle Namgyel (1306–1386), the author of a hundred volumes of religious writings. Many texts were originally composed as notes taken during lectures by famous teachers, and sometimes these texts were of inestimable value because of interlinear notes that were incorporated during study (Aldridge 1999b). The reputation of a distinguished scholar and possession of his texts and others conferred distinction upon a monastery or religious group or school.

Some lamas became known as "text-discoverers" or "revealers of treasure" because they produced compilations of rediscovered texts that had been hidden during political upheavals in the ninth century; these texts glorify the achievement of ancient kings. While some texts may indeed have been hidden and retrieved, some may have been composed for the legitimacy conferred by an ancient provenance. Real or quasi-rediscovered texts allowed new groups of monks to produce "refurbished literary works with [the] sanctity of earlier traditions" and all served the same function: "the creation of a national sentiment whether in state affairs or in matters of religion" (Snellgrove and Richardson 1986, 154). Possession and study of unique texts was also important in differentiating various "schools" of Tibetan Buddhism. For example, the Precious Treasury of Hidden Texts, editions of 25 or more volumes, was important to the Nyingmapa and Kargyupa schools. The famous Fivefold Set of Scrolls, rediscovered in the 1300s, is perhaps the most famous example of this kind of text.

Before woodblock printing came to Tibet, books were copied by hand, like manuscripts in Western medieval monasteries. While rarely distributed, particularly fine copies continued to be made by hand as late as the twentieth century. Woodblock printing was introduced in the 1400s, about the time that Europeans adopted movable metal type printing presses. The Tibetans became so attached to block printing, an early and laborious method in which seven to ten pages were reproduced per block, that it was not until the mid-twentieth century that they developed interest in any other method (Snellgrove and Richardson 1986). Even after the advent of woodblock printing, the format of Tibetan books remained the same: Each is composed of paper strips, approximately 4 inches high by 20 inches wide, covered by beautifully carved oblong wooden planks, preserving the style of the Indian palm-leaf texts.

While monasteries of any size could print charms and prayer flags, large monasteries had printing shops with woodblock presses and rooms housing tens of thousands of blocks. According to data collected in 1957, the Great Monastery of Derge had a collection of more than half a million woodblocks that was systematically deposited in more than ten halls (Alterman, Alterman, and Gewissler 1987). The use of such blocks made possible printing on demand. The bigger monasteries produced complete editions of the general collection, the *Kangyur.* Collections of works on philosophy, spiritual practice, medicine, astrology and other topics unique to a particular school's curriculum would be printed at the principal monastery and copies distributed to branches (Aldridge 1999b). For example, Dzogchen Monastery printed a core collection of books that were sent out to 200 affiliated monasteries. In addition, books were made to order; the purchaser had to supply ink and paper, and the monks were paid for the work. Books were usually not resold. Religious merit was acquired by printers, copyists, and the persons commissioning (and then possessing) the work (Zwalf 1981). Status and reputation increased for monasteries and temples with holdings of important blocks and texts. For example, the Nartong Monastery, founded in 1153, was famous for its woodblocks of the entire Buddhist canon, the Nartong edition, carved between 1730 and 1741. The Vairocana Chapel of the Pelkor Chode Monastery was known for its extremely large scripture written in gold ink on black paper.

A ninth-century stone inscription expresses an early reverence for religious learning that became a permanent feature of Tibetan culture: "The kings, grandsons and sons, from the time of their earliest age onwards, and even after they have assumed authority, should appoint teachers of religion from among the ordained monks, and should absorb as much religion as they can learn" (Snellgrove and Richardson 1986, 38). A monastery was seen as a school as well as a religious institution (Hicks 1988), and large monastic universities served as centers for learning for intellectuals and students from all over Central Asia. Each had between 3,000 to 5,000 students and a rigorous curriculum for monks aged eighteen to forty-five. A large monastic university had at least two colleges (distinguished by type of study), each with its own administration, faculty, textbooks, and houses (where the monks lived during training). Teachers were accorded special veneration because Tibetan Buddhists believed that doctrine and scriptures were valueless without controlled transmission by one qualified to assess the psychology and aptitude of the student and guide him through a personalized program (Zwalf 1981).

There were several schools of Buddhism, the main being the Gelugpa or Yellow Hats. Sera Monastery, one of three great Gelugpa monasteries near Lhasa, had more than 5,000 fully ordained monks, novices, and workers. Some monks devoted their entire life to study and spiritual discipline while others were non-literate administrators: A monk might be a cook, a treasurer, a policeman, a scholar, a teacher, a servant (Hicks 1988). The hierarchical order began with novices and progressed through monk, accomplished master, reincarnation, and *rinpoche*. High standards of scholarship, acquired from Indian monastic universities, were maintained. The student's main emphasis was on devoting himself wholeheartedly to a spiritual teacher and learning by heart considerable quantities of sacred literature. Monk scholars became repositories of doctrine, able to reproduce from memory any text or quotation that served the immediate discussion. They were tested, by means of formal debate, for competence in five branches of literature. Scholars memorized and debated for up to 20 years before standing for their final exams in the Doctor of Divinity or *Geshe* degree.

"The great miracle of Tibetan civilization was the zeal and competence which they showed for Indian Buddhism in all its varied forms," write distinguished Tibetan scholars David Snellgrove and Hugh Richardson (1986, 236). This intense focus, however, may have resulted in the sacrifice of other kinds of development, including modern technology and promotion of official mechanisms by which Tibet could have established itself as a recognized sovereign nation-state. The two authors assert that the price for this intensity may have been paid in Tibet's loss of independence. The Tibetans were simply unprepared for the aggressive, imperialistic demands of the modern world.

THE CHINESE TAKE CONTROL, 1950–1966

As large as the continent of Europe, Tibet is situated between India, China, and Russia. This position made it attractive to colonial powers, especially the British, who attempted to dominate it in the late 1800s. The British incursions were alarming to the Chinese, who claimed that Tibet was within China's sphere of influence (and even part of their empire), despite the fact that Tibet had maintained an independent identity for over hundreds of years and had borrowed much more culturally from India than from China. In 1904 a Chinese army was sent to counter British claims, and, subsequently representatives of the Manchu dynasty ruled Tibet for seven years, until the dynasty fell in 1911. In the ensuing disruption, the Chinese were expelled, and the Dalai Lama reaffirmed Tibet's independence. Yuan Shah-kai, who assumed leadership of China's new republic, ignored Tibet's declaration of independence and reasserted China's interest in Tibet by launching Sun Yat-sen's idea of the "five races of China," which claimed most of the major border regions (including Tibet and Mongolia) as provinces of China (Avedon 1997). This belief was retained by subsequent Chinese leaders, both Nationalist and Communist. However, because of internal preoccupations, civil wars, and the Sino-Japanese War of 1937–1945, the Chinese did not act again upon this notion, and Tibet was able to spend several decades in relative tranquility.

By 1949 the Communists had built a formidable war machine. After taking control in China, they proceeded to assert China's dominion over its "provinces." One of the first tasks the Communist Party undertook was to extend the border of modern China into the Himalayas, and one year after their takeover in China, the People's Liberation Army (PLA) invaded

Tibet. Impetus came from the same intense nationalism that had inspired the idea of the five provinces and behind which the Communists and Nationalists had rallied to drive out the Japanese Imperial Army in 1945. The red banner of the People's Republic of China depicted five stars, one of which represented Tibet's membership in the "great Chinese family" and Radio Peking announced definitively, "Tibet is part of China's territory and no foreign aggression will be tolerated; the Tibetan people are an inseparable part of the Chinese people. Aggressors who do not recognize this fact will shatter their skulls against the fist of the People's Liberation Army" (Donnet 1994, 64). From the Chinese point of view, the Communist government was merely seeking the reestablishment of historically unequivocal rights that they had been unable to exercise for some time (Heberer 1991).

Official justification for invasion also was rooted in Marxist/Communist philosophy, which prompted the belief that the Tibetan people, as victims of a feudal regime, were urgently awaiting revolution and that the Chinese were helping to facilitate internal rebellion and also to protect Tibet against imperialist machinations. In the Chinese media and among Party members, the former Tibetan government was consistently depicted as feudal and cruel, led by monks who sucked the blood of the people. As late as 1987, Chinese President Li Xiannian, during an official visit to France, referred to pre-Communist Tibet as inhabited by savages, a medieval society of serfs crying for intervention (Donnet 1994). For the next fifty years, the Chinese would represent their annexation as the Marxist liberation of the serfs and their occupation as part of a continuous history of Tibetan development and progress toward modernity. This, of course, is the same logic that Western colonial powers used in justifying their rule as having a civilizing effect on the natives in their dominions (Shakya 1999).

To most Tibetans, the invasion and continuing presence of the Chinese was blatant imperialism, motivated by a desire for Tibetan territory and natural resources. After all, in Chinese, Tibet was known as Xizang, "the Western Treasure House." During the invasion and thereafter, there was little the Tibetans could do to resist or expel the Chinese. Because of Tibet's physical isolation and lack of international recognition (a function of ongoing isolationist policies), there was little protest from the international community, and even less after Tibetan officials, sequestered in Beijing and under duress, signed the Seventeen Point Agreement, making Chinese control official. Though the treaty guaranteed the continuity of the existing political and social fabric of Tibet and declared that the religious beliefs, customs and habits of the Tibetan people would be respected

(Wangyal 1984), Chinese leaders soon instituted Sinicization and social-ization policies that invalidated or ignored Tibetan claims to human rights such as political self-determination and religious and cultural freedom.

At first, the People's Liberation Army was on its best behavior. Rather than instituting summary executions, moderate Chinese leaders sought to persuade (primarily through bribery) the ruling class of Tibet, the "patri-otic upper strata" (Shakya 1999, 93), into serving as the vanguard of a "peaceful Revolution" (Norbu 1987, 125). The post-invasion situation sta-bilized and the Dalai Lama, who had fled in December 1950, returned to Lhasa in May 1951, a fact which, in itself, may have supported the slower, relatively incremental changes instituted in Central Tibet. In that region, the presence of the Dalai Lama, whom the Chinese did not want to com-pletely alienate, was a check on immoderate radicalization. However, in the outlying areas of Kham and Amdo, the Chinese quickly abandoned discretion and reforms gained momentum. By the mid-1950s, refugees began to arrive in Lhasa bearing tales of repression and violence.

China's newly claimed frontier regions had 55 identified ethnic minor-ities and 67 million people, which amounted to less than 6 percent of the overall population of the Communist motherland (Donnet 1994). Con-certed Sinicization efforts were required to head off the possibility of rebellion and secession, so the Chinese concentrated first on acculturating minorities in those areas closest to China. In Tibet, this meant the prov-inces of Amdo and Kham. The Chinese actually treated the minorities in these areas in much the same way that they were treating their own Han population—conducting political meetings designed to cultivate class con-sciousness, confiscating personal possessions, initiating processes of col-lectivization, and weeding out dissenters. The difference was that, in China, the Communists were accepted as the legitimate governing force; they had free reign and encountered little organized resistance. In Tibet the people's allegiance was to the Dalai Lama, and they rejected the Chi-nese initiatives as illegitimate. Also, the Chinese were hampered by their ignorance of the nature of Tibet's society, persistent prejudice, and indif-ference to Tibetan resentment (Grunfeld 1996).

The fiercely independent border-Tibetans saw Communist reforms first and foremost as an attack on their value systems, and in their resistance, they united around their Buddhist faith. Rebellious activities began as early as 1951 and continued sporadically. In 1955, Beijing hard-liners, impatient with the pace of reforms, told the PLA to intensify disarmament of the fiercely independent nomads and farmers. They were to incite class discord through mandatory public struggle sessions (*thamzing*) and push forward the total collectivization of property. As a first step in claiming the 40 percent of land held by the monasteries, the Chinese began to accuse the clergy of stealing from the people, calling the monks "Red Thieves" and the lamas "Yellow Bandits." As the border Tibetans realized that their whole way of life was under attack, resistance mounted, and full-scale guerilla warfare erupted in Kham by 1956. The Chinese responded ferociously, and Tibetans were massacred, crucified, dismembered, beheaded, buried alive, burned and scalded to death, dragged to death behind horses, and forced to kill and sexually assault each other. Whole villages were obliterated. The Chinese attacked the monasteries as centers of resistance—and, indeed, many were sheltering refugees. Some monasteries went into siege mode, preparing to withstand ground attacks, but the Chinese simply bombed them into oblivion from the air. During the 1956 festivities for the Tibetan New Year, when the monasteries were full of pilgrims, the Chinese bombed Batang's 350-year-old Chode Gaden Phendeling Monastery and killed 2,000 people; they also razed a famous monastery in Lithang, built in 1580, and killed 4,000 monks, men, women, and children (Kewley 1990). Tibetan casualties during this period were high, but the Chinese also lost 40,000 troops in two years.

Refugees from Kham flooded into Lhasa, where the situation became very tense. The climax came in 1959 when the Dalai Lama fled again to India and Tibetans took to the streets of the capital in a short but bloody uprising that left thousands dead. Tibetans were no match for the well-armed Chinese troops who hunted them down in the streets and buildings of Lhasa. Many monuments and sacred buildings were damaged and destroyed. Ramoche Cathedral, a hallowed temple, was shelled and burned, as was the Chakpori, an ancient monastic medical college. Records and sacred books were destroyed at the Potala, the Dalai Lama's home. Central Cathedral, the most sacred shrine and a refuge for 10,000 people, was also shelled. Mortars and heavy artillery were fired at close range into the crowds around the Dalai Lama's summer palace. Bodies were stacked in piles and doused with kerosene; the pyre burned for three days. In 1966, guerrillas captured a Chinese convoy and confiscated PLA records revealing that by China's own account some 87,000 Tibetans were killed in the 1959 revolt (Avedon 1997). At the time, information was suppressed, and Beijing portrayed the fighting as but a minor disturbance.

The Chinese were merciless in crushing the revolt. Martial law was enforced in many areas and campaigns were launched to establish incontestable control over the population. The "Three Cleanlinesses" campaign focused on the "cleaning up" of reactionaries, arms, and hidden enemies of the people. The main object was to flush out all survivors sympathetic to the revolt (Patt 1992). The first step was to destroy any leadership

through extensive purges of the religious hierarchy and Tibetan aristocracy, who were branded monsters and demons. These groups were accused
of "reactionary rebellion to separate Tibet from the Motherland" (Norbu
1987, 197)—high treason by Chinese standards. The entire Tibetan army
was arrested and deported to labor camps, along with hundreds of thousands of Tibetan civilians. It is estimated that one-tenth of all adult males
were imprisoned during this era. Few people returned from the 166 camps
alive; an estimated 173,000 died in the coal mines alone (Margolin 1999).
Many were used like slaves to build highways, serve as miners, or work
on large-scale projects such as hydroelectric plants. In the border areas
near China, especially large numbers were arrested and those who survived would be held in custody for twenty years. These arrests were instrumental in dealing with present and future dissent, in clearing areas for
Chinese occupancy, and in providing a large pool of disposable slave
labor.

The radicals in Beijing used the uprising as a rationale for abandoning
the conciliatory policies by which the moderates had hoped to win over
the population in Central Tibet. The hard-liners seized the opportunity to
institute "democratic reforms" and put Tibet on the "socialist road by
destroying reactionary forces"—the existing religious and secular elite
(Donnet 1994, 38). The people reeled as the Chinese gave them "shock
after shock, blow upon blow, with no time to recover" (Norbu 1987, 219).
The shift in attitude was expressed succinctly by one Chinese General:
"We do not care what the Tibetan people want. We can always draft in
enough soldiers to make them do what *we* want" (as quoted in Hicks 1988,
69). What the Chinese seemed to want was a compliant or enslaved population. If a Tibetan died, that was one less recalcitrant to worry about. In
the prisons, a rough process of selection for the most dangerous work
assignments or for punishment or execution made absolute conformity
essential. According to one prisoner, "Those who held on to their ideas,
their nationalist feelings, their sympathy for the Tibetan people, those who
did not readily submit to Chinese reeducation, they were sent to do the
most dangerous work. The intention was gradually to eliminate these people" (Patt 1992, 225). After decimating the leadership, the Chinese replaced the Dalai Lama's government, and Tibet was partitioned into
controllable administrative units. The Tibetan provinces of Amdo and
Kham were divided up among the four Chinese provinces of Yunnan,
Sichuan, Gansu and Qinghia in a move that gutted the demographic, economic, and political importance of Tibet (Donnet 1994). "Tibet" became
the central, 500,000-square-mile Tibet Autonomous Region (TAR) within
the People's Republic of China. The TAR was divided into 72 counties,

seven administrative districts, and one municipality (Lhasa). In Lhasa, martial law was harshly enforced and movement was severely restricted. The city was divided into three areas and the boundaries so strictly maintained that family members living one mile apart often had no knowledge of one another's condition for as long as twenty years (Avedon 1997).

Using many of the techniques that they had developed to transform China and the Tibetan frontier areas, the Chinese launched all-out economic, social, and political campaigns to fully integrate Central Tibet into the People's Republic of China. They targeted traditional social and economic structures, and the ties of family and religion as they instituted socialism as the prime force in all aspects of life. With the radicals in command, any acknowledgement of separate status for national minorities, including the Tibetans, became unacceptable. National minorities, like all people in the China motherland, were subject to the dictatorship of the proletariat (a proletariat 95 percent Han Chinese) and opposition to the Chinese Communist Party was considered a capital offense, as was opposition to being Chinese or part of China (Smith 1996). Patterns that would endure throughout the century were set: Tibetan opposition was either discounted as the residue of anti-feudal sentimentalism, which would eventually wither away, or interpreted as dissent, an indicator of a dangerous reactionary rebelliousness that must be extinguished (Shakya 1999).

The Chinese directed a tremendous amount of effort to the development of socialist consciousness. Socialist terminology and texts were translated into Tibetan, and authorities tried to impose ideological correctness and adherence to Chinese interpretations of history and current events. The Chinese tried to win over the Tibetan people at rallies and meetings in which the cadres initiated condemnation of the evils of *Chitsog Nyinpa* (the old society) (Shakya 1999) and railed against the former Tibetan government, aristocratic estate owners, and the monasteries. The population was divided into six classes (manorial lords, manorial representatives, rich, middle class, poor, and reactionaries) (Paljor 1977) and forced to participate in *thamzing* denunciations and confessions. If Tibetans resisted these processes, the sessions could culminate in torture and death. In one collection of survivors' tales, a Tibetan said that *thamzings* were particularly galling in that the Chinese facilitators repeatedly claimed to be serving the Tibetans' best interests while often exhibiting condescension and physical repulsion toward the Tibetan people. They addressed the Tibetans using the word *Latseng,* meaning "waste or garbage" (Patt 1992) and may have been influenced by centuries-old images of the Tibetans as primitive and dirty. Belief in the superiority of their culture was so deeply embedded in Chinese consciousness that a paternalism verging on racism permeated the actions of the government and its officials. Ironically, while China's claims to Tibet were bolstered by a philosophy that defined as erroneous the practice of basing political sovereignty on ethnic identity, being a Han was obviously far more desirable than being a Tibetan; everyone was to conform to Chinese customs and speak Chinese. As the Chinese instituted policies to civilize the "ignorant" Tibetans and transform them into socialists and Chinese citizens, the relationship between the Tibetan and Han (Chinese) people, historically "abysmal," became exacerbated (Grunfeld 1996, 126) and, on the part of the Hans, chauvinistic (Wangyal 1984).

Daily life became very hard for the Tibetans. Many had to turn in their possessions, ostensibly to be redistributed to the "people" when in fact the most valuable items were sent to China. The good furniture and rugs were reserved for Han civilian and military personnel, and watches and clothing were sold to Chinese office workers (Avedon 1997). Tibetans were urged to increase agricultural production and make economic progress, to eat less and produce more. Many policies seemed intent on keeping the people so busy that they did not have the time or energy to act on their own (Patt 1992). The movement of nomads was restricted; farmers were put in cooperatives and assigned production quotas. Many Tibetans had to work on mindless projects apparently designed to oppress and intimidate them. There was no privacy and no free time as Tibetans of all ages were forced to perform long hours of exhausting fieldwork, followed by compulsory daily political meetings.

This repressive period after the 1959 revolt coincided with the radicals' Great Leap Forward reforms in China and the famines that killed millions of people. The same misguided policies were applied in Tibet: forced collectivization, the successive planting of second and third crops, hastily conceived irrigation and planting schemes, and the construction of useless canals. This reorganization of farming practices and the domestication of the nomads, whose way of life was essential in preserving ecological balance, upset centuries-old patterns of indigenous farming and resource-management techniques, and set up cycles of severe rationing and recurrent hunger. The late 1950s and early 1960s brought the first famines in Tibet's 2,000-year history. Food consumption by Tibetans dropped by two-thirds. Thousands starved to death, including at least 50 percent of the Tibetans living in Qinghia (Amdo), the province where the Dalai Lama was born (Becker 1996). Hunger lasted throughout the 1960s. Just as they had done in China, the radicals concealed problems and grossly exaggerated food production figures in order to avoid any hint of criticism of socialist theories.

Economic transformation required the seizure of land held by the monasteries; social transformation required shattering the architecture of Buddhism. The Chinese used the 1959 revolt to justify launching campaigns that targeted the monasteries and took the form of "three antis": anti-rebellion, anti-feudal privilege, anti-feudal systems of exploitation and oppression (Grunfeld 1996). Monks and lamas were accused of supporting the rebellion, both actively (by feeding, housing, and colluding with the rebels) and passively (by performing religious rituals and harboring evil intentions) (Norbu 1987). Learned monks, teachers, reincarnate lamas and administrators were tortured and arrested. Entire monastic communities were sent to the coal mines or to penal colonies. Monasteries that had not been bombed earlier were emptied of both residents and artifacts. Beginning in 1959, the destruction and desecration of rural monasteries in the day was supplemented by the looting of religious treasures at night. Truck after truck carried the artifacts of Tibet back to Beijing, and the antique markets in Hong Kong and Tokyo eventually became flooded with Tibetan objects. Throughout the first half of the 1960s, a Chinese-staffed Cultural Articles Preservation Commission inventoried the contents of all temples, monasteries, shrines, and government buildings. Units of Chinese civilians, including mineralogists and metallurgists, identified objects composed of precious gems and metals, assigned grades of value, and made lists of objects to be sent to China. In 1959 the number of active monasteries dropped from 6,200 to 1,700; the number of active monks went from 110,000 monks to 56,000 (Grunfeld 1996). By 1966 only 550 monasteries were still active; the number of monks had dropped to 6,900. Those monks who were not imprisoned were often forced to do physical labor and were unable to devote time to spiritual practices. The dissolution of the economic power base of the monasteries (and then the monasteries themselves) became the most significant social and political event in the history of Tibet since the introduction of Buddhism (Shakya 1999).

Because they could blame it on the short-term anarchy of Red Guards or radical elements, Beijing Party leaders have encouraged the myth that the monasteries were primarily destroyed during the Cultural Revolution (1966–1977). In reality, some of the worst destruction occurred after the revolt in 1959 when ethnocide first became Party policy. Visitors to Tibet in the 1980s often found bits of sacred scripture lying derelict in the fields and streets and were regaled with stories of how the Chinese in the late 1950s and early 1960s had desecrated the monasteries and chapels. After first removing religious items that were valuable, the Chinese destroyed the rest as publicly as possible. Wherever possible, Tibetans were forced to participate. The Chinese forced Tibetans to burn or shred sacred scriptures, mix them with manure, or lay them on the ground and walk on them. Tibetans had to break up the *mani* stones and use them to build toilets. Forcing the Tibetans themselves to desecrate the monasteries and religious objects was part of generalized campaigns to reduce resistance and identification with Tibetan culture. Because of their belief in reincarnation and the sanctity of life, Tibetans were forced to kill flies and other insects (the children, in particular, were assigned quotas and forced to turn in the bodies). Dogs, beloved by the Tibetans, were declared parasites on the economy and a hygienic risk and were stoned to death.

The practice of religion for any Tibetan became increasingly difficult as socialist reconstruction progressed. All religious festivals were banned and denounced as wasteful and indulgent (Batchelor 1987). Pilgrims were denied food rations for the duration of pilgrimages and were frequently subjected to *thamzing* on return (Hicks 1988). Religious people were ridiculed and humiliated and religious texts and objects were publicly destroyed and desecrated as the Chinese worked to reduce Buddhism to a much less central position in Tibetan life and society from which it could be shaken loose.

THE CULTURAL REVOLUTION, 1966–1976

In the years that followed, the Party repeatedly misinterpreted the Tibetans' fundamental rejection of Chinese rule for discontent with certain unpopular policies, and there was a persistent belief that all would be resolved with a new policy (Smith 1996). But instead, cycles of revolt, repression, and liberalization became self-perpetuating. As in China, policies concerning transformation to socialism varied with the ebb and flow of ideological extremism in the Communist Party in Beijing. When Mao and other hard-liners or radicals were in power, they emphasized socialist indoctrination and forced radical economic and social change: They pushed people into communes and initiated campaigns that incorporated high levels of violence and frequently caused disastrous economic problems. When the Party moderates were in power, change was approached incrementally, with more emphasis on economic growth and technological development. Every twist and turn of policy in China was reflected in the situation in Tibet. There, disagreement over the pace and means of social transformation was evident in the appearance and disappearance of "minority policies"—the moderates' vision of assimilation as a "knitting together" of nationalities with their "elder Han brother" (Avedon 1997, 224). The radicals, on the other hand, held that ethnic identity, as a product of bourgeois mentality, must be eradicated through forced assimilation.

In 1961 Party moderates began pulling China back from the disaster caused by the Great Leap Forward, but there was a lag time between the switch to more moderate policies in Beijing and their implementation in Tibet. Tibet's famine was prolonged. The moderates had just begun to promote relative liberalization as a solution to problems (and lingering hunger) in Tibet, when another radical push began within the Chinese Communist Party. In late 1964, an article appeared in the *Peking Review* stating that reactionary culture was a tool used by foreign and internal class enemies to poison the national minorities, undermine national unity, and sabotage the socialist revolution (Smith 1996). Therefore, an intensified program for the national minorities (Tibetans included) was necessary.

Soon it was apparent that the radicals, led by Mao, were poised for an all-out, no-holds barred battle to revolutionize China and all its territories. The new campaigns had two facets: the destruction of anything "old" (old ideology, culture, habits, customs) to make way for the "new" (Mao's new ideology, proletarian culture, Communist habits and customs), and the purging of moderate Party members and officials and all who had slowed the revolution. Minority cultures were regarded as a particular obstacle to propagation of Mao's thought. The simple fact that minorities in the border regions had a separate language and culture was considered reactionary (Avedon 1997). Communist administrators in minority areas were, to Party radicals, obviously reactionary because they had allowed any form of traditional cultural practices to continue. The stage was set for not only the deliberate destruction of Tibetan culture, but also collateral damage from a chaotic and violent power struggle between radicals, including Red Guards imported from China, and the local bureaucrats (relatively moderate) who were trying to maintain power.

During the first half of the Cultural Revolution, Chinese Party factions began fighting for control of the streets and major buildings of Tibet. The Tibetans were drawn into the conflicts, usually supporting the moderates, the Opposition Factions, who opposed wanton destruction. The army was eventually used to quell this quasi-civil war between factions. In 1969, a grass-roots revolt by the Tibetan people was also violently stifled by the troops. In the subsequent crackdown, "reforms" were instituted on a scale far surpassing (in both scope and inclusiveness) that of the past. Overall campaigns to revolutionize society were conducted much more vigorously in Tibet than in China proper. In 1970, 34 percent of the villages were organized in communes; in 1971, 60 percent; and by 1975, 2,000 communes existed and the whole of Tibet's rural population was locked into drudgery and political indoctrination (Shakya 1999).

In their effort to destroy traditional society, Maoists stepped up practices of fragmenting the population into manageable units for purposes of labor, indoctrination, and surveillance (Norbu 1997). Everyone registered for food and was assigned work points; everyone was organized into work units, which also functioned as centers for indoctrination. Access to food was linked to productivity and conformity, which were enforced by vicious *thamzing* sessions. The elderly and invalids who could not work received little or no rations and starved to death (Norbu 1987). The general per capita income was so low ($60 per year) that Tibet became the poorest nation on earth (Avedon 1997). The remnants of the former ruling elite— even those who had supported the Chinese—and intellectuals, defined in Tibet as anyone who was literate and therefore a member of the oppressive bourgeois class, were labeled *shamo nakpo,* "black hats," and either executed by a shot in the back of the head and sent to prison or labor camps (Kewley 1990).

During the Cultural Revolution Maoism was imposed over every last vestige of Buddhist society. Generalized suppression of religion became methodical. Anyone caught practicing religious rituals was classed as "an agent of the serf-owners" and deprived of grain coupons. Buddhists in Tibet were subject to the same public humiliation and violence as intellectuals in China proper—they were paraded through the streets in dunce hats, tortured, and abused. All religious articles were confiscated or destroyed. Prayer flags were replaced by Mao banners; images of the Dalai Lama were replaced by portraits of Mao, which were also installed in every house. In Lhasa's Ramoche Temple, which was badly damaged by Red Guards, the Chinese set up a temple to Mao Tse-tung and the ancient altars were decked with enormous pictures and statues of Mao. Twenty-eight thousand copies of Mao's *Little Red Book,* translated into Tibetan, were distributed ostensibly "in response to Tibetans' requests to study Mao's works" (Smith 1996, 544). People meeting on the street were to greet each other with an exchange of Mao quotations. Tibetans were coerced into repeatedly demonstrating their transfer of emotional allegiance from the Buddha to Mao.

People were attacked in the streets for wearing traditional clothes and long hair; they were required to don black Mao outfits and cut their hair short—or have it hacked off in public. In June 1966, Tibetans were mobilized to kill all the rats and rodents. Flowerpots were smashed and traditional folk decorative elements on Tibetan houses painted over. Street names were changed to reflect revolutionary themes. Loudspeakers blared Chinese songs and Maoist speeches twelve to fifteen hours per day. Tibetan writing was replaced by an officially sanctioned Tibetan-

Chinese "friendship language" that many couldn't understand. Names were changed to Chinese equivalents, and there was a drive to give Chinese names to all newborn Tibetan babies (Margolin 1999). Overall, a climate of social and physical brutality reigned, and mob violence, rape (Paljor 1977), public execution, mutilation, and scalding became fairly commonplace.

Radio Lhasa had predicted as early as February 1965, "a protracted, complicated and even violent struggle" to overcome the influence of the old society (Grunfeld 1996, 183). In China, the instrument for enforcing the Cultural Revolution, for smashing Chinese traditional culture in a final battle for the revolution, was the Red Guard, an army of fanatical university and middle-school students. The students, raised in a repressive Communist society, believed wholeheartedly that destroying the past, especially religion, to make room for Mao's thinking, was a noble undertaking. Since Tibet lacked a similar disaffiliated school-age cohort, some 8,000 Chinese Red Guards were sent to Tibet. Believing that Tibet was a stronghold for archaic beliefs and customs, they sought to liberate Tibetans from their barbarous and feudal past. And like radical Party members, the students rejected the idea of gradual assimilation and building on current foundations; they sought to scrape away anything old and make Tibet a clean slate upon which the Maoists could write. The Cultural Revolution began in Tibet on August 25, 1966, when, after a rally, Red Guards invaded the Central Cathedral, smashed images, defaced frescoes, and destroyed the revered treasures of centuries of Buddhism. The damage was particularly devastating because the cathedral had become a warehouse for countless artifacts from neighboring monasteries and because it contained both civil and religious records. For five days, scriptures and documents were burned in the courtyards. Tibet's holiest shrine (similar to the Vatican in Rome) was dubbed Guest House No. 5, and pigs were kept in the yard.

The Red Guards smashed and burned righteously, their orgy of vandalism obscuring the fact that the destruction of Tibetan culture had been building for years. Party members in Beijing and local officials encouraged Red Guard activities because they served *ongoing* policies of ethnocide. With the onset of the Cultural Revolution, the trucks that had been operating at night throughout the early 1960s to convey artifacts from rural monasteries to Beijing could operate blatantly even in populated areas as a final push was made to "mine" Tibet's portable wealth. Red Guards supervised while gold and silver images were collected, sometimes mashed as scrap, and removed to Beijing for release on the antique market or to be melted down into bullion. The scale of looting is mind numbing.

By 1973 one Beijing foundry had melted down 600 tons of Tibetan sculptures; in 1983 a recovery mission from Lhasa found 32 tons of Tibetan relics in the Chinese capital, including more than 13,000 statues and statuettes. The Red Guards seemed well schooled in their functions and had access to inventories, compiled by Chinese experts, that detailed the relative value of objects in the monasteries. Valuable images and artifacts, sometimes particularly valuable libraries, often were neatly packed and carried away before remaining objects, frescos, and the buildings were dynamited, knocked down, burned, or defaced.

The Red Guards were encouraged to destroy artifacts not considered worth exporting to China. Observers have commented that, despite the chaos they caused, the Red Guards often seemed highly disciplined (Harrer 1985). Chou-Enlai, who was responsible for preserving the Forbidden Palace in Beijing, ordered the Red Guards to spare certain historic buildings in Tibet—the reason that parts of buildings within thirteen monasteries (out of an estimated 6,000 in 1950) survived not only the post-1959 revolt initiatives, but also the Cultural Revolution. Kunsang Paljor (1977, 52), a Communist-Tibetan journalist who was then working for the *Tibet Daily,* later commented on patterns of "well-planned destruction" in which Red Guards often were sent to handle tasks that the local Chinese authorities were unable to handle. There was "method in this apparently mindless destruction: what was economically valuable was carted away, and what was historically connected with Imperial China was saved" (Norbu 1997, 276); those that were witness against this connection were destroyed. The fact that there was a pattern according to which objects and sites received some degree of protection is an indicator that Communist fanaticism was somewhat tempered by Han nationalism. In the weeklong pillage and defilement of the seventh-century Central Cathedral in Lhasa, only two chapels out of several hundred were spared. All statues, sacred texts, and objects were carried off or broken up—except the statue of Cakyamuni, which had been brought to Tibet by a Chinese princess (Margolin 1999).

Except for the few constraints mentioned above, the Red Guards were encouraged to destroy all signs of Buddhism and traditional Tibetan culture. Statues and frescoes (the texts of the illiterate) and printed scriptures, religious articles in their own right, were favored targets. The Guards usually committed their desecrations publicly and violently, often in the streets and marketplaces; religious texts were burned in giant bonfires in front of the temples. The Chinese students proudly declared themselves "a group of lawless revolutionary rebels [that] will wield the iron sweepers and swing the mighty cudgels to sweep the old world into a mess and bash people into complete confusion. . . . To rebel, to rebel, and to rebel through to the end in order to create a brightly red new world of this proletariat!" (Grunfeld 1996, 183). The Guards tried to enlist local Tibetan youth, but except for some members of the Communist Youth League from three middle schools in Lhasa, they failed to muster significant local support. But because vandalizing and destroying religious structures was supposed to be a "politically and psychologically cathartic act" (Smith 1996, 544), Tibetans were forced at gunpoint to demolish their own monasteries. The Chinese sometimes posed these public demonstrations of sacrilege as celebratory ceremonies and flew red flags and played drums, trumpets, and cymbals.

The processes of cultural destruction involved a curious mixture of vindictiveness, desecration, frugality, and manipulation. The pillars and beams of monasteries were removed from religious structures for use in Chinese quarters, and the wood-hungry Tibetans were allowed to salvage construction materials. Eyewitnesses interviewed by John Avedon (1997) for his book *In Exile From the Land of Snows* describe giant bonfires of scriptures. They said that those not incinerated were used as wrapping in Chinese shops, or as padding in shoes; ornate wooden book covers were made into floorboards, chairs, and tools. Another chronicler wrote of huge loads of scriptures that were brought into a prison and piled up; prisoners had to tear them into little pieces, dump the shredded pages into a drum of water, add mud, and thus prepare a mixture for use in plastering houses (Patt 1992). Clay images were ground up for use in streets, mixed with fertilizer, or made into bricks for use in public bathrooms. "The intention was not only to desecrate, but also to humiliate; to identify religion with the lowly and the vile. Predictably, holy Dharma texts were converted into toilet paper" (Donnet 1994, 82).

Eventually, most of the gutted monasteries were dynamited or shelled into rubble. "In a matter of months, there was nothing left but collapsed roofs, shattered walls, crumbled metal, crushed stones and shapeless, unrecognizable ruins . . . : inanimate ghost towns" (Donnet 1994, 82). The percentage of devastated monasteries grew to 99 percent. In most cases, the destruction involved the loss of written heritage. One scholar has declared that 60 percent of Tibet's philosophical, historical, and biographical literature had been burned (Rummel 1991). The ancient monastery of Bedroya Drofan Tana Noe-tsar Rigje Ling, with its historic and world-famous school of Tibetan medicine, was destroyed along with its records; a military prison and transmitter was built on the site (Kewley 1990). At the huge Sera Monastery, 95 percent of the statues and texts were destroyed along with 500-year-old frescoes; the rooms were then used for grain storage, stables, and prisons. A journalist in the 1980s recorded the comments of a monk surviving the destruction of the Dokhang Th'e Gelma monastery:

> More important than the building, which was indeed old, were the most beautiful scriptures painted in gold and silver on palm leaves. They were very ancient. Very special. But the Chinese came and tore them from the shelves they had lain on for hundreds of years and threw them on the fire they made in the middle of the temple. When some monks pleaded with the soldiers saying "Please don't. They are very old and mean everything to us," the Chinese pushed them to the floor and said, "Rubbish, religion is bourgeois poison!" They proceeded to pour kerosene on the priceless scriptures and then put a match to them as though they were useless refuse. "Now how," he asked me gently, "can we replace that?" (Kewley 1990, 208).

All over Tibet, printing presses and texts were broken up, burned, desecrated, and turned into waste. The ancient state printing house located below the Potala, known for producing magnificent large sacred books, was destroyed (Harrer 1985). Dzogchen Monastery along with its substantial printing press, wooden blocks, and library, was burnt to the ground (Aldridge 1999b). Also destroyed was Zhalu Monastery, renowned as the home of the brilliant scholar-abbot Buton Rinchen Drup, who had brought Tibetan Buddhism to full maturity by collecting and classifying all the texts of the *Tengyur*. His 227 hand-written tomes were burned, along with his pen and the hand-written originals of his collected works. According to Roger Hicks, it was not merely

> a question of destruction of religion: the losses to scholarship were also incalculable, because no more than a dozen copies of even a recent book might exist, while some libraries held thousand-year-old manuscripts copied from originals that no longer exist in India. It is not unrealistic to compare Chinese destruction of centres of learning in Tibet with the destruction of the library of Alexandria in AD 640; by comparison, the book-burning of the Inquisition or of the Nazis was the work of uncoordinated amateurs. (Hicks 1988, 78–79)

An estimated 85 percent of the nation's written materials and documents were destroyed (60 percent of its literature as mentioned earlier). Some were ancient, coming from the eighth century and written on palm leaves. But some were not even religious. Years after, Tibetans still had trouble understanding and accepting the losses and conveying this to Westerners.

One mused to a Western visitor: "Many were the documents of simple families recording details of their personal history, their births, their death, their marriages. Details of their land. . . . What possible use was their destruction to the Chinese? It was as though all your culture's old manuscripts written on parchment and with painted pictures in the margins, Gutenberg bibles and Domesday books were burned. That's what happened in Tibet" (Kewley 1990, 104).

TIBET AFTER THE CULTURAL REVOLUTION, 1976–2000

After Mao's death in 1976, control was again in the hands of Party moderates. The Communist Chinese Party (CCP) leadership acknowledged that "errors" had been made in Tibet during the Cultural Revolution, but dismissed the era as an aberration from normal practice and blamed the ultra-radical Gang of Four and the Red Guards. Without exception, all of China's official publications stated that Tibet did not suffer any more than the rest of China and that the Cultural Revolution in Tibet was not a case of one nationality pitted against another but a campaign by counter-revolutionary groups against the people of all nationalities (Donnet 1994). Since Tibet was under military rule and sealed off from the world, few voices contradicted the Party line.

The moderates engineered a shift from rigid Maoist orthodoxy to a more flexible and pragmatic plan to win over the minorities—similar to earlier policies of natural acculturation—and a relatively relaxed period ensued from the late 1970s until 1987. Officials pulled back from enforcing class struggle; they disbanded communes, cut back on taxes, and allowed a certain degree of religious freedom and cultural revival. Tibetans were given modest funds to repair the most important cultural sites, and some historic and religious artifacts were returned from China. A gradual return to relative normalcy occurred.

Tibetan studies advanced as a scholarly subject in China. In a subtle way, the Chinese literature on Tibet continued earlier, more blatant campaigns that the Chinese had maintained since their takeover. In the 1960s they had set up a Museum of the Tibetan Revolution across from the Potala, and there presented dioramas of fabricated feudal atrocities and scenes from "the glorious uprising in 1950," thus trying to pose their invasion as an effort to support a local revolution. Torture instruments and bones and skin taken from the corpses of "assassinated serfs" were displayed to illustrate a society the Chinese typified as brutal and medieval; treasures from the Potala were exhibited as proof of the decadence of the

Dalai Lama and the religious establishment. Whether from a political need to legitimize their invasion as "liberation" and to divert attention from current conditions, or from a psychological need to demonize Tibetan society in order to justify its destruction—or from both, the Chinese continually characterized the old Tibet as a lurid hell on earth. The fabricated and garish displays were used to promote the Chinese as liberators and to support a "correct" interpretation of history: that Tibet always had been part of China. The control of all media and destruction of Buddhist sites and texts from the late 1950s through the mid-1970s were part of a process of eradicating any materials that contradicted Communist hegemony. After the Cultural Revolution, the Museum was quietly removed and China implemented more mainstream techniques for establishing and disseminating claims to sovereignty over Tibet. The Communist-oriented Tibetan-studies initiative existed, in part, to contradict a huge publishing campaign launched by the Government of Tibet in Exile. The Chinese published or reprinted many books on Tibet—*A Catalogue of Chinese Publication in Tibet Studies (1992–1995)* listed 700 books (most printed in Western book style, not Tibetan) dealing with philosophy, religion, politics, law, history, archeology, geography, astronomy, art, and so on (Aldridge 1999a). These books were mostly for Chinese readers or for foreign tourists allowed into Tibet in the 1980s and 1990s. In a sense, the books, and China's Institute of Tibetology, acknowledged that Tibet had had a culture of some dignity, but undermined any claims to independent identity.

Some politically correct and literate Tibetans were able to write and publish texts approved by the Party, and reprints were made of some of the ancient manuscripts banned and destroyed during the Cultural Revolution. Dictionaries, grammars, word lists, and other works that had been started during the conciliatory period in the 1950s and miraculously saved from destruction in the Cultural Revolution began to be published (Aldridge 1999b). Some libraries that had been hauled away in convoys from major monastic centers, and thus saved, were taken out of storage, catalogued, indexed, and microfilmed (Aldridge 1999b). Tibetans themselves came up with funding to print a few books in the traditional style (Aldridge 1999a). The Gye-Me (the Lower Tantric College), which had been completely desecrated during the Cultural Revolution and turned into housing, was reopened in 1985 with 35 monks who began some woodblock printing of the *Tengyur.* Books began to reappear, and various surviving religious texts could be seen in some of the chapels and public buildings. The Chinese returned a superb edition of the *Kangyur,* taken from Tara Chapel in 1959; the fifth Dalai Lama had commissioned the 114-volume set, bound in sandalwood with ivory ends and written in gold ink. A new medical center in Lhasa opened in 1980 and had shelves with the complete *Kangyur* and *Tengyur* and a collection of the principal medical treatises of Tibet (Batchelor 1987).

Little systematic collection work has been done on compiling a comprehensive bibliography of indigenous Tibetan books. Cate Hutton (1997), an American Library Association fellow assigned to Tibet for nine months in 1993 and 1994, reported that Lhasa was one of only a few regional capitals in China without a functioning institution equivalent to a state library. Hutton learned of several magnificent but uncataloged collections of old and rare books. A trip to Sakya Monastery revealed, in the beam of a flashlight, an approximately 60-foot high mound of books visible through the dust and obviously untouched for years. Significantly, the pile was draped with the "white, silky offering scarves called '*kha-ta*' that are often used to indicate respect for sacred objects" (Hutton 1997, 31). Little is known about what other books may be warehoused in surviving monasteries, but reports sometimes surface of "Tibetan books [that have been] ignored, sometimes forgotten about or hidden away . . ." (Aldridge 1999b); inquiries by both Chinese and Western scholars are met with distrust. The existence of a private library within a home, composed of books hidden during times of repression, is still rarely acknowledged. Efforts to identify, catalogue, reprint, and preserve Tibetan texts often flounder on the fear of the caretakers and owners, and with good reason. In 1997 the Communists initiated a campaign against the Dalai Lama and sent teams of officials to even the most remote monasteries and nunneries to expunge references to the Dalai Lama from Buddhist texts. Again, books and archives were destroyed (Craig 1999).

The religious freedom granted Tibetans was but a facade of the Buddhist faith, and on the whole, the Communists tended to trivialize Buddhism. The people were allowed to resume practices such as making prostrations, circumambulating places of worship, burning incense, and turning prayer wheels, but the propagation of Buddhist teachings was either banned or severely controlled. In 1987 the exiled Dalai Lama made this statement: "The so-called religious freedom in Tibet today amounts to permitting our people to worship and practice religion in a merely ritualistic and devotional way. There are both direct and indirect restrictions on the teaching and study of Buddhist philosophy. Buddhism, thus, is being reduced to blind faith which is exactly how the Communist Chinese view and define religion" (as quoted in Government of Tibet in Exile 1999, 5). Also restricted were the activities of the fewer than 7,000 monks and nuns who survived the Cultural Revolution. Only a small number of monks were permitted to occupy the shattered monasteries, even the ten designated as historical sites that had been allowed to escape with some intact buildings: Sera formerly had 7,997 monks, but now was allowed only 300; Drepung had had 10,000 and now had 400 (Government of Tibet in Exile 1999). Few resources were provided to allow monasteries to function as educational and learning centers. Instead, they are marginally supported as historical sites and cultural museums—attractions for the controlled tourism that the Chinese allowed in the 1980s. Monks were instructed to collect fees and to charge for posing for photographs. Their daily routines served as the religious equivalent of living-history performances. Even in the shells of the great monastic universities, the monks functioned not as intellectuals and teachers, but as caretakers and exhibits. In any event, continuation of the intense teacher-learner process of Buddhism was impossible given the lack of resources, constraints on the monks, and the fact that the new acolytes were only allowed to be admitted to monasteries if they convinced the authorities that they were politically correct, "upright, patriotic young people . . . who have reached a certain level of cultural development" (Government of Tibet in Exile 1999, 6). They had to be willing to accept the leadership of the Party and government, support socialism, and safeguard national and ethnic unity.

While Tibetan culture experienced a degree of revival, the people began to see an acceleration of China's neo- or liberation-colonialism. In the interests of industrializing and meeting the needs of their huge mainland population, China was rapidly stripping Tibet of its natural resources. Clear-cutting of Tibet's forests provided China with $54 billion worth of lumber between 1959 and 1985, and cost Tibet fully one-half of its ancient forests. Deforestation led to erosion and siltation of major rivers. Converting marginal lands to agriculture led to desertification. Gashes appeared in the mountains as ore was extracted by the tons. Sheep and yak, mainstays of rural society, were killed for export to various Arab countries (Pema 1997) and wild animals, for centuries protected by religious laws, were slaughtered for the hides and meat or for the amusement of Chinese hunters. Animals including the Himalayan blue bear, the snow leopard, the Himalayan monkey, gazelles, and wild asses were hunted almost to extinction.

To add insult to injury, Tibetans often have been used as slave labor on dangerous highway, railway, hydroelectric, and mining projects that provided the infrastructure for extracting resources for use by the Chinese, rarely by Tibetans. They certainly had no control over their land as Tibet was turned into "merely a piece of punctuation at the end of a long, complicated Han Chinese sentence of environmental catastrophe" (Schell 1991, 203). Millions of Chinese settlers poured in and were given preferential treatment across the board—employment, housing, medicine, and education. Chinese, who controlled commerce as well as everything else, ran most businesses. Lhasa was overwhelmed with ugly, new concrete buildings reserved for the Chinese, while Tibetan historic areas were leveled. Economically, Tibet became a Third World region within a Third World country (Kewley 1990) and Tibetans, the "last of the least" (Donnet 1994, 147).

After the horrors of the first twenty years under Communist rule, even small improvements were welcomed, but Tibetans continued on a long slide into marginalization under an emerging system of apartheid (Ennals 1991). Schools were provided for the Chinese children, but any education provided to Tibetan students was conducted in Chinese in substandard schools and with poorly trained teachers who denigrated Tibetan culture. The illiteracy rate for Tibet was as high as 80 percent. In a 1988 document, the Chinese government admitted that 50 percent of Tibetan children did not attend school, but in many areas that figure was grossly inflated; in Qinghai only 11.2 percent went (Donnet 1994). Under Chinese law, Tibetans were forbidden to listen to any foreign-language broadcasts or read foreign newspapers, magazines, or books. In the 1980s, one Tibetan lamented: "It's not only censorship, it's more: it's China's deliberate policy to keep our people ignorant—not only about our rights, but about the outside world. . . . Most of us have never even seen a map. The Chinese are trying to turn us into living vegetables. Much easier to manipulate an entire population that way" (Kewley 1990, 193). Tibetans who could read were restricted to the Tibet version of the "China Daily" and texts produced by the Chinese. Discussing the propensity for the Communists to suppress information damaging to their image and ideology, Adrian Abbotts, a Buddhist scholar and the author of *Naked Spirits: A Journey into Occupied Tibet,* raised this question: ". . . What is Truth? It always seemed to me quite a good question really. The subjectivity required for its construction makes it very easy to manipulate, when you control the information" (Abbotts 1997, 14). The legitimacy of China's claim to Tibet rested on the twin pillars of military occupation and the imposition of a rigid control over the media and cultural and political apparatuses. In regard to libraries, Hutton, the American Library Fellow who visited for nine months in 1993–4, summed it up: "most Tibetans [she met] had never heard the word 'library,' much less visited one" (Hutton 1997, 31).

By the mid-1980s, most of the salient features of colonial domination were present: forcible occupation and the use of armed force to crush resistance; exploitation of natural resources; discrimination based on racial, linguistic, and cultural differences; deprivation of legal rights, including due process, human rights, freedom of religion, speech, and assembly, and freedom from arbitrary arrest; exclusion of indigenous peoples from government except in nominal positions; disproportionate standards of life distinguishing colonizers from colonized; and population transfer to reduce Tibetans to an insignificant minority in their own land (Bohana 1991). "Tibet has been made into a colony, not just in the legal and political sense, but in the tradition of the colonial lords of the dim past. Colonialism is not always the same, but the worst form is that which justifies its acts with the development of the subjugated country" (Van Walt Van Praag 1991, 62).

Disagreements between Party moderates and hard-liners continued to cause shifts in policy in Tibet, but while the factions disagreed over the pace and intensity of socialist transformation, both groups always maintained that China's occupation was a "liberation" and its initiatives carried out in the interest of the Tibetans. Certainly, Party members never criticized the regime as a whole. Thus, an incident in 1980 rocked the leadership. Hu Yaobang, the Chinese Communist Party General Secretary, went on a fact-finding tour of Tibet and was shocked at the poverty and the dissolution of Tibet's economic self-sufficiency into complete dependence. In an amazing breach of Party solidarity, the Secretary, apparently overwhelmed at the poverty, misery, discrimination, and segregation between Hans and Tibetans, cried out in shame against a situation that he described as "colonialism pure and simple" (Margolin 1999, 546). Hu made a public self-criticism of himself and the Party and chastised local officials: "The Central Government has spent several billions in Tibet, how did you spend it? Did you throw it in the Tsangpo river? . . . . [O]ur Party has let the Tibetan people down. We feel very bad! The sole purpose of our Communist Party is to work for the happiness of people, to do good things for them. We have worked nearly thirty years, but the life of the Tibetan people has not been notably improved. Are we not to blame?" (as quoted in Donnet 1994, 97).

Hu and others brought about some reforms, but by 1987 their policies gave way to a new "leftist wind," manifested as an Anti-Bourgeois Liberalization Campaign. Hu was removed from his position and soon after died in disgrace. His criticisms of Chinese policies in Tibet were held up as an example of an "ideological laxity" that threatened political stability by opening the door to spiritual pollution by western capitalists and humanist ideologies (Smith 1996). Within China itself the massacre of protestors in Tiananmen Square on June 4, 1989, illustrated the government's determination to maintain control and reject critical analysis of Party policies. Rioting in Tibet in 1987, 1988, and 1989 received less publicity, but was also deadly. During three days of rioting in Lhasa in 1989, the Tibetans, led by monks and nuns, demonstrated a fusion of religious freedom with Tibetan nationalism and identity. The Chinese leaders in Tibet, who had been complacent about post-Cultural Revolution liberalization initiatives, including those fostered by Yaobang, seemed stunned by the explosive protests, and reacted aggressively, initiating martial law and radicalizing their policies. But the people simply were not prepared to accept officially defined limits to the new freedom of religion (Shakya 1999). The decade of relative liberalization had allowed Tibetans a breathing period, a time in which unresolved basic issues such as legitimacy could revive (Norbu 1997), and the demonstrations continued throughout the 1990s.

With the relative relaxation in the post-Cultural Revolution era and the opening of Tibet to limited tourism in 1982, the Chinese monopoly on information was broken. Tibetans learned for the first time that refugees under the leadership of the Dalai Lama had developed the thriving Government of Tibet in Exile in Dharamsala, India, and were promoting the interests of Tibetan human rights worldwide. Besides creating a political structure for a Tibetan nation, this community was preserving and modernizing Tibetan culture. Knowledge of the existence of a Tibet governed by the Dalai Lama gave hope and purpose to indigenous rebellions against the Chinese and fanned an independence movement. Although fueled by resentment over the miserable plight of Tibet after forty years of occupation, the inspiration for Tibetan resistance did seem to arise spontaneously from identification with the Dalai Lama, who was an enduring symbol of Tibetan religion, civilization, and cultural sovereignty. Certainly, the Chinese blamed the ongoing unrest on his influence; in 1995, they passed sweeping new restrictions on religious practices in which even possession of a photo of the Dalai Lama became illegal (Abbotts 1997). In 1996, armed searches of private homes led to more riots. The participation of monks in strikes caused the monasteries to be sealed off by troops, and the Famous Ganden Monastery was completely closed after a shooting occurred. China announced the implementation of a fifteen-year plan to eradicate the Dalai Lama as a recognizable figure in Tibet. As late as fall 2000, American newspapers were reporting that Chinese troops were still raiding homes in search of religious articles.

TIBETAN CULTURE IN EXILE

Indeed, something remarkable had occurred in India. When 100,000 people poured out of Tibet, most of them between 1959 and 1963, many died on the perilous trip out and from disease and hunger during the first years. Survivors worked on road gangs in India, where conditions were brutal and, often, fatal. However, the Dalai Lama mobilized support and created a simple but viable community in Dharamsala where attention eventually turned from physical survival to cultural reconstruction. The Dalai Lama discarded archaic ceremonial traditions and focused on keeping alive key cultural activities: the performing arts, literature, science, religion, and crafts that produced saleable items (Avedon 1997). Based on the belief that survival as a people depended on cultural vitality, a series of cultural institutes, each with the focus on both preservation of Tibetan identity and education for a purposeful future, were established: first the Tibetan Dance and Drama Society, then the Tibetan Medical Center, and, in 1971, the Library of Tibetan Works and Archives (LTWA), which sought to secure Tibet's written heritage.

Many refugees had dragged religious artifacts over the Himalayas with them and, because the written and spoken word of the Buddha is the core of all Buddhist culture, entire libraries were brought out of Tibet (Aldridge 1999b). These books were gathered together, and the road camps were scoured for scriptures. Because of the critical role of the teacher in Buddhist learning and traditions of memorizing texts, a search was also made for scholars, and they were removed from deadly work conditions. Of Tibet's 600,000 monks, only 7,000 made it into exile along with only a few hundred of the 4,000 incarnate lamas. Preserving the scholars within this group was essential because many could be considered as living texts; for every scholar who died building roads, centuries of learning were lost (Avedon 1997).

Along with gathering resources and protecting scholars, book production was begun and the Tibetans began lithographing more than 200 major works with stone and ink. Beginning in 1962 and continuing for two decades, a United States' Library of Congress program in India reprinted 2,800 Tibetan classics that represented thirteen centuries of Tibetan literature. The Tibetans adapted the typewriter and modern typesetting processes, but Tibetan orthography presented problems. The development of computers and, in the 1990s, TTPS, a Tibetan "desktop publishing system," would ultimately offer the potential for easier storage and retrieval and make possible the printing on demand once offered by woodblocks (Alterman, Alterman, and Gewissler 1987).

By the year 2000, the collection of the LTWA had grown to 80,000 manuscripts, books, and documents (Government of Tibet in Exile 2000), including the estimated 40 percent of Tibet's literature that was saved (Avedon 1997). The library also contains 6,000 photographs; several thousand legal and social documents in Tibetan, some dating as far back as the tenth century; and 15,000 hours of taped interviews with senior Tibetans. Both scholars and the general public are granted access to the collection, which supports the education of new generations, the collection and preservation of Tibetan texts and manuscripts, and initiatives to disseminate information about Tibet through international information networks set up by the Government of Tibet in Exile. These networks provide basic information for monographs and articles that expose Chinese actions as ethnocide and genocide and enlist international support for Tibetan rights.

In 1959, 1961, and 1965, the International Commission of Jurists' reports had condemned China for perpetrating genocide in Tibet, and in 1961 and 1965 the United Nations recognized and reaffirmed the right of the Tibetans to self-determination. However, Tibet was not a popular issue globally in either the 1960s or 1970s. It was not until 1980, when the Dalai Lama began to travel the world lobbying for human rights in Tibet, that the situation reached the international public. His intellect and moral force earned him a Nobel Peace Prize in 1989. Books, articles, and documentaries publicizing the plight of Tibetans and their right to cultural sovereignty were also highly effective in turning public opinion against China by the 1990s.

CONCLUSIONS

When China took over Tibet, it was faced with a society in which religion was practiced with intensity comparable to that of Communism itself. When applied with all the explicitness, systematization, and urgency of political ideology, religion indeed becomes ideology—that is, a belief system based on a transforming idea and organized into behavioral regulations. Many of the great revolutions in history have been driven by religion. And all modern ideologies, including Communism, have had to deal with displacing religion and traditional forms of ethics as the organizing forces behind social, cultural, and political behavior. Indeed, after the 1950 annexation, Party officials declared that Communism and religion could not coexist. Mao himself said, "To be sure religion is a poison. It has two big faults: it attacks race and the country's progress is held up. Tibet and Mongolia were both poisoned by religion" (As quoted in Pema 1997, 165). From the beginning of occupation on, the Chinese believed that their ideology was indisputably transcendent and superior and saw the Buddhism of Tibet as a form of primitive, reactionary, and oppressive blind faith that could and should be replaced. After all, they were rooting out alternative ethical and moral value systems in China itself, casting aside their own past and traditions as so much detritus. But in China, the government was sponsoring a revolution (ostensibly as arising from the people) in a country shattered by almost a century of political violence and turmoil; what success they had was a function of the exhaustion of the people and, in some cases, the desire for radical change. In Tibet, the Communists underestimated the society's homogeneity and cultural attachment to Buddhism; the Tibetans were much more than an ethnic group, and Tibet was not so much a political entity, as it was a civilization that had evolved over time into a whole. The Tibetans had not experienced the societal trauma that made groups open to political and social change, and thus the Chinese were attempting to bring a revolution to an immensely stable, integrated society that was devoted to a worldview that clashed utterly with that of the Chinese.

To the Chinese, economics were the root cause of life's misfortunes, and the corrupt feudal society of Tibet had to be transformed by the socialist redistribution of wealth. In contrast, the Tibetans, as Buddhists, felt that economic solutions and constructions were irrelevant, as earthly existence was by nature unsatisfactory (Avedon 1991). Committed to the pursuit of enlightenment, Tibetans believed that struggle over material things could never bring liberation because "in the end they leave the human heart untouched, alienated and confused" (Patt 1992, 35). Scientific and economic theories might offer ways to manage the material world, but could not substitute for knowledge of the transcendent. Further, Buddhism was the source of Tibetans' greatest pride: Their development of Buddhism and preservation and advancement of the canon was the gift they offered to the "mental civilization" of the world (Library of Tibetan Works and Archives 2000, 1). Deadlock was inevitable.

In an ironic revelation of the flaws of their ideology, which explicitly abhorred imperialism, the Chinese Communists emerged as colonialists *par excellence.* With socialist liberation as a rationalization, they zealously practiced the politics of communism *and* nationalism, militarism, and racism—ideologies that clashed in Tibet with a belief system of equal strength. The Chinese government's commitment to the Sinicization of Tibet was a commitment to the destruction of everything that distinguished Tibetans from the Chinese, everything that made them unique. Perhaps because the Chinese found the chasm between their notions of religion, culture, language, history, and political ethos and that of the Tibetans entirely unbridgeable, Sinicization became a program of forced extinction—the only way to "liberate" Tibet being to destroy it (Patt 1992). Certainly the violent and cumulative implementation of their policies brought them to genocide. A pattern emerges when one compares the fate of Tibetans with other religious groups. Phuntsog Wangyal (1984) has pointed out an interesting parallel between the Communists' destruction of Buddhist Tibetans and the Nazis' destruction of the Jewish race because of their inability to disassociate the Jewish people from Judaism. While not extending the logic to its fullest extent (the *final* extermination of a race), the Chinese, nevertheless, resorted to mass murder because they could not accept that to be Tibetan meant to be Buddhist. In their attempt to destroy religion, they destroyed too many Tibetans.

Decimated also was the spiritual sophistication of the lamas, the environmental knowledge of the nomads and farmers, the nuances of Tibetan medicine, and a large portion of the written records of a seminal culture. Like much of their natural environment, the Tibetans have become an endangered species. The damage to Tibetan civilization must be seen as a severe blow to the world's cultural diversity and vitality.

REFERENCES

Abbotts, Adrian. 1997. *Naked Spirits: A Journey into Occupied Tibet.* Edinburgh: Canongate Books.

Aldridge, Stephen. 1999a. "A Look At Tibetan Books." [http://www.khamaid.org/programs/culture/books.htm]. May 1999.

Aldridge, Stephen. 1999b. "Discovery and Preservation of Ancient Tibetan Manuscripts." [http://www.khamaid.org/programs/culture/text.htm]. December 1999.

Alterman, Benjamin, Deborah Alterman, and Laura L. Gewissler. 1987. "From Woodblock to Silicon Chip: The Transmission of Tibetan Language." *Printing History* 9 (1):15–26.

Apte, Robert Z., and Andres R. Edwards. 1998. *Tibet: Enduring Spirit, Exploited Land.* Santa Fe, New Mexico: Heartsfire Books.

Atisha, Tenzin Phuntsok. 1991. "The Tibetan Approach to Ecology." In *The Anguish of Tibet*, eds. Petra K. Kelly, Gerta Bastian, and Pat Aiello. Berkeley: Parallax Press, 222–6.

Avedon, John. F. 1991. "In Exile from the Land of Snows." In *The Anguish of Tibet*, eds. Petra K. Kelly, Gert Bastian, and Pat Aiello. Berkeley, California: Parallax Press, 14–30.

Avedon, John F. 1997. *In Exile from the Land of Snows: The Definitive Account of the Dalai Lama and Tibet Since the Chinese Conquest.* New York: Harper Collins.

Batchelor, Stephen. 1987. *The Tibet Guide.* London: Wisdom Publications.

Becker, Jasper. 1996. *Hungry Ghosts: Mao's Secret Famine.* New York: Henry Holt.

Bohana, Michele. 1991. "U.S. Foreign Policy and the Violation of Tibet." In *The Anguish of Tibet*, eds. Petra K. Kelly, Gert Bastian, and Pat Aiello. Berkeley, California: Parallax Press, 83–91.

Craig, Mary. 1999. *Tears of Blood: A Cry for Tibet*. Washington, D.C.: Counterpoint.

Donnet, Pierre-Antoine. 1994. *Tibet: Survival in Question*, trans. Tica Broch. London: Zed Books.

Ennals, David. 1991. "Tibet: A New Colony." In *The Anguish of Tibet*, eds. Petra K. Kelly, Gert Bastian, and Pat Aiello. Berkeley, California: Parallax Press, 65–67.

Government of Tibet in Exile. 1999. "Religion and National Identity." [http://www.tibet.com/WhitePaper/white7.html]. December 1999.

Government of Tibet in Exile. 2000. "The Library of Tibetan Works and Archives." [http://www.tibet.com/ltwa.htm]. March 2000.

Grunfeld, A. Tom. 1996. *The Making of Modern Tibet*. Rev. ed. Armonk, New York: M.E. Sharpe.

Gyaltag, Gyaltsen. 1991. "From Monarchy to Democracy: An Historical Overview." In *The Anguish of Tibet*, eds. Petra K. Kelly, Gert Bastian, and Pat Aiello. Berkeley, California: Parallax Press, 3–13.

Harrer, Heinrich. 1985. *Return to Tibet*, trans. Ewald Osers. New York: Schocken Books.

Heberer, Thomas. 1991. "Tibet and the Chinese Concept of Nationhood." In *The Anguish of Tibet*, eds. Petra K. Kelly, Gert Bastian, and Pat Aiello. Berkeley, California: Parallax Press, 47–52.

Hicks, Roger. 1988. *Hidden Tibet: The Land and Its People*. Shaftesbury, Dorset: Element.

Hutton, Cate. 1997. "High-Altitude Librarianship: The Adventures of an ALA Library Fellow in Tibet." *Information Technology and Libraries* 16 (1):30–33.

Kewley, Vanya. 1990. *Tibet: Behind the Ice Curtain*. London: Grafton Books.

Library of Tibetan Works and Archives. 2000. "A Brief History of Library of Tibetan Works and Archives." [http://www.chocodog.com/ltwa/ltwbhis.htm]. February 2000.

Margolin, Jean-Louis. 1999. "China: A Long March into Night." In *The Black Book of Communism: Crimes, Terror, Repression*, eds. Stephane Courtois, Nicolas Werth, Jean-Louis Panne, Andrzej Paczkowski, Karel Bartosek, and Jean-Louis Margolin, trans. Jonathan Murphy and Mark Kramer. Cambridge, Massachusetts: Harvard University Press.

Norbu, Dawa. 1987. *Red Star Over Tibet*. 2nd ed. New York: Envoy Press.

Norbu, Dawa. 1997. *Tibet: The Road Ahead*. London: Rider.

Paljor, Kunsang. 1977. *Tibet: The Undying Flame*. New Delhi, India: Model Press.

Patt, David. 1992. *A Strange Liberation: Tibetan Lives in Chinese Hands*. Ithaca, New York: Snow Lion Publications.

Pema, Jetsun with Gilles Van Grasdorff. 1997. *Tibet: My Story, An Autobiography.* Shaftesbury, Dorset: Element.

Rummel, R.J. 1991. *China's Bloody Century: Genocide and Mass Murder Since 1900.* New Brunswick, New Jersey: Transaction Publishers.

Schell, Orville. 1991. "Chinese Attitudes to Conservation and to Tibet." In *The Anguish of Tibet,* eds. Petra K. Kelly, Gert Bastian, and Pat Aiello. Berkeley, California: Parallax Press, 199–206.

Shakya, Tsering. 1999. *The Dragon in the Land of Snows: A History of Modern Tibet since 1947.* New York: Columbia University Press.

Smith, Warren W. Jr. 1996. *Tibetan Nation: A History of Tibetan Nationalism and Sino-Tibetan Relations.* Boulder, Colorado: Westview Press.

Snellgrove, David, and Hugh Richardson. 1986. *A Cultural History of Tibet.* Boston: Shambhala.

Van Walt Van Praag, Michael. 1991. "Tibet: An Occupied Country." In *The Anguish of Tibet*, eds. Petra K. Kelly, Gert Bastian, and Pat Aiello. Berkeley, California: Parallax Press, 60–64.

Wangyal, Phuntsog. 1984. "Tibet: A Case of Eradication of Religion Leading to Genocide." In *Toward the Understanding and Prevention of Genocide. Proceedings of the International Conference on the Holocaust and Genocide*, ed. Israel W. Charny. Boulder, Colorado: Westview Press, 119–126.

Zwalf, W. 1981. *Heritage of Tibet.* London: British Museum Publications.

Chapter 9

THE COLLISION OF IDEAS

"Utopias have their value—nothing so wonderfully expands the imaginative horizons of human potentialities—but as guides to conduct they can prove literally fatal. Heraclitus was right, things cannot stand still."

(Berlin 1991, 15)

In the most general sense, one could say that the ultra-nationalists and Communists of the twentieth century effectively replaced traditional systems of ethics and morality by a single means: the leveraging of ideology. Nationalism and socialism, in themselves compelling belief systems, were transformed by merciless leaders into totalistic dogmas that reduced what is sacred to a single notion of predestined collective potential. Familial loyalties were subordinated to loyalty to the state. A sociopolitical environment was engineered to snuff out alternative ideas. Violence was instituted as necessary, and even desirable, in the quest to maintain the totalitarian structures that would deliver a purified and transformed society.

Fueling the impulse toward violence was the ideologues' conviction that enemies—animate or inanimate, a person, even a book—surrounded them. When a book's content contradicted an ideologue's dominance over ideas and seemed to support cosmopolitanism, democracy, or humanism, that book was labeled a tool of the enemy and in itself, a dangerous thing. Such a book, therefore, became a candidate for censorship, which ran the gamut from blacklisting to burning or pulping. Similarly, when libraries were identified as hindering ideological transformation and impeding progress toward the desired utopia, they were attacked and sometimes eliminated, along with their human possessors. Perhaps the most astonishing part of this phenomenon was the inclusion of a nation's own possessions as enemies to the cause. The Nazis first censored and destroyed those *German* books that they considered problematic, then destroyed the books of those they considered pathological (the Jews), inferior (the Poles), and resistant (the British). When ideological fervor intensified in China, the Communist radicals destroyed classic *Chinese* texts and intellectuals and in Tibet, both texts and resistant Tibetans. With progress narrowly defined as achieving ideological goals, print materials often came to be associated with cultural or political intransigence and their destruction a war effort on the same two fronts. The violence and public nature of destruction often obscured the fact that the ruin was a practical means of destroying information that contradicted the myths of the regime or substantiated the claims of other ethnic or political groups to resources and territory.

Books were destroyed as part of the process of homogenizing discourse, suppressing individualism in the interest of the collective, and co-opting or purging the intellectuals. The goal of extremist regimes was complete control, and books and libraries were compromised by their association with humanism, the creed of enemy democracies. Indeed, the twentieth-century ideologues despised humanists, who valued books and libraries for precisely those qualities that pitted them against ideologues. Regardless of their individual agendas, books ultimately, by their very existence and coexistence with the entirety of the world's print literature, support individualism, pluralism, creativity, rationalism, freedom of information, critical thinking, and intellectual freedom. The ideologue must reject traditional knowledge in order to look to the future, while the humanist actively seeks inspiration from the past. Humanists believe that written materials are fundamental to the maintenance and progress of culture; ideologues seek to politicize and overturn existing culture. Ideologues view libraries as problematic, their potential as instruments of indoctrination compromised by their humanistic or reactionary nature and ability to pose alternate realities or ideas. World War II was fought between ideologues and humanists, and books and libraries played no small role. The jubilant Nazi book burnings and the ensuing wartime devastation of cultural institutions throughout the world resulted in the United Nations' orientation toward the preservation of humanism. The cultivation of a world in which cultural resources are safe became a declared goal of both democratic nations and the international community that coalesced around the need for peace.

Democratic humanism in theory and as an ideal for practice was the polar opposite of extremist programs. Humanists sought incremental social progress through democratic processes rather than quick and radical changes because they knew that humans pay high costs during times of rapid change. Ideologues sought instantaneous revolution, regardless of the human costs; their sole concern was with the collective. For them, ideology was the measure of all things; for humanists, human well-being was the measure. Far from mindless of community issues, humanists promote human worth and individual development because they believe that the intellectual, spiritual, and ethical development of each individual enriches society. Ideologues view individual growth as progress toward becoming the "new man"—a being who, where adherence to strict orthodoxy is enforced, is essentially a pliant tool of the state. Since individualism and independent thinking are highly suspect, books are problematic because of their potential to engage the mind, introduce cognitive dissonance, or merely entertain and distract. There are, of course, pressures to conform in democracies but rarely at such a grand cost to intellectual freedom and pluralism. In democracies, the public library celebrates these values and provides access to information for decision-making. In totalitarian societies, the public library is typically a tool for the dissemination and inculcation of the ideology of the state. In comparison to the closed systems under totalitarian regimes, democracies are relatively open societies and, to some degree, engage in the process of critical introspection. Their books and libraries serve as conduits for the information necessary for that process.

When ideologues purge books and libraries, they are expressing a battle over these very ideas: their ideology against humanism and its support of pluralism. Since extremist regimes demand that commitment to the ideology be absolute, there is no room for alternative creeds, particularly humanism with its anti-dogmatic roots. For example, the Serbs practiced a clerical-nationalist ideology with an anti-Western idolization of the nation and hostility toward democracy and Western humanism: "We do not want a Europe without God nor a pseudo-humanist Europe where, man, instead of god, is enthroned," declared a Serbian leader (Anzulovic 1999, 125). Twentieth-century extremist regimes understood that humanism had to be extinguished internally as well as externally, but this was a difficult task because humanist principles permeated existing cultural and educational institutions. Libraries, for example, supported modern scholarship

and technology by preserving and disseminating the information necessary for scientific inquiry, technological development, and the systematic
advancement of knowledge. These functions, which made libraries the
quintessential representation of humanism, were problematic for extremists. For example, Chinese Communist radicals of the 1960s and 1970s
wanted industrialization based not on scientific and technological expertise but on revolutionary will and zeal. Libraries suffered as a conse-
quence. The Nazis sought to rationalize racism, and German libraries
flourished only when they aligned with this goal.

Extremists need to control humanist institutions and transform them
from cultural resources into political tools, part of the overall machine of
the revolution. Ideologues censor and then reconstruct their own libraries
and those of conquered enemies, or they destroy books or entire libraries
outright because they fear the connection between libraries and alternate
belief systems, especially humanism, which allow for pluralism. Books
and libraries are destroyed not only because of their functions within a
society, but because, by the twentieth century, books, libraries, and all
intellectual pursuits had become clearly linked to humanism. Their destruction was part of an overall system of eliminating the influence of
humanism in the sociopolitical arena, particularly as concerned intellectuals, scholarship, science, history, and foreign relations.

INTELLECTUALS AND SCHOLARSHIP

Twentieth-century intellectuals ran the spectrum from intellectual-as-
humanist to intellectual-as-ideologue or -revolutionary. Their precursors
(the secular intellectuals of the post-Enlightenment period) also expressed
both tendencies. Having rejected organized religion in order to pursue
their own ideas, eighteenth- and nineteenth-century scholars went on to
elevate their ideas to the status of dogma, a suitable foundation for later
ideological extremism. For the past 200 years, the rise of the secular intellectual has been a powerful influence in the shaping of the modern
world. Displacing religious authority, intellectuals donned the cloak of
moral rectitude and assumed the role of telling mankind how to conduct
its affairs.

Paul Johnson, in his provocative book *Intellectuals* (1988), posits the
theory that a new breed of thinkers secularized the task of diagnosing
society's problems, subjecting traditional prescriptive codes to principles
of their own devising, and prescribing radical changes; they realized that
the products of their intellect could be used to replace the existing order

and transform society. The nineteenth-century romantic poet Shelley, for instance, believed that society was rotten and that intellectuals occupied a privileged position in reconstructing society. Many of the writers of the 1800s wanted to use ideas to fight against injustice, oppression, conformism, moral blindness, egoism, cruelty, servility, poverty, and despair and bring about an opposite state, a "reign of truth, love, honesty, justice, security . . . decency, independence, freedom, spiritual fulfillment" (Berlin 1991, 3). What these secular intellectuals did not know was that their ideas would shape modern society for both good and bad, and would come to form the basis for the ideological storms of the next century. "The doctrines of Enlightenment and social science, touted to liberate man from the tyranny of the priesthood, would soon establish their own tyranny" (Boorstin 1998, 225). While professing a love for humanity in general these writers tended to put ideas—often heartless—*before* people, preparing the way for the fanatical regimes of the 1900s. Like many intellectuals, Shelley's personal life was a shambles; Johnson (1988, 48) describes him as "capable of feeling for, in the abstract, the whole of suffering humanity, yet finding it manifestly impossible, not once but scores, hundreds of times, to penetrate imaginatively the minds and hearts of all those people with whom he had daily dealings." This is precisely the dynamic that emerged in Communist revolutions between the regime and the people.

Shelley and other nineteenth-century figures had been preceded by Jean-Jacques Rousseau (1712–1778), who had proposed that state-sponsored cultural engineering would inculcate virtue, that the perfect state would operate under laws made by the general will, and the general will would have moral authority and always be righteous. Rousseau believed that those who control a people's opinion also control its actions; according to Johnson (1988), Rousseau's ideological offspring was the totalitarian state, an interesting assessment in light of the closed societies that were the product of twentieth-century totalitarianism. As the nineteenth century progressed, intellectuals prepared the way for extremism by treating groups as embodied ideas rather than as flesh-and-blood human beings. Playwright Henrik Ibsen believed that an enlightened minority would always lead mankind in a desirable direction; of course, autocratic party members would eventually lead mankind into an abyss. Desk-bound and remote from those in whose name he called for revolution, Karl Marx boldly evolved powerful theories that set different goals for humanism, moving it away from its focus on the individual (Johnson 1988). An undertone of violence in his work foreshadowed the later pitiless imposition of revolutionary ideas by elite vanguards.

A split in intellectual currents occurred between those who sought to incorporate the tenets of the Enlightenment into a liberal scholarship based on objectivity and intellectual freedom and those who, although secular, operated as true believers, in the sense that they were more concerned with supporting personal theories than arriving at objective truth. Johnson (1988) argues that Tolstoy, in his role as prophet, distorted the record in *War and Peace* to prove his theory of how history works. Marx deliberately falsified facts to prove his theses, and in Johnson's opinion "his work reflects a disregard for truth which at times amounts to contempt" (Johnson 1988, 69). These works set the precedent for the scholarship of those who became part of twentieth-century revolutionary machines (Nazis, Communists, Iraqis, Serbs) and used research and pseudo-analysis to support extremist regimes, intellectualize prejudice, and buoy propaganda that justified aggression. The intellectual-as-ideologue operated in direct contradiction to mainstream modern liberal humanistic scholarship.

Certainly, intellectuals and their scholarship have directed the battle between democratic and liberal humanism and extremist ideologies, an important element in twentieth-century libricide. Through their works, intellectuals have the dual potential to either maintain the status quo or dismantle it through the application of critical thinking. Extremist regimes know that intellectuals, when brought into correct political alignment, exercise a positive influence by supporting and legitimizing their policies. When not aligned with the regime, intellectuals may engineer revolutions and provide the theoretical support for opposing belief systems, and thus, pose a potential threat to any existing order. Therefore, highly authoritarian or totalitarian regimes subject intellectuals to processes of neutralization: co-option or social and professional ostracism, exile, imprisonment, even execution.

The fate of intellectuals under each regime has been addressed throughout this book because, as the primary users of texts and, indeed, living representations of those texts, their fates often paralleled those of books and libraries. In Nazi Germany, scholars were forced to choose between ostracism and inactivity, exile, conciliation, or active participation in Nazi programs. Many, in fact, became enthusiastic proponents of National Socialism. They legitimized Nazi racial prejudices through distorted scholarship and used the educational and intellectual apparatus to homogenize consciousness and institute National Socialism as the dominant form of scholarly discourse. Intellectuals in Iraq and Serbia served similar functions: Those who didn't go into exile became enthusiastic spokesmen for the regime. Fulfilling the humanistic function of scholars (exercising critical intelligence, engaging in objective research as witnesses to truth, embodying freedom of thought, exercising moral responsibility and imagination) was impossible for them. In both countries, the media and all intellectual avenues were sealed off from outside input, and ultra-nationalist rhetoric and premises became self-perpetuating. Intellectuals prepared the way for the aggressive moves of both Saddam Hussein and Slobodan Milosevic by engaging in the discourse of war and supplying propaganda that fueled hostility and legitimized paranoia. Thus, intellectuals were accomplices in the collapse of rational politics.

The situation was slightly different in Communist China. The Party, on the whole, was anti-intellectual, and many scholars were killed in the early days of the Communist takeover. Even those willing to cooperate were viewed with suspicion and subjected to discrimination. While Party moderates knew that industrialization required an educated class, the radicals under Mao depended on will and ideological fervor rather than scientific and technological expertise. Nevertheless, intellectuals were held responsible for lack of progress toward social transformation and, like libraries, were subject to the fortunes of the radicals. Communist regimes generally considered educated people to have a curse upon them—intellectuals failed to understand life and were cut off from the people (Kundera 1981).

Intellectuals were considered innately dangerous, particularly those in the arts. A Polish writer, Czeslaw Milosz, summed up the writer's "choice" concerning "socialist realism":

> There is not, as some think, merely an esthetic theory to which the writer, the musician, the painter or the theatrical producer is obliged to adhere. On the contrary, it involves by implication the whole Leninist-Stalinist doctrine. . . . It is concerned with the beliefs which lie at the foundation of human existence. In the field of literature it forbids what has in every age been the writer's essential task—to look at the world from his own independent viewpoint, to tell the truth as he sees it, and so to keep watch and ward in the interest of society as a whole. It preaches a proper attitude of doubt in regard to a merely formal system of ethics but itself makes all judgment of values dependent upon the interest of the dictatorship. Human sufferings are drowned in the trumpet-blare: the orchestra in the concentration camp; and I, as a poet, had my place already marked out for me among the first violins (Milosz 1990, xi–xii).

Under extremist regimes, all writing serves the purpose of indoctrination. Intellectual honesty, including objective consideration of evidence, becomes a farce as conforming intellectuals scramble to stay within specified frames of reference; conclusions precede evidence, rather than the evidence leading to findings (Lin 1991). The humanistic emphasis on clarity, accuracy, and fair-mindedness is stood on end. "The end of this kind of thinking is obedience without questions, belief without inquiry, and loyalty by a uniform will, uniform ideas, and uniform actions" (Lin 1991, 18).

Overall, the twentieth-century institutionalization of political violence by extremists endangered intellectuals as well as books because the ideologues' supremacy over ideas had to be absolute. The extremists discussed in this book cleverly merged ideas with violence, and although they were demagogues and thugs, their personal agendas and ideological imperatives were so interwoven that their classification as ideologues is valid, especially in the cases of Hitler and Mao. With Saddam and Milosevic, ideology was more obviously a cover for a lust for power. The first order of business in establishing a new order is the elimination of dissent and leaders of the opposition. The Nazis imprisoned and killed Jewish intellectuals first, then Jews in general. In Poland, thousands of educated Poles were massacred as the first step toward the eventual enslavement and genocide of the entire population. After the capture of a town in Bosnia, the Serbs' execution of Muslim professionals (doctors, lawyers, judges, teachers, politicians) became standard practice. Party radicals executed thousands of Chinese intellectuals in 1949 and subjected those remaining intellectuals to imprisonment, violence, and death in intermittent campaigns. In Tibet, the Chinese ultimately exterminated most of the educated classes—the monks, government officials, and uncooperative aristocrats.

Conforming intellectuals, denied freedom from involuntary subjective control, undergo a particular kind of extinguishment that is often expressed as apathy (Milosz 1990). Extremists knew:

> [t]he most neuralgic points of the doctrine are philosophy, literature, the history of art, and literary criticism; those are the points where man in his unfortunate complexity enters the equation. The difference of a tiny fraction in the premises yields dizzying differences after the calculation is completed. A deviation from the line in the evaluation of some work of art may become the leaven of a political upheaval. . . . [I]t becomes obvious that intellectual terror is a principle that Leninism-Stalinism can never forsake, even if it should achieve victory on a world scale. The enemy, in a potential form, will *always* be there. . . . [Even from 1 percent deviation,] a new church can rise. (Milosz 1990, 213–214)

At stake is the ideology's possession of each person and ability to transform all individuals into a collective, manipulable mass. To be correct—

indeed, to survive—in the homogenized society required by ideologues, one had to replace "I" with "we." As one writer said of the Communist regime in Yugoslavia, "[t]he consequences of using the first person singular were often unpleasant. You stuck out; you risked being labeled an 'anarchic element' (not even a person), perhaps even a dissident. For that you would be sacked, so you used it sparingly and at your own risk. This was called self-censorship" (Drukulic 1996, 3). The extinguishing of all differences creates a spiritual and ethical vacuum that opens the way for a kind of cultural autism. Erasing memory becomes easy: You destroy books, culture, history; someone writes new books, manufactures a new culture, and invents a new history; and before long "the nation will begin to forget what it is and what it was. The world around it will forget even faster. . . . Or is it true that a nation cannot cross a desert of organized forgetting?" (Kundera 1981, 159). All too often, extremism collapses and leaves the devastated individual the task of reconstructing an "I" and society with the task of resurrecting a usable past and stories that point people towards standards and positive actions (Hoffman 1993). In these times, books and libraries provide solace and sustenance, not to mention "an opportunity for critical self-evaluation based on the mistakes of earlier generations" (Debeljak 1994, 19).

Books and libraries have very little place in the culture of lies that rests on a dichotomization of "us" versus "them" (Ugresic 1998, viii), binary terms that justify the destruction of other groups. If genocide is defined as the mass murder of members of a group, then the wholesale extermination of literate classes can certainly be thus classified—and when the violence reaches books and libraries, we face a form of ethnocide that falls under the same classification. An international community that endorses liberal humanistic principles has begun to combat ethnocide (including libricide) because, like genocide, such actions transgress civilized boundaries and constitute crimes against humanity.

HUMANISM AND THE INTERNATIONALISTS

With the age of Enlightenment came a general awareness that the destruction of cultural objects and institutions is wrong, both for its violence and for its representation of the loss of the "common property of mankind—its inheritance from the past, or its means of subsistence and enrichment in the present" (Best 1980, 65). In 1758 legal scholar Emheric de Vattel's *The Law of Nations* introduced the principle: For whatever cause a country is ravaged, those edifices which do honor to human society must be spared; to do otherwise is to declare oneself an enemy of mankind

(Kaye 1997). Twentieth-century French intellectual Andre Malraux proposed that a general shift in consciousness occurred around 1870, when
humanity realized that while other cultures, such as that of Egypt, had
known only the societies directly preceding them, modern societies possessed an awareness of being the sum of all the others—the first planetary
civilization (Boorstin 1998). This realization may have been the byproduct
of reactions throughout the 1800s to particularly gratuitous incidents of
cultural destruction. The devastation by British troops of Washington,
D.C., in 1814, especially the burning of the Capitol building and the national library, was internationally condemned. Napoleon's systematic looting of cultural property in occupied territories precipitated a series of
precedent-setting regulatory conventions and codes. The 1815 Convention
of Paris ordered the return of items pilfered by the French to the country
of origin and established that looting of cultural property was contrary to
the principles of justice (Kaye 1997). During the American Civil War, the
1863 Lieber Code, perhaps the first known attempt to codify the principles
of cultural protection, specified that soldiers must respect institutions such
as churches, schools, and libraries (Kaye 1997). By the early twentieth
century, these principles were given impetus by internationalism, the
translation of humanist values into a global ethos. The Hague Convention
of 1907 (also known as the "Convention Respecting the Laws and Customs of War on Land") formalized protection to cultural property during
war and forbade looting of and destruction or willful damage to religious,
cultural, or educational institutions.

However, after the Hague Convention, incipient trends toward internationalism faltered as intensely nationalistic sentiments built and exploded into world war. The Germans, staunch nationalists, established the
precedent of destruction of cultural artifacts as a tool of modern war when,
in 1914, they deliberately burned the ancient university library at Louvain,
Belgium, and experimented with other terrorist acts against the population.
Louvain was an iconic event that signaled the arrival of new wartime
tactics based on the notions that breaking the will of the enemy population
was key to victory.

In 1935, internationalism was again a factor in the Roerich Pact, also
known as the "Treaty on the Protection of Artistic and Scientific Institutions and Historic Monuments." Twenty-one American nations signed this
agreement and promised to respect enemy cultural institutions during war.
In Europe, throughout the 1930s, the League of Nations drafted but failed
to formalize conventions that dealt with definitions, obligations, and issues
such as post-war repatriation of cultural objects. Instead, the unresolved

conflicts, bitterness, and economic trauma of the post-World War I years provided the perfect catalyst for various nationalistic beliefs to develop into ideologies that glorified violence. When World War II broke out, the influence of extreme ideologies, given full reign, would result in cataclysmic human and cultural losses. The burning of Louvain, so devastating at the time, foreshadowed the deliberate destruction of cultural sites and artifacts in World War II, including the Baedeker raids on Britain and ethnocidal attacks within occupied territories (such as the German initiatives in Eastern Europe and Japanese attacks in China and the Philippines). Innovations in methods of war and technical advancements in weaponry, combined with intense militarism, led to total war; the logic of total war in which all possible means must be used and no targets are exempt, plus the stakes involved, led the Allies to engage in carpet bombing that added to the unparalleled destruction. Posed as a struggle for the survival of opposing ways of life (democracy versus fanatical nationalism), war was brought to the heart of dueling nations. World War II added a new chapter to the havoc to culture that was wreaked internally and externally by the repression, conflicts, and wars initiated by totalitarian regimes. Throughout the century, the peace sought by internationalists proved elusive.

However, the systematized violence, perpetrated by both the right and left, did result in successful postwar collaborations in developing a more effective institutional base for internationalism. The Allies became the primary sponsors of the United Nations, founded in 1945 to take on the task of creating a world system committed to peace. Humanism became the guiding creed. The UN soon took steps to protect cultural heritage through UNESCO (the United Nations Educational, Scientific, and Cultural Organization). Founded on the premise that "wars are created in the minds of men," this agency promotes the defense of peace through universal access to education, science, culture, and knowledge (Campbell 1989, 223). Among its many initiatives were its development of the World Heritage List, which identifies and protects outstanding world cultural sites, and a relatively new program, begun in 1992, called "Memory of the World," designed to preserve endangered documentary items of importance to specific regions and groups and promote appreciation of all cultures. This program, styled as preventing "collective amnesia," concerns itself with the preservation, in any medium, of manuscripts and other rare and valuable documents in libraries and archives ("Memory of the World Programme" 1994). The UN promotes the free flow of information and supports fifty worldwide information systems that collect and circulate data with the goal of increasing the world's problem-solving capacities (Boulding 1988).

Systems that preserve, generate, and disseminate knowledge were supplemented by a series of idealistic efforts by the United Nations' General
Assembly to reform international relations by formulating a system of
international law. Of primary concern was protecting the right to life and
this took the form of the Genocide Convention; other rights were spelled
out by the Universal Declaration of Human Rights. The latter provided
for, among other rights, the right to hold and express opinions and the
right to receive and impart information and ideas through any media and
regardless of frontiers. To protect material, including cultural monuments
and artifacts, the UN passed a series of international agreements including
the 1954 Hague Convention for the Protection of Cultural Property in the
Event of Armed Conflict. The Hague Convention proscribed the destruction of monuments and manuscripts, books and other objects of artistic,
historical, or archaeological interest, as well as scientific collections, large
libraries, and archives during war. However, it failed to put in place mechanisms of deterrence. The convention stated that damage to cultural property belonging to any people whatsoever was damage to the heritage of
all mankind, since each people contributes to world culture (Detling
1993). In 1970, a new UNESCO convention prohibited the illicit transport
and transfer-of-ownership of cultural property, specifically referring to
property of artistic interest or relating to history, including engravings,
prints, lithographs, books, documents, rare manuscripts and incunabula.
This agreement states that "the interchange of cultural property among
nations for scientific, cultural and educational purposes increases the
knowledge of the civilization of Man, enriches the cultural life of all
peoples and inspires mutual respect and appreciation among nations" (Detling 1993, 51).

Tension has always existed between the *structure* of the United Nations,
which favors the sovereign state (and thus legitimizes regimes, regardless
of their policies), and the body's *philosophy,* internationalism, which promotes humanist values, human rights (including freedom of choice, religion, information, and culture), global connectedness, and a common
human culture. The prerogatives of sovereignty exist uneasily within the
framework of human rights and cultural security. If the international community's cultural heritage is the sum of all national heritages and humanity
is the party of interest, independent of national arrangements, then in
theory, cultural artifacts and institutions belong to all people (Merryman
1986). Species identification supersedes classifications based on geographical or religious divisions; thus, nations and factions that destroy the
culture of "enemy" groups destroy the cultural inheritance of all (Boylan
1993). According to that thought, regimes must not threaten peace and

civilization by destroying those objects that "form a yoke that holds us all together" (Tanselle 1991, 31). Still, despite official international opprobrium, sovereign national regimes that have breached these conventions within their own borders or territories of influence have, for the most part, gone unchecked.

Each case history in this book has demonstrated that extremists have targeted texts both as the material embodiment of specific enemies and as symbols of broader antithetical forces: the spread of cosmopolitanism, democracy, humanism, internationalism, and processes of secularization. Recent events continue to demonstrate this tendency. For example, a New York Times article—dateline: Kabul, Afghanistan, February 2002—features a picture of a bullet-riddled English language encyclopedia; the caption reads "The Taliban commonly shot books, like this one at Kabul University" (Burns 2002, 12). Cultural destruction in Afghanistan has demonstrated that as the United Nations and universalists intensify efforts to preserve local cultural objects—for example, designating sites and objects as the "protected" heritage of the world—they may actually be setting them up as targets for disaffiliated groups. Art historian Dario Gamboni (2001) perceptively hypothesizes that the Taliban destruction of the ancient Bamiyan Buddhas of Afghanistan occurred, in addition to religious motivations, because the religious leaders resented ostracism by an international community that was at the same time expressing concern for the Buddhas' preservation. Destroying the Buddhas amounted to a provocative affirmation of their sovereignty and, simultaneously, the rejection of international values. Tellingly, a Taliban official, after the destruction, declared that the decision to destroy the "idols" was made "in a reaction of rage after a foreign delegation offered money to preserve the ancient works at a time when a million Afghans faced starvation" (Gamboni 2001, 11). Gamboni (2001, 11) believes that: "The Taliban's disingenuous expression of surprise at the outrage caused by their act—Mullah Omar was quoted as making the typically iconoclastic statement, 'we're only breaking stones'—can also be understood as a criticism of Western materialism. This criticism is typical of a movement that . . . 'draws vitality from the perceived evils of foreign cultural imperialism.'" The rise of the Taliban and their creation of a totalitarian world, ruled by dogma and violence, aptly illustrate the destructive potential of religious fundamentalism implemented as state ideology. It is not surprising that Afghanistan's books and libraries suffered tremendous damage during Taliban rule. This type of disaffiliation and aggression, which found further action in the destruction of American symbols and sources of power—the World Trade Center and Pentagon—may make cultural symbols increasingly vulnerable. Unfortunately, modern technology and communications has invested extremists with the capability of carrying their ideologies and spleen to the core of all nations.

Internationalists, usually humanistic in orientation, embrace plurality and support the preservation of books and libraries because of the witness they bear, the counterforce they exert against extremists' pursuits of conformity, orthodoxy, and ideological domination. Octavio Paz, the Nobel prize-winning Mexican poet and essayist, captures the essence of the basic tenet underlying efforts to preserve all cultures: "What sets worlds in motion is the interplay of differences, their attractions and repulsions. Life is plurality, death is uniformity. By suppressing differences and peculiarities, by eliminating different civilizations and cultures, progress weakens life and favors death. The ideal of a single civilization for everyone . . . impoverishes and mutilates us. Every view of the world that becomes extinct, every culture that disappears, diminishes a possibility of life" (as quoted in Marsella and Yamada 2000, 22). Perhaps the greatest testament to a commitment to plurality was the Convention on the Prevention and Punishment of the Crime of Genocide passed by the UN in 1948. It made the prevention of the mass extermination of any group an overriding moral imperative for the international community (Gourevitch 1998). This convention, designed to "liberate mankind from such an odious scourge," made genocide a crime under international law (Chalk and Jonassohn 1990, 44). While emphasizing the right to life, the Convention has been interpreted as implying a basic right to cultural identity as well. But by failing to honor the promise of international action against genocide, except on rare occasions, the UN demonstrates that it has yet failed to reckon with the tension between sovereignty and internationalism. While internationalism provides a rallying point for amity in principle, an increasingly unfriendly world has hosted more than 100 substantial armed conflicts since World War II. With 200 independent states and 8,000 ethnic and cultural groups that now want to be recognized as "nations," the incidence of violence and cultural destruction has risen sharply in the resulting clash of interests. In many cases, the collapse of political order within a state has resulted in chaos and anarchy. Historian Eric Hobsbawm (1997) attributes this breakdown to the steady dismantling of the defenses against barbarism erected by the civilization of the Enlightenment. Nonetheless, the UN persists in promoting internationalism and has intermittently intensified efforts to protect vulnerable populations and cultures.

The critical self-reflective revision of social practices is an essential part of modern institutions (Giddens 1990). The Genocide Convention, the Hague Convention, and others have been key efforts to incorporate exactly that, to erect girders in scaffolding upon which to construct a global civil society. Internationalism promises to provide ideals for current and future generations. After all, the essence of policymaking is the struggle over ideas capable of inspiring collective action (Stone 1997). To paraphrase Milovan Djilas, in politics more than in anything else, moral indignation is the catalyst for change (as quoted in Leys 1977). Ideas can result in decreased tolerance for a practice. For example, the rejection of slavery in the nineteenth century eventually resulted in its being virtually eliminated. Internationalists have urged regimes and individuals to recognize the broader consequences of their choices and consider social costs and harmful effects, but overall, the destruction of culture remains a persistent problem—the interests of specific nations and regimes pitted against the general interest.

The discrepancy between international values and those of individual tribes or nations impedes consensus (beyond lip-service) with respect to the destruction of cultural artifacts. It is unclear whether humanists and internationalists alone perceive the destruction of books and libraries to be in violation of the social contract or whether there is a level of consensus across value systems. In other words, is the preservation of culture a universal objective or is it specific to Western sensibilities? If the former, then should this objective be left to the discretion of individual states? Ironically, the UN as a whole condemns the destruction of books and libraries while some of its own extremist members persist in such destruction. Certainly, divisions over responsibility and accountability for genocide and libricide are bound to exist. Where genocide is concerned, despite the moral gravity of the crime, it is difficult to assign individual responsibility and almost impossible to punish the state. Where the destruction of culture is concerned, perpetrators are also often under the direction of their government, and therefore, rarely held personally responsible. It is nearly impossible to hold individuals accountable for their actions when their governments can dodge responsibility.

The question remains as to whether there exists sufficient international consensus against the destruction of books and libraries to warrant their prohibition and the enforcement of accountability. International law offers a way to delegitimize rogue regimes, heighten awareness of the consequences of the destruction of culture, and enforce accountability. In 1992 the UN General Assembly issued the Declaration on the Rights of Persons Belonging to National or Ethnic, Religious or Linguistic Minorities. This resolution committed signatories to develop public information programs on cultural and ethnic diversity and the importance of respecting all cultures (Boylan 1993). But, of course, education alone is not enough to

prevent errant nations from acting on their ideas. A tightening of international sanctions was the direct result of the implosion of Yugoslavia in
the 1990s. In a move designed to provide an accountability mechanism
for the Genocide Convention, the UN convened a criminal tribunal to
investigate Serbian war crimes in Bosnia. In 1999 this tribunal indicted
Milosevic for war crimes, including the destruction of cultural sites. In
the same year, accountability for destruction of culture was also addressed
by a new protocol of the Hague Convention. This protocol provides for
the "exceptional protection" of significant sites, monuments, and institutions, limits the parameters for justifying destruction on the basis of military necessity, and designates new categories of war crimes. Extradition
for "cultural" war crimes is now possible under international jurisdiction
regarding the most serious crimes (Boylan 1999).

As in other contemporary crises, idealists were reminded by the events
in Yugoslavia of the precariousness of civilization, defined, in one of its
aspects, by Aldous Huxley (1961, 230) as "a systematic withholding from
individuals of certain occasions for barbarous behavior." Because of the
international community's ineffectual responses, civilization as defined by
Huxley failed and Serbia's behavior produced political disaster and, more
significantly, moral debacle. The crisis in Yugoslavia demonstrated the
limits of contemporary liberal internationalism (Pfaff 1993) in the face of
sovereignty, nationalism, and tribalism. Optimism concerning the doctrine
of cooperative security, a principle pillar of global governance (whereby
force is renounced, all come to the aid of the attacked, and concern is
taken for cultural and social dimensions), was significantly dampened
(Evans 1998). Bosnia was the UN's Vietnam, or as romantics might respond, it is better explained as the UN's Munich—a failure of collective
nerve and will (Thakur 1998). The presumption of global values was
exposed as shaky (Groom 1998) and the promise of the UN charter, which
had established legitimacy on the basis of "We the peoples of the United
Nations," was blighted. Bosnia represented the antithesis of almost 200
years of halting progress toward a common culture and heritage for all
humanity, instead offering fragmented constructions of culture according
to narrow nationalistic, religious, linguistic, and ethnic terms (Boylan
1993). In Bosnia, a "vision of a world order based on universal values
had succumbed . . . to the paralysis of isolation" (Gutman 1993, xlii). The
Bosnian conflict showed once again how the canon of international law
was, in reality, not a universal standard (Ali and Lifschultz 1993). The
prospect of a synergistic society flickered as the global community stood
by and watched the destruction of Bosnia's people, books, and libraries.

The fact that so much cultural destruction had to occur in Yugoslavia before the UN mobilized to intervene and assert even a rudimentary measure of legal accountability demonstrates that social systems always lag in responding to society's demands and crisis is thus endemic (Tehranian 1990). But ideas carried to excess—as in Bosnia, where ethnic cleansing was practiced on a secular, multi-ethnic population—create a powerful backlash (Ali and Lifschultz 1993). By the end of the 1990s, there was a general change of public temperament with respect to the role of nationalism and the nation-state in international relations (Kohn 1968). The way governments treated their people became less a simple political issue of sovereignty and more of a human-rights issue, thus moving within the provenance of international concern. With less than one-half of 1 percent of all people in the world living in monoethnic states, the need to consider minority interests had become imperative (Zimmerman 1999). To succeed in accommodating to each other's differences, the peoples of the world are faced with the necessity of persevering in condemning excessive political and cultural aggression and devising policies and mechanisms of control (Edgerton 1992).

The paradox of this realization involves ideas. While gathering all the people into a common entity, a world society, the most scrupulous attention must be paid to a humanistic emphasis on individual choice. The brotherhood of "one world" cannot be based on a claustrophobic, orthodox ideology, yet must provide a framework of basic beliefs that animate tolerance and curb destructive impulses. "Humanism does not consist in saying: 'No animal could have done what we have done,' but in declaring 'We have refused to do what the beast within us willed us to do, and we wish to rediscover Man wherever we discover that which seeks to crush him to the dust'" (Malraux 1978, 642). Democratic humanism is perhaps the strongest existing weapon to combat the kidnapping of belief systems and the misuse of their potential for energizing and uniting societies. Defining the glory of mankind as the exclusive prerogative of any one nation or group is antithetical to humanism. As the great European writer Miroslav Krleza suggests, "a box of lead letters . . . [is] all that man has so far thought up in defense of human dignity" (as quoted in Ugresic 1998, 268).

Preserving the libraries of the world is preserving witness to the greatness of mankind. The assemblage of many masterpieces—from which, nevertheless, so many are missing—conjures up in the mind's eye *all* the world's masterpieces. "How indeed could this mutilated possible fail to evoke the whole gamut of the possible?" Malraux (1978, 15) asked with respect to art museums; but the observation is equally applicable to libraries. As long as it holds any books at all, a library represents the whole of human knowledge, and with that immeasurably precious legacy, the possibility for progress and human transcendence.

REFERENCES

Ali, Rabia, and Lawrence Lifschultz. 1993. "In Plain View." In *Why Bosnia? Writings on the Balkan War,* eds. Rabia Ali and Lawrence Lifschultz. Stony Creek, Connecticut: The Pamphleteer's Press, xi–lv.

Anzulovic, Branimir. 1999. *Heavenly Serbia: From Myth to Genocide.* New York: New York University Press.

Berlin, Isaiah. 1991. *The Crooked Timber of Humanity: Chapters in the History of Ideas,* ed. Henry Hardy. New York: Alfred A. Knopf.

Best, Geoffrey. 1980. *Humanity in Warfare.* New York: Columbia University Press.

Boorstin, Daniel J. 1998. *The Seekers: The Story of Man's Continuing Quest to Understand His World.* New York: Random House.

Boulding, Elise. 1988. *Building a Global Civic Culture: Education for an Interdependent World.* Syracuse, New York: Syracuse University Press.

Boylan, Patrick. 1999. "New International Treaty to Strengthen Protection of Cultural Property in the Event of Armed Conflict, The Hague, 15–26 March 1999." *IFLA Journal* 25 (4):246–248.

Boylan, Patrick. 1993. "Thinking the Unthinkable." *ICOM News* [International Council of Museums] 48 (1):3–5.

Burns, John F. 2002. "For Women in Kabul, This Test is Welcome." *The New York Times,* 10 February, sec. 1, p. 12.

Campbell, Harry. 1989. "Libraries in War, Peace and Revolution." *Canadian Library Journal* 46 (4):223–224.

Chalk, Frank, and Kurt Jonassohn. 1990. *The History and Sociology of Genocide: Analyses and Case Studies.* New Haven, Connecticut: Yale University Press.

Debeljak, Ales. 1994. *Twilight of the Idols: Recollections of a Lost Yugoslavia,* trans. Michael Biggins. Fredonia, New York: White Pine Press.

Detling, Karen. 1993. "Eternal Silence: The Destruction of Cultural Property in Yugoslavia." *Maryland Journal of International Law and Trade* 17 (1):41–75.

Drukulic, Slavenka. 1996. *Café Europa: Life after Communism.* New York: Penguin Books.

Edgerton, Robert B. 1992. *Sick Societies: Challenging the Myth of Primitive Harmony.* New York: The Free Press.

Evans, Gareth. 1998 "Cooperating for Peace." In *Past Imperfect, Future Uncertain: The United Nations at Fifty*, ed. Ramesh Thakur. London: Macmillan Press, 33–46.

Gamboni, Dario. 2001. "World Heritage: Shield or Target." *Conservation, The GCI Newsletter* 16 (2): 5–11.

Giddens, Anthony. 1990. *Consequences of Modernity.* Stanford, California: University of California Press.

Gourevitch, Philip. 1998. *We Wish To Inform You That Tomorrow We Will Be Killed With Our Families: Stories From Rwanda.* New York: Farrar Straus and Giroux.

Groom, A.J.R. 1998. "Global Governance and the United Nations." In *Past Imperfect, Future Uncertain: The United Nations at Fifty,* ed. Ramesh Thakur. London: Macmillan Press, 219–242.

Gutman, Roy. 1993. *A Witness to Genocide: The 1993 Pulitzer Prize-winning Dispatches on the "Ethnic Cleansing" of Bosnia.* New York: Macmillan.

Hobsbawm, Eric. 1997. *On History.* New York: The New Press.

Hoffman, Eva. 1993. *Exit Into History: A Journey Through the New Eastern Europe.* New York: Penguin Books.

Huxley, Aldous. 1961. *The Devils of Loudun.* London: Chatto & Windus.

Johnson, Paul. 1988. *Intellectuals.* New York: HarperPerennial.

Kaye, Lawrence M. 1997. "Laws in Force at the Dawn of World War II: International Conventions and National Laws." In *The Spoils of War: World War II and Its Aftermath: The Loss, Reappearance, and Recovery of Cultural Property*, ed. Elizabeth Simpson. New York: Harry N. Abrams, 101–105.

Kohn, Hans. 1968. "Nationalism." In *International Encyclopedia of the Social Sciences*, ed. David Sills. Vol. 11. New York: MacMillan Company and the Free Press, 63–69.

Kundera, Milan. 1981. *The Book of Laughter and Forgetting,* trans. Michael Henry Heim. New York: Alfred A. Knopf.

Leys, Simon. 1977. *Chinese Shadows.* New York: Viking Press.

Lin, Jing. 1991. *The Red Guards' Path to Violence: Political, Educational and Psychological Factors.* New York: Praeger.

Malraux, André. 1978. *The Voices of Silence,* trans. Stuart Gilbert. Princeton, New Jersey: Princeton University Press.

Marsella, Anthony J., and Ann Marie Yamada. 2000. "Culture and Mental Health: An Introduction and Overview of Foundations, Concepts, and Issues." In *The Handbook of Multicultural Mental Health: Assessment and Treatment of Diverse Populations*, eds. I. Cuellar and F. Paniagua. New York: Academic Press, 3–24.

"Memory of the World Programme." 1994. *IFLA Journal* 20 (3):350–356.

Merryman, John Henry. 1986. "Two Ways of Thinking about Cultural Property." *American Journal of International Law* 80 (4):831–853.

Milosz, Czeslaw. 1990. *The Captive Mind,* trans. Jane Zielonko. New York: Vintage Books.

Pfaff, William. 1993. *The Wrath of Nations: Civilization and the Furies of Nationalism.* New York: Simon and Schuster.

Stone, Deborah. 1997. *Policy Paradox: The Art of Political Decision Making.*
    New York: W.W. Norton.
Tanselle, G. Thomas. 1991. *Libraries, Museums, and Reading.* The 6th Sol. M.
    Malkin Lecture in Bibliography presented December 17, 1990, Columbia
    University. New York: Book Arts Press.
Tehranian, Majid. 1990. *Technologies of Power: Information Machines and Dem-
    ocratic Prospects.* Norwood, New Jersey: Ablex Publishing.
Thakur, Ramesh. 1998. "Introduction." In *Past Imperfect, Future Uncertain: The
    United Nations at Fifty,* ed. Ramesh Thakur. London: Macmillan Press,
    1–14.
Ugresic, Dubravka. 1998. *The Culture of Lies: Antipolitical Essays.* University
    Park, Pennsylvania: Pennsylvania State University Press.
Zimmerman, Warren. 1999. *Origins of a Catastrophe: Yugoslavia and Its De-
    stroyers.* New York: Times Books.

INDEX

About the Author

REBECCA KNUTH is an Associate Professor, Library and Information Science Program, University of Hawaii.